ESSENTIAL LEGAL KNOWLEDGE AND WRITING SKILLS

ESSENTIAL LEGAL KNOWLEDGE AND WRITING SKILLS

Foundations of Law for Every Profession

MARYELLEN MALEY

CAROL KRUEGER-BROPHY

FRANK R. TORTORELLA

CAROLINA ACADEMIC PRESS
Durham, North Carolina

Library of Congress Cataloging-in-Publication Data

Names: Maley, Maryellen, author. | Krueger-Brophy, Carol, author. | Tortorella, Frank R., author.
Title: Essential legal knowledge and writing skills : foundations of law for every profession / Maryellen Maley, Carol Krueger-Brophy, and Frank R. Tortorella.
Description: Durham, North Carolina : Carolina Academic Press, 2024. | Includes bibliographical references and index.
Identifiers: LCCN 2024040226 | ISBN 9781531017132 (paperback) | ISBN 9781531019396 (ebook)
Subjects: LCSH: Law--Methodology. | Legal composition. | Legal ethics. | Practice of law.
Classification: LCC K212 .M353 2024 | DDC 340.023--dc23/eng/20240828
LC record available at https://lccn.loc.gov/2024040226

Carolina Academic Press
700 Kent Street
Durham, North Carolina 27701
(919) 489-7486
www.cap-press.com

Printed in the United States of America

To John, Jeff, Michael, Erin, Taylor, Dora, Jack, Monica, Ryan, Ethan, Emmett, and The Six with boundless love. How did I get so incredibly lucky to share my life with you? Teaghlach!

—MEM

To Sean, Ryan, and Erin: With gratitude for all your love and support; you are my foundation and my why.

—CKB

To my high school teachers who inspired excellence: Avis Leabman, Carol Gavoorian O'Brien, and Marguerite Picillo-Gonsalves.

—FRT

Contents

About the Authors

MARYELLEN MALEY, BA, BSN, JD, received her law degree from Loyola University Chicago School of Law where she was a member of Law Review. Prior to law school she received a BSN in Nursing and a BA in English Literature. Maryellen worked as a nurse for several years. She then attended law school after which she worked as a healthcare attorney at a large Chicago law firm. She next worked as regulatory counsel at a University of Chicago Hospital, and as a Senior Health Policy Analyst at the American Academy of Pediatrics. She was also a research rep for LexisNexis at Notre Dame, University of Chicago, and Loyola. She is certified in mediation from Chicago's Center for Conflict Resolution and Harvard Law School.

Maryellen began teaching legal writing to 1Ls at Loyola in 2005. In 2008 she was the first person to teach in Loyola's Beazley Institute for Health Law and Policy's online Master of Jurisprudence program. She created and taught the Introduction to Legal Studies and Legal Writing Course, Introduction to Legal Research Course, and the Capstone Thesis Course. As the Director of the Online Writing Program she hired and mentored approximately 20 adjunct writing professors per semester. Having retired from her full-time faculty position, she is teaching as an adjunct professor and is pursuing an MA in Bioethics from Loyola's Neiswanger Institute for Bioethics & Healthcare Leadership.

CAROL KRUEGER-BROPHY, DPT, JD, MSW attended law school at the University of Michigan where she served as the research and development editor of the University of Michigan Journal of Law Reform. Following an internship in the Health Legislation Unit of the World Health Organization, she joined the health law group at Vedder, Price, Kaufman, and Kammholz.

Carol co-authored a textbook entitled *Legal and Ethical Issues in Physical Therapy*. She was an adjunct faculty member at Belmont University for seventeen years, teaching healthcare ethics to graduate physical therapy students. She was an adjunct faculty member at the Beazley Institute for Health Law and Policy at the Loyola University School of law for eight years. She has maintained an interest in the intersection of medicine, law, and ethics, teaching courses in ethics and jurisprudence to physical therapists. Carol has recently embarked on a third career as a behavioral health counselor.

FRANK R. TORTORELLA, MBA, JD, FACHE, is the executive director for patient experience at the University of Texas MD Anderson Cancer Center in Houston. He previously served as vice president of accreditation, regulation, and certification and vice president of clinical support services. Prior to joining MD Anderson, Tortorella served as vice president of finance and vice president of ambulatory care at Advocate Illinois Masonic Medical Center in Chicago. He holds a Bachelor of Arts degree from Harvard University, a Master of Business Administration degree with a specialization in healthcare administration from the University of Chicago, and a Juris Doctor degree with a concentration in health law from Loyola University Chicago. Tortorella is also an adjunct professor at the Beazley Institute for Health Law and Policy at the Loyola University Chicago School of Law. He has served as a Baldrige examiner at the state and national level and has presented on healthcare operations at national professional conferences and co-authored multiple articles in peer reviewed journals on healthcare operations. He is the editor of the book entitled *Leading Ancillary and Support Departments to Higher Performance: The New Service Imperative for Patient Care.*

Preface

If we want to feel an undying passion for our work, if we want to feel we are contributing to something bigger than ourselves, we all need to know our WHY.

—Simon Sinek[1]

Why Pursue Legal Studies?

Why are you pursuing the study of law? Are you hoping to get a promotion in your current job? Does your work require legal knowledge? Are you looking for a new career? Your "why" is important because it informs the direction of your future studies. As you begin your legal education, a solid foundation will serve you well.

Understanding the fundamentals of law and improving your writing skills are beneficial for several reasons. They...

- Provide tools that increase your value in the workplace.
- Improve your problem-solving skills.
- Strengthen your analytical skills.
- Enhance your communication skills.
- Inform your citizenship.

This text supports those benefits by providing an easy-to-read guide to the fundamentals. If you need a review of the United States legal system, Chapter Two offers important details on the trial court system and our government's structure and function. Chapter Three provides detailed guidance and specific strategies to read and analyze legal cases. Learning to read and analyze legal cases is fundamental to understanding how the law develops. A clear and concise guide to interpreting statutes and regulations is found in Chapters Four and Five.

1. Simon Sinek, David Mead, & Peter Docker, Find Your Why: A Practical Guide for Discovering Purpose for You and Your Team (2017).

This book provides a solid foundation for students who want to gain knowledge of the law for current or future employment. Many employees, in a wide variety of employment sectors, would benefit by expanding their legal knowledge. Most also recognize the importance of learning to express complex legal issues clearly and convincingly.

There are other texts that provide guidance on legal studies. Two important things separate this book from many others. One is its focus on regulatory law. The reason for this focus is best explained by Professor Kevin M. Stack:

> We live in an era of regulation, but our jurisprudence has fallen behind. Despite the central place that regulations occupy in our law, their interpretation has garnered little focused consideration, especially in comparison to the lavish attention devoted to statutory interpretation.[2]

It is this era of regulation that makes the study of regulatory law vitally important to the master of legal studies student. Much of the law that demands compliance in the workplace requires an in-depth knowledge of regulatory law. Chapter Five, therefore, provides focused consideration of regulatory law.

The other notable distinction in this text is its heavy emphasis on writing. Many business leaders, business magazines, and business schools rank skillful writing among the most important qualities in predicting job success and security. A 2018 FORBES article titled *Why Mastering Writing Skills Can Help Future-Proof Your Career* highlighted the following study: "[A]ccording to a Conference Board survey of 431 human resources professionals, writing is one of the biggest employee skill gaps."[3]

Another study echoes the employer call for employees with good writing skills:

> Recent research proves that written communication skills are at the top of employers' wish lists. According to the National Association of Colleges and Employers, **73.4% of employers** want a candidate with strong written communication skills. Written communication was the number three most desired quality overall, behind leadership skills and ability to work as a team member.[4]

This book, therefore, provides three chapters on writing. Chapter Six explains how to produce good writing. Chapter Seven presents the characteristics of legal writing and analysis. Chapter Eight sets forth the qualities of good business writing.

Finally, Chapters Nine and Ten address ethics and the unauthorized practice of law.

---

2. Kevin M. Stack, *Interpreting Regulations*, 111 MICH. L. REV. 355 (2012).

3. G. Solomon, *Why Mastering Writing Skills Can Help Future-Proof Your Career*, FORBES (2018, August 9). The Conference Board, established in 1916, is a business organization with many business members in over sixty countries. It regularly conducts business-related research.

4. K. Moore, *Study: 73% of Employers Want Candidates with This Skill*, INC.COM (2016, April 7) (emphasis added).

The Master of Legal Studies Degree

Let's take a minute to think about what you plan to do with this education. Whether you are a human resource specialist, a risk manager, a compliance officer (and the list goes on), it is advantageous for you to be familiar with the law that governs your profession. Below you will find a list of just a few professionals who could benefit from a master of legal studies degree.

- Accountant
- Bank official
- Chief executive officer
- Chief financial officer
- Chief operating officer
- Compliance specialist
- Contract administrator
- Financial consultant
- Head nurse
- Hospital administrator
- Human resource manager, analyst, generalist
- Paralegal
- Portfolio manager
- Pharmacist
- Physician
- Police officer
- Policy analyst
- Real estate agent
- Risk manager
- Social worker

Whatever your profession, ESSENTIAL LEGAL KNOWLEDGE AND WRITING SKILLS: FOUNDATIONS OF LAW FOR EVERY PROFESSION will give you an edge in the classroom and the workplace. The material presented, the granular, step-by-step guidance, and the exercises included in each chapter provide the education you need on your road to legal literacy. The text also incorporates student feedback and lessons learned in the authors' combined thirty years of experience teaching legal masters students. We use this experience to provide a straightforward, valuable, and, dare we say, enjoyable learning experience.

Finally, this degree holds several different titles: master of jurisprudence, juris master, master of legal studies, master of science in law, and likely others. Throughout this text we use the term master of legal studies, but we are referring to all these degrees. Regardless of the degree you are seeking and the specific focus of your program, the foundation and knowledge that you need to succeed are the same. This textbook provides you with that knowledge and foundation, and our hope is that it also provides inspiration as you focus on the law.

PART I

INTRODUCTION TO THE LAW

CHAPTER ONE

The Law

> *The end of law is not to abolish or restrain, but to preserve and enlarge freedom.*
>
> —John Locke[1]

Do you agree with John Locke? As you contemplate that question, let's think about the law itself. Where does the law come from? How does the law affect society? What role does the law play in our civil discourse? We explore these ideas below.

§1.1 Law and Society

The law is an important aspect of life for every person who lives in a community. It sets forth the guidelines and rules for living together harmoniously. As society has become more complex, our rules and regulations have followed suit, requiring familiarity and, increasingly, critical inquiry. Perhaps the need for legal knowledge is not obvious in all situations. We would caution readers, however, to remember the adage that ignorance of the law is not a defense. We are bound, therefore, to know the law and follow the law.

The complexity of society, though, takes us even one step further. In almost every occupation, the law shows itself. We cannot be ignorant of the rules and regulations that pertain to our jobs. It is, therefore, not only from interest that we study the law, but we are also compelled to do so.

§1.2 Where Do Our Laws Come From?

Rules governing human behavior date back to ancient times. As far back as 3000 B.C.E., the Egyptians had a centralized court system with judges to administer justice.[2] There are many concepts from centuries ago that provide the very foundation of our system of government today. For example, Cicero, the Roman philosopher and lawyer, delineated three parts of the law: legislative, administrative, and judi-

1. John Locke, Two treatises of government (1821), 234.
2. V. Calvi & S. Coleman, American Law and Legal Systems (2008, 6th ed.), 20.

cial.[3] When the Framers signed our Constitution in 1787, these concepts were not new. For example, the Framers looked to the system of checks and balances in the constitution of the Iroquois Confederacy in drafting the US Constitution. The contribution of the Iroquois was recognized in a 1988 Congressional joint resolution noting that George Washington and Benjamin Franklin greatly admired "the concepts of the Six Nations of the Iroquois Confederacy and that the confederation of the original Thirteen Colonies into one republic was influenced by the political system developed by the Iroquois Confederacy as were many of the democratic principles which were incorporated into the Constitution itself."[4]

These represent just a few of the many ideas that influenced the Framers of our Constitution. As our laws develop, concepts from past societies and philosophers arise in our discourse and notions of humanity. One such concept is that of natural law.

§1.3 Law and Morality

Natural law has been a topic of interest and debate since ancient times. Many believe that Aristotle supported the concept; others disagree.[5] The Stoics, Thomas Aquinas, John Locke, and many others have defined and discussed natural law.[6] For our purposes, we will use the natural law definition stated as "moral principles that are objectively valid and discoverable by reason."[7]

While a legal right, sometimes referred to as positive law, is granted to an individual by society or by a government, natural law is yours just because you are a human being. It doesn't require adoption of a law by society. In the seventeenth century, John Locke counted life, liberty, and property among natural laws and argued that no one ought to harm another in his life, health, liberty, or possessions.[8] While initially a philosophical concept, you may now see reference to natural law as a rationale for legal decisions. In fact, natural law is cited in more than 1,400 United States Supreme Court and state supreme court decisions.[9]

---

3. V. Calvi & S. Coleman, AMERICAN LAW AND LEGAL SYSTEMS (2008, 6th ed.), 20, 22.

4. https://www.govtrack.us/congress/bills/100/hconres331/text. See also Gerald Murphy, *About the Iroquois Constitution*, in MODERN HISTORY SOURCEBOOK: THE CONSTITUTION OF THE IROQUOIS CONFEDERACY, https://sourcebooks.fordham.edu/mod/iroquois.asp, drawing on the work of Arthur C. Parker, archeologist of the state museum of New York in 1915 (Arthur C. Parker, THE CONSTITUTION OF THE FIVE NATIONS, https://babel.hathitrust.org/cgi/pt?id=loc.ark:/13960/t9x06q92m&view=1up&seq=28).

5. E. Tracz, *Is Natural Law a Public Good?* 25 CARDOZO J. EQUAL RTS. & SOC. JUST. (2018), 43, 46.

6. G. Duke, *Aristotle and Natural Law*, 82 THE REVIEW OF POLITICS 1 (2020), 1–23, https://doi.org/10.1017/S0034670519000743.

7. P. Soper, *Some Natural Confusions About Natural Law*, 90 MICH. L. REV. (1992), 2393, 2394.

8. S. Heyman, *The First Duty of Government: Protection, Liberty, and the Fourteenth Amendment*, 41 DUKE L. J. (1991), 507, 514–15.

9. John Makdisi, *A Thomistic Perspective on Natural Law Reasoning in the Supreme Courts*, 45 OHIO N. U. L. REV. (2019), 301, 302.

This concept of natural law is also found in the Preamble of the Declaration of Independence: "We hold these truths to be self-evident, that all men are created equal, that they are endowed by their Creator certain unalienable Rights, that among these are Life, Liberty, and the pursuit of Happiness."

Many issues in studying the law are grounded in natural law. One of the hot political topics today is the idea of universal health care. Is health care a natural right? Does a person have a right to health care in the United States? Should it be considered an inalienable right? If not a right, is it a benefit we wish to provide to all citizens? What about non-citizens?

Does a person have a right to die or take his or her own life? Does a person have a right to assist a loved one who is about to die or who is suffering greatly? Are these the kinds of rights our government was set up to protect? Are they benefits or prohibitions? These are the interesting, but difficult, questions we, as a society, must consider and debate.

§1.4 Civic Mindedness and Civil Discourse

"Our American values are not luxuries, but necessities—not the salt in our bread but the bread itself. Our common vision of a free and just society is our greatest source of cohesion."[10] Historically, we know that the inalienable rights promised in our Constitution did not extend to all. For example, the rights of women were considered but expressly rejected by the Constitutional Congress. The issue of coverture was adopted from the English system. Coverture meant that any property owned by a woman was transferred to her husband upon marriage and that she was legally his chattel or possession; the woman lost her legal identity.[11] This concept was not set aside in the new Constitution, despite the fact that Abigail Adams expressly wrote to her husband, John, at the time of the Constitutional Congress regarding the issue of coverture:

> In the new Code of Laws which I suppose it will be necessary for you to make I desire you would Remember the Ladies, and be more generous and favorable to them than your ancestors. Do not put such unlimited power into the hands of the Husbands.[12]

---

10. President Jimmy Carter's farewell address, January 14, 1981, https://www.jimmycarterlibrary.gov/the-carters/selected-speeches/president-jimmy-carters-farewell-address.

11. *Barber v. Barber*, 62 U.S. 582 (1858), quoting Coke and Blackstone.

12. Letter from Abigail Adams to John Adams dated March 31, 1776, in Adams family correspondence, volume 1, http://www.masshist.org/publications/adams-papers/view?id=AFC01d244. John is reputed to have replied: "I cannot but laugh." http://staging.nyhistory.org/sites/default/files/newfiles/cwh-curriculum/Module%201/Resources/Resource%201%20Couverture.pdf?_ga=2.229562655.265847452.1591739158-1326616086.1591739158.

So, in learning about the law, it is important to be mindful of the past as we look to a brighter future. In doing so, analyzing and discussing societal values is an important aspect of studying the law. As Michael J. Sandel tells us in his thought-provoking book, JUSTICE: WHAT'S THE RIGHT THING TO DO?, mutual respect is supported by our willingness to engage in civil discourse:

> A more robust public engagement with our moral disagreements could provide a stronger, not a weaker, basis for mutual respect.... There is no guarantee that public deliberation about hard moral questions will lead in any given situation to agreement—or even to appreciation for the moral and religious views of others.... But we cannot know until we try. A politics of moral engagement is not only a more inspiring ideal than a politics of avoidance. It is also a more promising basis for a just society.[13]

Pause for Reflection Discourse in a **pluralistic society** . . .

- What are the advantages of a pluralistic society?
- What are the challenges of a pluralistic society?
- Why do Democrats and Republicans in Congress often find it difficult to compromise?
- Why do people sometimes find it difficult to really hear a divergent point of view?
- What skills are necessary to have a true exchange of ideas?

As you continue through this book, reflect on some of the ideas presented in this chapter. Do our laws "preserve and enlarge [our] freedom" as John Locke had hoped? How does our government succeed or fail in consensus-building? Where does morality fit into the laws of a just society? Consider your own civic mindedness. In what ways might it compel you to become more involved in your community?

This text offers opportunities for critical inquiry and civil discourse to foster a sense of civic mindedness. Civic mindedness is "a person's inclination or disposition to be knowledgeable of and involved in the community, and to have a commitment to act upon a sense of responsibility as a member of that community."[14] In particular, we focus on the following skills as delineated by Steinberg, Hatcher, and Bringle:

- Communication and Listening: ability to communicate (written and oral) with others, as well as listen to divergent points of view.

13. M. Sandel, *Justice, What's the Right Thing to Do* (2009), 268–69.

14. H. A. Weiss, T. Hahn, & K. Norris, CIVIC-MINDED GRADUATE 2.0: ASSESSMENT TOOLBOX (2017); Kathryn S. Steinberg, Julie A. Hatcher, & Robert G. Bringle, *Civic-Minded Graduate: A North Star*, MICHIGAN JOURNAL OF COMMUNITY SERVICE LEARNING (2011), 19–33.

- Diversity: understanding the importance of, and the ability to work with, others from diverse backgrounds; also appreciation of and sensitivity to diversity in a pluralistic society.
- Consensus-Building: ability to work with others, including those with diverse opinions, and work across differences to come to an agreement or solve a problem. [15]

Pause for Reflection Let's consider an application. Suppose you are with a group of individuals who want to have a meal at a restaurant. One group wants to try a new restaurant that features international fusion cuisine; another group prefers a restaurant chain where the menu is predictable and familiar. How do you decide? You might consider taking a vote with majority rule, or you may list all the pros and cons of each and then decide. You might let each side lobby for their choice. You may opt to break off into two groups. Would you feel differently if you knew that one individual has a severe allergic reaction to certain spices? While this is a trivial example, now imagine you are a city council member determining whether to allow a confined animal feeding operation (CAFO) in your community. CAFOs are factory farms in which large numbers of animals are confined for extended periods of time. It will supply jobs but may affect property values or even the health of local residents. Or you are a state legislator determining budget priorities—do you build the new sports arena or allocate funds for new infrastructure to supply potable water to an impoverished area?

Finally, when studying the law, it is important to ask yourself where does the authority come from? If a law is morally wrong or impinges on a natural right, one may feel justified or even compelled toward civil discourse about the appropriateness of the law and its moral underpinnings. So, throughout this book and throughout your studies, consider asking yourself: Where does the authority behind the law come from? Is it just? How does the law affect society? How does it impact individuals that have been historically marginalized?

§1.5 Constitutional Authority

In considering where the authority behind the law comes from, we turn our attention to our Constitution. The United States Constitution is the supreme law of the land. In setting up our government with the Constitution as the pinnacle, rather than a person at the helm, the Framers followed the principle that the rule of law is better than the rule of any individual. We are a government of laws, not of men. Unlike countries where the king is law, Thomas Paine told us in COMMON SENSE: "In America law is King."[16]

---

15. Steinberg et al., *Civic-Minded Graduate*, 22.

16. J. Bessler, *The Rule of Law: A Necessary Pillar of Free and Democratic Societies for Protecting Human Rights*, 61 SANTA CLARA L. REV. (2021), 467, 500.

Our country was established to provide power to the people. Escaping from tyranny, the Framers created a governmental structure intended to protect against power becoming too centralized. You will recall from your high school or college studies the separation of powers doctrine, the basis of this concept. The government was separated into three branches, and each plays an important part in the law of the United States.

We note that the first three articles of the Constitution set forth the three branches of government:

Article I	The Legislative Branch
Article II	The Executive Branch
Article III	The Judicial Branch
Article IV	is devoted to the states.

We next turn to Chapter Two and examine how these three branches of government are structured and how they function. We address each branch of government in constitutional order beginning with Article I and the legislative branch.

EXERCISES

1. Take some time to ponder and write down your why for selecting this course of study.
2. Scan the list of professionals that might benefit from legal studies. Can you think of others? As you continue your studies, reflect on additional directions that you might explore with your new knowledge.
3. Consider a conversation that you have had recently with someone with whom you disagreed. Perhaps you argued aggressively for your point of view. Did you hear the other person's perspective? Why or why not? Can you think of ways the conversation could have gone differently? Are these skills you would like to hone?

CHAPTER TWO

Government Structure and Function

§2.1 The Legislative Branch

Article I: "All legislative Powers herein granted shall be vested in a Congress of the United States, which shall consist of a Senate and House of Representatives."[1]

The Constitution is the foundational document for our government structure, describing the functions of the legislative, executive, and judicial branches that will be discussed in this chapter. We will start with the legislative branch. In 1776, John Adams said:

> As good government is an empire of laws, how shall your laws be made? In a large society, inhabiting an extensive country, it is impossible that the whole should assemble to make laws. The first necessary step, then, is to depute power from the many to a few of the most wise and good.[2]

John Adams also recognized, however, that even "the most wise and good" will make mistakes at times and a system of checks and balances is needed for accountability.

> A single assembly is liable to all the vices, follies, and frailties of an individual; subject to fits of humor, starts of passion, flights of enthusiasm, partialities, or prejudice, and consequently productive of hasty results and absurd judgments. And all these errors ought to be corrected and defects supplied by some controlling power.[3]

There is a complex interplay among the judicial, legislative, and executive branches in our system of checks and balances. Consider the workings of an aviation team—a pilot, a copilot, and the control tower. Each must perform a unique role while paying attention to the advice of the other two in order for the flight to be successful. A copilot hesitant to point out a pilot's error is not fulfilling the job requirements. The pilot and copilot must respond appropriately to the directions of

1. US Constitution (1787, 1992), https://www.archives.gov/founding-docs/constitution.
2. https://billofrightsinstitute.org/founding-documents/founders-quotes/.
3. John Adams, THOUGHTS ON GOVERNMENT, April 1776," *Founders Online*, National Archives, https://founders.archives.gov/documents/Adams/06-04-02-0026-0004. [Original source: *The Adams Papers*, Papers of John Adams, vol. 4, *February–August 1776*, ed. Robert J. Taylor. Cambridge, MA: Harvard University Press, 1979, pp. 86–93.]

the control tower. The pilot must lead and set the course. Successful teamwork requires cooperation, clear roles, and a balance of authority. Similarly in government, each branch must have clearly delineated roles to avoid conflict and duplication. Partisan politics can make this necessary teamwork a challenge.

§ 2.1.1 How Laws Are Made

Before we dive into a study of the law, we need to reflect on how laws are made and who is entrusted with that responsibility. The answer is actually more complex than you might think. At the federal level, the United States Congress enacts statutes, subject to approval by the president, under the Constitutional authority of the necessary and proper clause in Article I quoted in § 2.1.2. Statutes may be clarified and implemented through regulations by a relevant executive agency and/or interpreted by judges through case law (see Chapter Three).

Pause for Reflection To begin to appreciate the complex task of drafting the laws that govern a nation, consider this simple scenario. A large municipal park is the pride of Smalltown, USA, a midwestern college town. Dogwood Park contains hiking and biking trails, a pond and a playground. The mayor's office, the parks and recreation department, the onsite park ranger, the police, and the local newspaper all receive complaints about all-terrain vehicles (ATVs) and motorbikes on the trails that pose safety hazards to walkers and cyclists. Draft a rule to address the problem.[4]

How did you do? Perhaps you went with something like "No ATVs or motorbikes in the park." This would mean that a resident cannot ride her motorbike into the park and park it in the parking lot. Perhaps "No ATVs and motorbikes on the trails." Better, but now the mayor's office receives calls about students on motorized scooters cutting through the park to get to class. The rule is broadened to "No motorized vehicles on the trails." Disability rights advocates point out that this excludes motorized wheelchairs and scooters. It can be difficult to address the needs of each relevant stakeholder even with a matter as simple as a park rule. How then does the US Congress enact laws that consider and address the needs of all?

§ 2.1.2 Congress: Structure and Roles

Under Article I, Section 8 of the Constitution, Congress has the power "to make all Laws which shall be necessary and proper for carrying into Execution the foregoing Powers, and all other Powers vested by this Constitution in the Government of the United States, or any Department or Officer thereof."[5] This is often called the Necessary and Proper Clause.

---

4. Based on a hypothetical posed by H. L. A. Hart, *Positivism and the Separation of Law and Morals*, 71 HARVARD LAW REVIEW 4 (1958), 593–629.

5. US Constitution (1787, 1992), https://www.archives.gov/founding-docs/constitution.

Congress, as we know, is bicameral, meaning it has two bodies or chambers—the Senate and the House of Representatives. Each has a distinct set of powers and responsibilities. The two portions of Congress were set up set up differently to represent represent the people of their states.

a. The Senate

The Senate is comprised of one hundred members, two from each state. The term of a senator is six years, and approximately one-third of the Senate is up for reelection every two years. Interestingly, the process of electing senators began in 1913 with the ratification of the Seventeenth Amendment; prior to that they were appointed by each state. Governors continue to appoint senators in cases of a vacancy prior to an election cycle. To be eligible to serve in the Senate, an individual must be at least thirty years old, have been a citizen for at least nine years, and inhabit the state they represent.

The equal number of senators from each state ensures that each state has equal representation, regardless of size. The vice president presides over the Senate. Some legislative matters are unique to the Senate; these include ratifying treaties and confirming Supreme Court justices, federal judges, cabinet members, ambassadors, and other federal executive officials. In addition, the Senate conducts trials for individuals impeached by the House of Representatives.

b. The House of Representatives

In contrast, the House of Representatives is established according to the population of a state as determined by census; the more populous states have more representatives. There are 435 voting members. In addition, six US territories have nonvoting participation rights; these include Puerto Rico, Guam, the US Virgin Islands, American Samoa, the Northern Mariana Islands, and the District of Columbia. These nonvoting members may participate and vote in committees, and introduce legislation. A congressional term is two years. In order to be eligible to serve in the House, an individual must be at least twenty-five years old, have been a citizen for at least seven years, and inhabit the Congressional district they represent.

One of the unique features built into our system is that under the Constitution, the House of Representatives must introduce all revenue and appropriations bills. The Senate may reject or amend them.

c. Federal and State Legislative Roles: Introduction

While Article I clearly vests legislative powers in the United States Congress, we know that state legislatures also have legislative powers. Article I, Section 8 grants specific enumerated powers to the federal government, including the right to coin money, regulate commerce, raise and maintain armed forces, declare war, and establish a post office; all other powers are to be reserved to the states. The federal government's role has expanded over the years, initially through cases involving interstate and foreign commerce that required interpretation of the commerce clause. In general, if a federal law conflicts with a state law, under the supremacy clause of the Constitution, the federal law rules. The appropriate balance of power between the federal government and the states was debated during the Constitutional Congress and remains a hot topic today. The trend has been to centralize matters that pertain to all Americans at the federal level (such as care for the environment and discrimination law) while allowing states to determine their own laws, regulations, and practices on other matters based on regional variations in needs, resources, and values (for example, setting state speed limits). Over the years, there have been trends toward and away from centralization of power reflective of political and philosophical differences, power struggles, case law, and budgetary considerations, making this a dynamic area for study. Consider, for example, Professor Clark's comments on **federalism** in an analysis of Medicaid, a joint federal/state initiative.

> Medicaid is a central focus of the enduring debate about federal health policy. It is also a persistent target of federalism-based accusations that the federal government is infringing on states' sovereignty in the area of health care. These accusations have been used to advance proposals to reduce Medicaid funding, roll back entitlements, and shift greater responsibility to the states—all in the name of protecting state power and increasing state flexibility. Such proposals have existed since Medicaid's creation, but the 2016 elections have reinvigorated calls for Medicaid retrenchment as part of the plan to repeal and replace the Affordable Care Act.[6]

We will return to the topic of balance of power and federalism in our consideration of the role of state governments in § 2.4.

§ 2.1.3 Publication of Statutes

In both the Senate and the House, once a proposed piece of legislation is introduced, it is assigned to a committee for further research, debate, and development. In the 115th Congress (2017–2018), the House of Representatives had 20 standing committees, 97 subcommittees, and 1 select committee. The Senate had 16 standing committees, 68 subcommittees, and 4 select committees. There were also four joint committees.[7] It is up to the committee chair to bring the proposed legislation to the floor for a vote (or not). In order to become law, both the House and Senate must

---

6. B. Clark, *Medicaid Access & State Flexibility: Negotiating Federalism*, 17 Hous. J. Health L. & Pol'y (2017), 241. See also J. Davis Mortenson & N. Bagley, *Delegation at the Founding*, 121 Columbia Law Review (2021), 277–368, https://columbialawreview.org/wp-content/uploads/2021/03/Mortenson-Bagley-Delegation_at_the_Founding.pdf.

7. *Committee Types and Roles*, Congressional Research Service, https://crsreports.congress.gov/product/pdf/RS/98-241/20.

approve a proposed piece of legislation, and it must be signed by the president. If the president vetoes a law, a two-thirds majority vote of the House and Senate is required to overturn the veto.

Before enactment, proposed legislation is known as a bill or resolution; once signed into law by the president, it is an act. You will see reference to HB 131 for House Bill 131 that originated in the House or S 252 to designate Senate Bill 252 originating in the Senate. These may be the same law, but are identified differently and located in different places, which can be confusing, posing a challenge to legal researchers.

a. Session Laws

Session laws are a collection of all the statutes enacted by a legislature in a single session. These are often difficult to research as they are organized in sequence in the order that they were enacted in Congress, rather than by subject. For example, the Americans with Disabilities Act (ADA), S 933, became Public Law 101-336. This refers to the 101st session of Congress and the 336th matter adopted.

b. Codified Statutes

Codified law refers to the same statutes that have subsequently been organized and published by topic, including the official code and annotated codes.

c. The Official Code

The Official Code contains the statutes as adopted and nothing more, and is the form that is required in court proceedings. The ADA is identified as 42 U.S.C. ch. 126 Section 12101 et seq. Here the ADA appears in context, in Section 42 of the US Code that addresses Public Health and Welfare.

d. The Annotated Codes

Annotated codes, in contrast, have accompanying material such as historical references, related case notes, regulation cross references, and secondary authority references (such as legal treatises and law review articles) to supplement interpretation of the statutes. These supplemental materials directing readers to other sources are written by staff attorneys employed by the publisher (such as LexisNexis and Westlaw) and are often very helpful but not official sources. The original intents and purposes section of the ADA, for example, as annotated on Thomson Reuters Westlaw Edge under 42 U.S.C.A. Section 12101, contains context and analysis references to 225 law review commentaries, 281 ALR Library references, 388 encyclopedia sources, 109 forms, and 673 treatises and practice aids. Additionally, Westlaw points to 102,957 citing references. These references are to the intents and purpose section alone, which is itself only three pages long. Chapter Four, which covers statutory analysis, will help you better understand how to read and interpret these multiple sources.

§ 2.1.4 Legislative, Judicial, and Executive Branches—Checks and Balances

Our Constitutional system of checks and balances involves a sometimes nuanced separation of powers between the judicial, legislative, and executive branches. Congressional action is subject to review by the courts, as established in a landmark Supreme Court case, *Marbury v. Madison* (1803).[8] In that case, Chief Justice Marshall stated:

> Should Congress, in the execution of its powers, adopt measures which are prohibited by the Constitution, or should Congress, under the pretext of executing its powers, pass laws for the accomplishment of objects not intrusted [*sic*] to the Government, it would become the painful duty of this tribunal, should a case requiring such a decision come before it, to say that such an act was not the law of the land.

In addition, while Congress is the primary legislative body, much of the detail of laws is "fleshed out" in regulations overseen by the executive branch. We turn to an examination of this branch in § 2.2.

Pause for Reflection Let's return to Smalltown and the motorized vehicle problem. (§ 2.1.1 Pause for Reflection). In drafting a rule, someone must consider the needs of each of the stakeholders and decide the best implementation strategies. Who will write the rule? Is the department in charge of the space involved in tailoring the rule? What should the penalties be? Consider, for example, a fine and/or removal from the park. Who enforces it? Is there an avenue for appeal? How is the rule conveyed to park users? Is there a sign? If so, how large, how many, and where? What language(s) should the sign(s) be in? What is the cost of this initiative? We begin to broaden the picture beyond the linguistic difficulties of drafting a law to the pragmatic considerations of budgets, interpretation, enforcement, and checks and balances.

In Smalltown, municipal codes are typically drafted by the city council; the mayor has a nonvoting seat on the council but can break ties. Codes are broadly written, and the department in the relevant area (in this case, parks and recreation) decides on the interpretation of the code for their area. The park ranger enforces the rule, overseen by the park commissioner. If a resident wishes to appeal the fine, the mayor considers the appeal. As we move forward to sections that address the remaining branches of government, consider how each of the players outlined above (city council, mayor, parks and recreation department, park ranger, park commissioner) might correspond to members of the legislative, executive, and judicial branches.

---

8. *Marbury v. Madison*, 5 U.S. 137 (1803), https://www.oyez.org/cases/1789-1850/5us137.

EXERCISES

1. Describe the differences and similarities between the roles of the Senate and the House of Representatives.
2. What steps does a bill go through before becoming law?
3. What is the difference between session laws and codified statutes? What are the research implications?
4. Who is responsible for writing the annotations in the U.S.C.A.? Are they official sources?
5. List four overarching considerations in drafting legislation.

§2.2 The Executive Branch

Article II: "The executive Power shall be vested in a President of the United States of America."[9]

The executive branch is comprised of the president, vice president, cabinet members, and administrative agencies. Its primary roles are implementation and enforcement of the law. However, the role of the executive branch in creating and interpreting the law has changed significantly over the years and been the subject of debate and litigation.[10] As the quotes below illustrate, one particularly dynamic and controversial area is the degree of rulemaking and adjudication conducted by regulatory agencies.

> At present, the vast and bloated executive branch—existing through its alphabet soup of agencies such as the EPA, IRS, DOE, ATF, and the like—intrudes into virtually every aspect of American life. It regulates your workplace, your home, your car, and your kids' school. It's staffed by legions of bureaucrats who enjoy job security that private-sector employees can only dream of, and it's granted legal authority by the Supreme Court to interpret its own governing statutes and expand the scope of its own authority. In its own spheres of influence, it often acts as legislator, prosecutor, and judge. —David French, NATIONAL REVIEW, February 24, 2017[11]

> The regulatory state is deeply misunderstood. No one denies the importance of federal agencies in formulating the rules that shape the modern economy and civil society. But the regulatory state is not, as its critics maintain, an illegitimate "Fourth Branch" of government, operating on its own. It is, instead,

---

9. US Constitution (1787, 1992), https://www.archives.gov/founding-docs/constitution.

10. F. Easterbrook, *Presidential Lawmaking Powers*, WASHINGTON UNIVERSITY LAW QUARTERLY 68 (1990), 533–60, https://chicagounbound.uchicago.edu/cgi/viewcontent.cgi?article=1476&context=journal_articles.

11. As quoted in https://ballotpedia.org/Quotes_about_the_administrative_state.

a vital function of government, which is part of the executive branch (though not within the White House), and is subject to numerous constitutional checks and balances. —Paul Verkuil, REALCLEARPOLICY, October 25, 2016[12]

§2.2.1 Executive Branch Leaders

a. President

The president oversees the executive branch including cabinet level departments as well as over fifty commissions and regulatory agencies.

Bills adopted by Congress are presented to the president for signature. If the president vetoes a particular bill, a two-thirds majority vote of Congress is required to override the veto. The president may enter into treaties; these must be ratified by a two-thirds vote of Congress.

The president may also issue executive orders. Executive orders have been issued on a wide array of topics ranging from labor rights to national security and foreign relations. The use of executive orders has varied widely across presidents and periods of history. The record for most executive orders while in office is 3,721, by Franklin D. Roosevelt; in recent years, the number has varied from 166 issued by George Bush to 381 by Ronald Reagan.[13]

As an example, in 2020 President Trump signed an executive order entitled Executive Order on Safe Policing for Safe Communities[14] outlining his recommendations regarding credentialing and certification, information sharing, and policies to address mental health, homelessness, and addiction issues. The executive order suggests a coordinated effort to prioritize resources to implement community support models, to be carried out by the secretary of health and human services in consultation with the attorney general and the director of the Office of Management and Budget. The executive order also directs the attorney general to craft legislative recommendations to be submitted to Congress regarding enhanced law enforcement practices and building community engagement. We see how the order coordinates various departments and agencies within the executive branch and envisions recommendations for review by the legislative branch.

An executive order may be rescinded by a subsequent administration or overturned judicially if found to be unconstitutional. In 2018, the Supreme Court upheld an executive order by President Trump, overturning the lower court that had found the order to be unconstitutional.[15]

---

12. As quoted in https://ballotpedia.org/Quotes_about_the_administrative_state.

13. The American Presidency Project, UC Santa Barbara, https://www.presidency.ucsb.edu/statistics/data/executive-orders.

14. Safe Policing for Safe Communities, https://www.federalregister.gov/documents/2020/06/19/2020-13449/safe-policing-for-safe-communities.

15. *Trump v. Hawaii*, 138 S. Ct. 2392 (2018), https://www.oyez.org/cases/2017/17-965 (order regarding travel bans from certain countries).

Article II expressly appoints the president as the commander in chief of the armed services. The president also nominates ambassadors and Supreme Court justices, with the "advice and consent" of the Senate.

b. Vice President

The vice president presides over the Senate; however, the vice president has no vote on pending legislation unless there is a tie. Presiding over joint sessions of Congress is another duty of the vice president. The vice president may perform additional executive functions at the request of the president.

c. Cabinet

The president appoints and oversees the heads of the fifteen executive departments. These individuals are members of the advisory board known as the cabinet. These cabinet-level departments are the:

Department of Agriculture

Department of Commerce

Department of Defense

Department of Education

Department of Energy

Department of Health and Human Services

Department of Homeland Security

Department of Housing and Urban Development

Department of the Interior

Department of Justice

Department of Labor

Department of State

Department of Transportation

Department of the Treasury

Department of Veterans Affairs

In addition to the department heads, the cabinet includes "the White House Chief of Staff, the US Ambassador to the United Nations, the Director of National Intelligence, and the US Trade Representative, as well as the heads of the Environmental Protection Agency, Office of Management and Budget, Council of Economic Advisers, Office of Science and Technology Policy, and Small Business Administration."[16] Under Article II, Section 2 of the Constitution, the cabinet members advise the president on any subject on which she requests information.

---

16. *The Cabinet*, https://www.whitehouse.gov/administration/cabinet/.

FIGURE 2.1

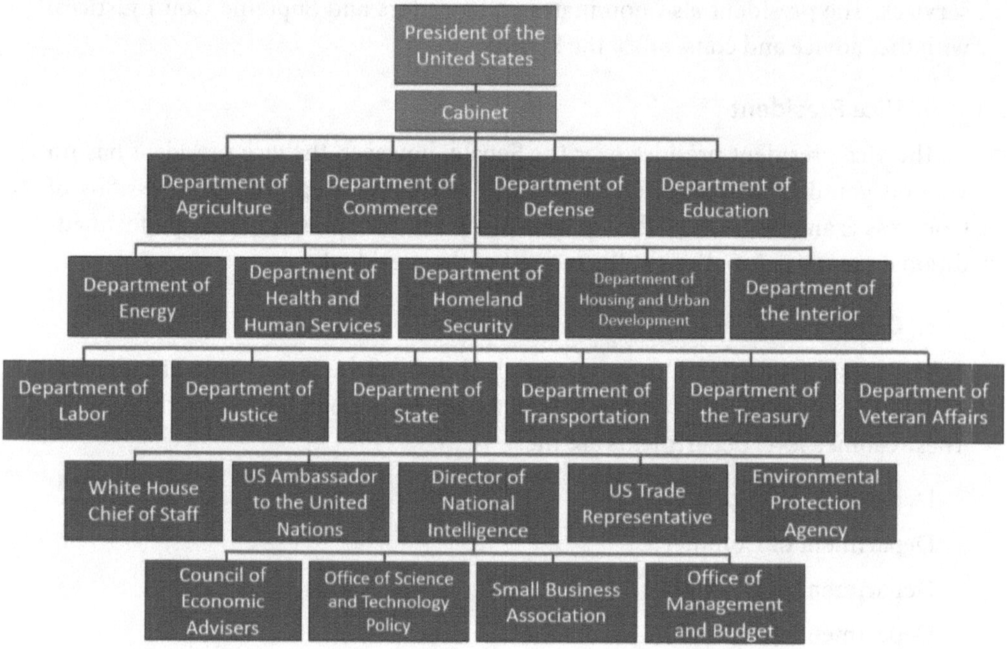

§2.2.2 Administrative Agencies

Pause for Reflection To set the stage for our introduction to administrative law, consider the following scenario.

Shanika Lytle is the compliance officer at a major medical device company that focuses on medical devices for use in surgery with an emphasis on orthopedics. John Stark is an electrical and computer engineer and a recent addition to the research and development team. Late one evening, as she is leaving the office, Shanika overhears John talking on the phone. "I have been toying with an app that could really be a moneymaker but I think we need to move on it quickly. It's not what we do around here so I think I'm good to go after it on my own. Gofundme might be the best option to get us capital, and if we market it not as a medical device but fitness related we can get around the FDA requirements that hold things up for so long around here. Let's meet for drinks; I can tell you more and you can decide if you're in." Shanika is troubled; John is an excellent engineer and has already been a contributor to several projects, but she is not sure where the line is drawn on individual development efforts. She is also concerned about his plan to "get around the FDA requirements."

a. Types of Administrative Agencies

Executive departments are headed by each of the members of the cabinet. Examples would be the Department of Labor and the Department of Education. Each department may have separate agencies that report to it, and the organization and scope may be quite complex. For example, the Department of Health and Human Services (HHS) "has 12 operating divisions, including nine agencies in the US Public Health Service and three human services agencies."[17] These include the Centers for Disease Control and Prevention (CDC), the Centers for Medicare and Medicaid Services (CMS), the Food and Drug Administration (FDA), the Health Resources and Services Administration (HRSA), and the Indian Health Service (IHS). Agency budgets are significant. "HHS proposes $144.3 billion in discretionary and $1.7 trillion in mandatory proposed budget authority for FY 2024."[18]

There are numerous additional federal agencies, including independent agencies, commissions, boards, and quasi-official agencies. Each of these plays a distinct role. Independent agencies include a wide variety of entities, including the Federal Trade Commission, the Social Security Administration, the National Labor Relations Board, and the Environmental Protection Agency. Boards, commissions, and committees may be convened for a specific (often investigative) purpose to gather and report information regarding a particular topic. They may include investigative hearings to assist in the research process. Federal executive boards are composed of local senior-level federal agency officials and are charged with strengthening management and administration of federal agencies located outside of Washington, DC. They are overseen by the director of the Office of Personnel Management who reports directly to the president. It may surprise you to know that 85 percent of federal employees work outside of Washington.[19]

b. Administrative Agency Rulemaking

Executive departments and agencies implement the laws enacted by Congress in their respective areas. Agencies issue regulations to provide clarification and specificity to statutes and may hold hearings in quasi-judicial proceedings. The regulation and enforcement power of administrative agencies may be quite extensive; consider, for example, enforcement actions taken by the Internal Revenue Service or regulations issued by the Food and Drug Administration. An interesting question is the extent to which Congress or the president can control or shape the actions of administrative agencies.

The Congressional Research Service, which advises Congress on these matters, stated in 2018:

> In general, an agency has only that authority which has been delegated to it by Congress. Thus, Congress can control a federal agency by detailing its jurisdiction and authority, setting policy goals for the agency to accomplish in the exercise of that authority, and choosing whether it may regulate the

---

17. https://www.hhs.gov/about/agencies/hhs-agencies-and-offices/index.html.
18. https://www.hhs.gov/about/budget/fy2024/index.html.
19. *Frequently Asked Questions*, Office of Personnel Management, https://www.feb.gov/faqs/.

public.[20] Similarly, Congress may choose to grant an agency the authority to issue legislative rules, enforce violations of law, or to adjudicate claims made to the agency.[21] The more precise a delegation, the less discretion is afforded to the agency in its execution of its delegated authority.[22,23]

Let's begin by examining how agencies make law and how that authority was transferred to them by Congress through the Administrative Procedures Act (APA). Some administrative agencies also have a judicial function through specialized administrative courts. The APA also defines the scope of judicial review of administrative actions; we will explore the structure and function of the court system in § 2.3.

i. Authority: Administrative Procedures Act

The Administrative Procedures Act was enacted in 1946 to establish how administrative agencies operate.[24] Its four basic purposes are to inform the public about procedures and proposed rules, to allow for public comment on those rules, to ensure standardized procedures for rulemaking and administrative proceedings, and to establish a standard for judicial review of administrative determinations.[25] Under this delegation of authority by Congress through the APA, administrative agencies have a quasi-lawmaking role through the enactment of rules, both formal and informal.

ii. Formal Rulemaking

Formal rulemaking requires a hearing, may include witnesses, and is subject to certain rules and procedures.[26] The hearing is presided over by an administrative law judge (ALJ) or a panel of ALJs. This is a seldom-used provision of the APA. Consider the following: "Although the APA provides for formal rulemaking, the Supreme Court largely put an end to it forty years ago in *United States v. Florida East Coast*

---

20. See J. R. Deshazo & J. Freeman, *The Congressional Competition to Control Delegated Power*, 81 Tex. L. Rev. (2003), 1443, 1456, https://papers.ssrn.com/sol3/papers.cfm?abstract_id=324482.

21. See, for example, 12 U.S.C. § 5512(a) (granting the Consumer Financial Protection Bureau the authority to "administer, enforce, and otherwise implement" delegated authority); 42 U.S.C. § 405(b)(1) (granting the Commissioner of the Social Security Administration the authority to "make findings of fact, and decisions as to the rights of any individual applying for a [benefits] payment").

22. See J. M. Beermann, *Congressional Administration*, 43 San Diego Law Review (2006), 61, 77–78 ("A key formal method Congress employs to control executive discretion is to nip discretion in the bud by legislating with precision.").

23. *Congress's Authority to Influence and Control Executive Branch Agencies*, The Congressional Research Service (December 19, 2018), R45442, https://fas.org/sgp/crs/misc/R45442.pdf.

24. Administrative practice: general provisions, 5 U.S.C. ch. 5, subch. I § 500 et seq.

25. *Attorney General's Manual on the Administrative Procedure Act, US Department of Justice (1947), Florida State University College of Law. Archived from* the original *on September 4, 2006*, https://web.archive.org/web/20060915202809/http://www.law.fsu.edu/library/admin/1947i.html.

26. This text presents a simplified version of agency rulemaking.

Railway Co."[27] Professor Nielson asserts that the practice of formal rulemaking has largely "been forgotten." He notes that:

The American Bar Association's Section on Administrative Law and Regulatory Practice, for instance, has recently declared that it has "not identified a single scholarly article written in the past thirty years that expresses regret about the retreat from formal rulemaking."[28]

iii. Informal Rulemaking

Most agencies use informal rulemaking in creating regulations. These often begin with an act of Congress, requesting an agency to create regulations on a particular subject.[29] In informal rulemaking, proposed rules are published and subject to public scrutiny in a process known as notice and comment. The Federal Register Act (FRA), adopted in 1935, outlines the process of enacting federal regulations. In procedures adopted under the FRA, proposed administrative rules are published in the Federal Register[30] along with supporting data. This is termed a Notice of Proposed Rulemaking and requires a period for public comment. This enables the public and industry representatives likely to be affected by the rule the opportunity to review, reflect, and respond to the proposed rule. Notice and comment is intended to enrich the process, provide a voice to the public, and help administrative officials become aware of unintended consequences of a particular rule. The period for comment varies; typically 30 to 60 days, it can be as long as 180 days for a particularly complex rule.

For example, a rule issued by the Office of Civil Rights, Department of Health and Human Services (HHS) in 2016 under the administration of President Obama extended the protections of the Patient Protection and Affordable Care Act (ACA) to transgender individuals.[31] This was overturned in 2020 by a new rule issued by HHS[32] under the Trump administration that explicitly removes those protections.

---

27. A. Nielson, *In Defense of Formal Rulemaking*, 75 Ohio State L. Rev. 2 (2014), 237–92, 239, https://papers.ssrn.com/sol3/papers.cfm?abstract_id=2322062, citing *United States v. Fla. E. Coast Ry. Co.*, 410 U.S. 224, 237–38 (1973).

28. A. Nielson, *In Defense of Formal Rulemaking*, 75 Ohio State L. Rev. 2 (2014), 237–92, 240, https://papers.ssrn.com/sol3/papers.cfm?abstract_id=2322062, citing *Am. Bar Ass'n, Section of Admin. Law & Regulatory Practice* (October 24, 2011). Comments on H.R. 3010, The Regulatory Accountability Act of 2011, at 21, https://administrativelawreview.org/wp-content/uploads/sites/2/2014/04/American-Bar-Association-Section-of-Administrative-Law-and-Regulatory-Practice.pdf.

29. See, generally, M. P. Carey, *The Federal Rulemaking Process: An Overview*, The Congressional Research Service (June 17, 2013), https://fas.org/sgp/crs/misc/RL32240.pdf.

30. Federal Register and Code of Federal Regulations, 44 U.S.C. Chapter 15, https://www.archives.gov/federal-register/laws/federal-register.

31. Nondiscrimination in Health Programs and Activities, 81 FR 31375, 45 CFR 92 implementing Section 1557 of the ACA, https://www.federalregister.gov/documents/2016/05/18/2016-11458/nondiscrimination-in-health-programs-and-activities.

32. Nondiscrimination in Health Programs and Health Education Programs of Activities, Delegation of Authority, https://www.federalregister.gov/documents/2020/06/19/2020-11758/nondis-

Both rules were published in the Federal Register for notice and comment prior to issuance of the final rule. More recently, the Biden administration has issued proposed rules to reinstate these Section 1557 protections to comply with a Supreme Court ruling, and they have been published in the Federal Register (see § 2.3.1 for additional discussion of the *Bostock* case).[33]

Once public commentary has been received, the rule is finalized. The final rule as amended is published in the Federal Register. The Federal Register is published daily. A useful source of information for legal researchers are source notes, including the preamble that is found before the actual rule. It contains information about the problem addressed by the rule, its basis and purpose, the legal authority used to issue the rule, how the Code of Federal Regulations (CFR) will be changed to reflect the rule, and a summary of comments received during the notice and comment period.

After the final rule as amended is published, necessary changes are then made to the CFR. The CFR contains the rules of the federal agencies, divided into fifty titles, generally by subject matter, often linked to the issuing agency, and further subdivided into chapters.

Let's look at an example of the interplay between the roles of Congress, executive agencies, and the Department of Justice in enacting and interpreting law. In November 2019, William Beaumont Hospital in Royal Oak, Michigan, entered into a **settlement agreement** with the Department of Justice, US Attorney's Office regarding the services provided to deaf patients who use American sign language as their primary form of communication.[34] The case stemmed from allegations that William Beaumont Hospital failed to make available qualified sign language interpreters, inappropriately relied on the patient's family as interpreters, and relied on faulty video remote interpreting services despite connectivity issues and problems with the patient's vision and mobility that prevented seeing the screen, making communication ineffective.

The Americans with Disabilities Act of 1990 (ADA) enacted by Congress provides for communication services to deaf individuals through auxiliary aids and services. The law states:

> Sec. 12103. Additional definitions. As used in this chapter (1) Auxiliary aids and services. The term "auxiliary aids and services" includes (A) qualified in-

---

crimination-in-health-and-health-education-programs-or-activities-delegation-of-authority.

33. Nondiscrimination in Health Programs and Activities, https://www.federalregister.gov/documents/2022/08/04/2022-16217/nondiscrimination-in-health-programs-and-activities. https://www.hhs.gov/civil-rights/for-individuals/section-1557/index.html. *Bostock v. Clayton County, Altitude Express v. Zarda and Moore, Harris Funeral Homes v. EEOC*, 590 U.S. ___ (2020), https://www.oyez.org/cases/2019/17-1618.

34. Voluntary Resolution Agreement under the Americans with Disabilities Act between the United States of America and William Beaumont Hospital, DJ # 202-37-210, https://www.ada.gov/beaumont_hospital_sa.html.

> terpreters or other effective methods of making aurally delivered materials available to individuals with hearing impairments.[35]

The law was further refined through regulations published by the Justice Department in the Federal Register that expanded on this definition to include the use of video remote interpreting services.

> (f) ***Video remote interpreting (VRI) services.*** A public accommodation that chooses to provide qualified interpreters via VRI service shall ensure that it provides—
>
> > (1) Real-time, full-motion video and audio over a dedicated high-speed, wide-bandwidth video connection or wireless connection that delivers high-quality video images that do not produce lags, choppy, blurry, or grainy images, or irregular pauses in communication;
> >
> > (2) A sharply delineated image that is large enough to display the interpreter's face, arms, hands, and fingers, and the participating individual's face, arms, hands, and fingers, regardless of his or her body position;
> >
> > (3) A clear, audible transmission of voices; and
> >
> > (4) Adequate training to users of the technology and other involved individuals so that they may quickly and efficiently set up and operate the VRI.[36]

We see how the regulations describe in more detail the concept that the legislators enacted. The regulatory language was expressly quoted in the Beaumont settlement agreement.

The case was brought in 2017. When brought to the appellate court, the Eleventh Circuit reversed the trial court's **summary judgment**[37] for the defendant hospital, finding that Plaintiffs had **legal standing**[38] in this case "given ... we conclude that Plaintiffs' numerous visits to Defendants' facilities and the wealth of evidence showing repeated VRI malfunctions. Plaintiffs have Article III standing to proceed with

---

35. Americans with Disabilities Act of 1990 (ADA), 42 U.S.C. 126 Section 12103(1) (including changes made by the ADA Amendments Act of 2008 (P.L. 110-325), effective January 1, 2009), https://uscode.house.gov/view.xhtml?path=/prelim@title42/chapter126&edition=prelim.

36. Auxiliary Aids and Services, 28 C.F.R. § 36.303(f), as amended by AG Order No. 3181-2010, 75 FR 56253, Sept. 15, 2010, https://www.federalregister.gov/documents/2010/09/15/2010-21824/nondiscrimination-on-the-basis-of-disability-by-public-accommodations-and-in-commercial-facilities. AG Order 3779-2016, 81 FR 87378, Dec. 2, 2016, https://www.federalregister.gov/documents/2016/12/02/2016-28644/nondiscrimination-on-the-basis-of-disability-by-public-accommodations-movie-theaters-movie.

37. The definitions of the words that appear in bold letters throughout the text can be found in the glossary at the back of the book.

38. Legal standing means that the plaintiff has legal capacity to bring a particular suit, usually by showing that they have a stake in the outcome of the case.

their claims for injunctive relief."[39] As the case proceeded through the courts, the defendant hospitals again raised the issue of standing on the grounds that they had changed their policies and procedures regarding interpreters to remove the impediment to effective communication; on each of plaintiff's subsequent visits to the hospital she was granted an interpreter.[40] On this basis the Eleventh Circuit affirmed the defendant hospital's motion regarding standing as the case was now moot. We see the power of law to effect real change in policies and procedures that impact people's lives. Legal interpretation flows from legislation, to regulation, to the attorney general, and back and forth between the trial and appellate courts, for determination of its application to an actual fact set.

c. Administrative Agency Hearings

Disputes involving administrative law are handled in specialized courts by administrative law judges, or ALJs. **Administrative law** is the body of law that regulates government agencies.

Let's consider an example. Recall that the Centers for Medicare and Medicaid Services (CMS) is under the Department of Health and Human Services (HHS). If a Medicare Advantage Plan enrollee wants to contest a coverage determination, she can turn for guidance to the 106-page *Parts C & D Enrollee Grievances, Organization/Coverage Determinations*, an Appeals Guidance document effective January 1, 2020.[41] Then subject to a threshold for the amount in controversy, the appeal procedures may include a "plan reconsideration or redetermination (also referred to as a level 1 appeal), a reconsideration by an independent review entity (IRE), adjudication by an Administrative Law Judge (ALJ) or attorney adjudicator, review by the Medicare Appeals Council (Council), and judicial review."[42]

As suggested by the Guidance document quoted above and the Congressional Research Service referenced below, the determinations of ALJs may also be reviewable by courts under the APA.

> Agencies administer their delegated authority in a variety of ways, including by promulgating rules and regulations that bind the public, advising regulated parties of an agency's enforcement priorities via guidance documents, bringing enforcement actions against private individuals or corporations for

39. *Silva v. Baptist Health S. Fla, Inc.*, 856 F.3d 824, at 842 (11th Cir. 2017), https://casetext.com/case/silva-v-baptist-health-s-fla-inc-4.

40. *Silva v. Baptist Health S. Fla, Inc.*, No. 19-12386 (11th Cir. Dec. 3, 2020), https://casetext.com/case/silva-v-baptist-health-s-fla-inc-6.

41. *Enrollee Grievances, Organization/Coverage Determinations*, an Appeals Guidance document, https://www.cms.gov/Medicare/Appeals-and-Grievances/MMCAG/Downloads/Parts-C-and-D-Enrollee-Grievances-Organization-Coverage-Determinations-and-Appeals-Guidance.pdf.

42. Enrollee Grievances, Organization/Coverage Determinations, an Appeals Guidance document, https://www.cms.gov/Medicare/Appeals-and-Grievances/MMCAG/Downloads/Parts-C-and-D-Enrollee-Grievances-Organization-Coverage-Determinations-and-Appeals-Guidance.pdf.

violation of a statute or regulation, and determining whether to grant a benefit or license. These agency actions, in turn, often generate questions about the legitimacy of an agency's decision. Individuals affected by an agency decision can sometimes challenge that action in federal court as violating a legal requirement.[43]

Legal determination of whether an ALJ decision is appealable in court involves consideration of numerous factors, many of which are beyond the scope of this work. (These include but are not limited to the subject matter or **cause of action**, whether a particular entity has sovereign immunity, whether a threshold amount in controversy is met, when the action is brought, and jurisdictional issues.[44]) We examine some of these issues, such as jurisdiction, in our next section that addresses the judicial branch.

d. Sanctions

Administrative agencies vary in the type of sanctions (penalties) they may impose, and a full examination of this topic is beyond the scope of this work. However, it is important for students of the law to become familiar with the penalties that may be imposed by agencies that operate within their sphere of employment to assist with calculation of risk through analysis of the relevant statutes and regulations.

Pause for Reflection As an example, let's return to John Stark and his "fitness app" from §2.2.2. We are not offering an opinion on whether the app would be considered a device.[45] However, the FDA has several sanctions at its disposal in regulating medical devices, depending on the scope of the infraction and the damage inflicted on the public. John would be advised to do his homework thoroughly before proceeding to market without FDA approval. Can you identify any laws that might impact his plan? The Federal Trade Commission has created a tool, the Mobile Health App Interactive Tool, "meant to help you figure out the federal regulatory, privacy, and security laws and regulations that may apply. (Hint: More than one may apply.[46])"

---

43. J. P. Cole, *An Introduction to Judicial Review of Federal Agency Action*, Congressional Research Service (December 7, 2016), 1–25, 1, https://fas.org/sgp/crs/misc/R44699.pdf.

44. J. P. Cole, *An Introduction to Judicial Review of Federal Agency Action*, Congressional Research Service (December 7, 2016), 1–25, https://fas.org/sgp/crs/misc/R44699.pdf.

45. See FDA News release, "FDA clears mobile medical app to help those with opioid use disorder stay in recovery programs," December 10, 2018, https://www.fda.gov/news-events/press-announcements/fda-clears-mobile-medical-app-help-those-opioid-use-disorder-stay-recovery-programs; and N. Wetsman, *When It Comes to Fitness Trackers and Health Apps, the FDA Says You Figure It Out*, Popular Science (October 4, 2019), https://www.popsci.com/fda-regulations-fitness-trackers-apps/ (suggesting the FDA only plans to regulate apps it thinks are risky).

46. Federal Trade Commission, Mobile Health App Interactive Tool, https://www.ftc.gov/business-guidance/resources/mobile-health-apps-interactive-tool.

EXERCISES

1. Describe how administrative agencies engage in quasi-lawmaking functions.
2. Explain the function of the notice and comment requirement for administrative rulemaking.
3. What are executive orders and how are they modified?
4. Where can a legal researcher turn to find administrative agency regulations, both proposed and final?

§2.3 The Judicial Branch

Article III: "The judicial power of the United States, shall be vested in one Supreme Court, and in such inferior courts as the Congress may from time to time ordain and establish."[47]

As we have seen, there is interplay among the branches of government. The legislative branch enacts the laws, and the executive branch implements and enforces the laws. Article III establishes the third branch of government, the judicial branch. The judicial branch interprets the law through court cases.

"[W]hen government bureaus and agencies go awry, which are adjuncts of the legislative or executive branches, the people flee to the third branch, their courts, for solace and justice."[48]

The principles arising from judicial interpretation of statutes, regulations, and prior cases are referred to as **case law. Common law** addresses judge-made law only, or cases. You will often see the terms common law and case law used interchangeably.

To appreciate how judicial interpretation fits into the legal landscape, a student of the law must understand the overarching structure of the court system. This governs how far reaching a judicial determination may be in terms of **precedent.** ***Stare decisis*** is the legal term for the notion that courts must follow preceding cases; prior decisions may either be binding on a court or merely persuasive. If a prior case involves similar facts and is from the same court or a higher court in the same jurisdiction, it is binding precedent; otherwise, a court may look to a similar case as a guideline but is not bound by its ruling. A judge is not bound by rulings in other jurisdictions.

Even when a court's ruling is binding on a lower court, attorneys for the parties will argue over its applicability in a particular case. This provides the opportunity for lawyers to argue how similar their case is to the preceding one if the outcome was favorable, or to point out the distinctions between the cases if they do not want the

47. US Constitution (1787, 1992), https://www.archives.gov/founding-docs/constitution.

48. Justice J. Henderson, Supreme Court of South Dakota, dissenting from *Heritage of Yankton, Inc. v. South Dakota Dep't of Health*, 432 N.W.2d 68, 77 (S.D. 1988), https://law.justia.com/cases/south-dakota/supreme-court/1988/15992-1.html.

court to follow the earlier ruling. In reaching a decision, courts will look not only to other court cases, but to additional relevant sources of law.

Let's turn now to the structure of the federal court system.

§2.3.1 Structure of the Federal Court System

a. Trial Courts

i. US District Courts

Legal proceedings begin at the trial court level, known in the federal system as district courts. The district court determines questions of fact, what happened in a particular case, questions of law, and the application of the law to the facts. The district court is the only level that uses a jury. In some cases, trials are conducted with a judge and no jury; these are called bench trials.

ii. Specialty Courts

Because of their technical complexity, some cases require the specialized knowledge of judges well versed in the underlying law and subject matter. For example, the US has specialty courts to handle matters of patent, bankruptcy, and international trade, as well as military courts that have jurisdiction over military service members. In addition, the US Court of Federal Claims is a trial court created to hear cases involving monetary claims against the US government. Traditionally, matters involving Native Americans living on reservations have been handled in specialty courts established under tribal authority known as tribal courts. Where no tribal court exists, cases are conducted in special federal courts known as courts of Indian offenses operated by the Bureau of Indian Affairs (BIA).[49]

b. Appellate Courts

i. US Circuit Court of Appeals

The next level of court is the appellate court, known at the federal level as the circuit court of appeals. The party that loses at the lower court level may appeal to the relevant appellate court. Typically appeals concern a question of law rather than fact. In very rare instances, an appellate court may overturn a fact determination by a lower court; this is because the trial court judge is in a better position to weigh the evidence and assess witness testimony. Circuit courts are comprised of three judges and do not use a jury. Circuit court judges are nominated by the president and confirmed by the Senate and have a lifetime appointment. The circuit courts are divided regionally across the country according to population.[50] See Figure 2.1. For example, the Seventh Circuit handles cases from Indiana, Illinois, and Wisconsin.

---

49. Courts of Indian Offenses and Law and Order Code, 25 C.F.R. Part 11, https://www.ecfr.gov/current/title-25/chapter-I/subchapter-B/part-11. State Jurisdiction over offenses committed by or against Indians in the Indian country, 18 U.S.C. § 1162, https://codes.findlaw.com/us/title-18-crimes-and-criminal-procedure/18-usc-sect-1162/.

50. https://www.uscourts.gov/sites/default/files/u.s._federal_courts_circuit_map_1.pdf.

FIGURE 2.2

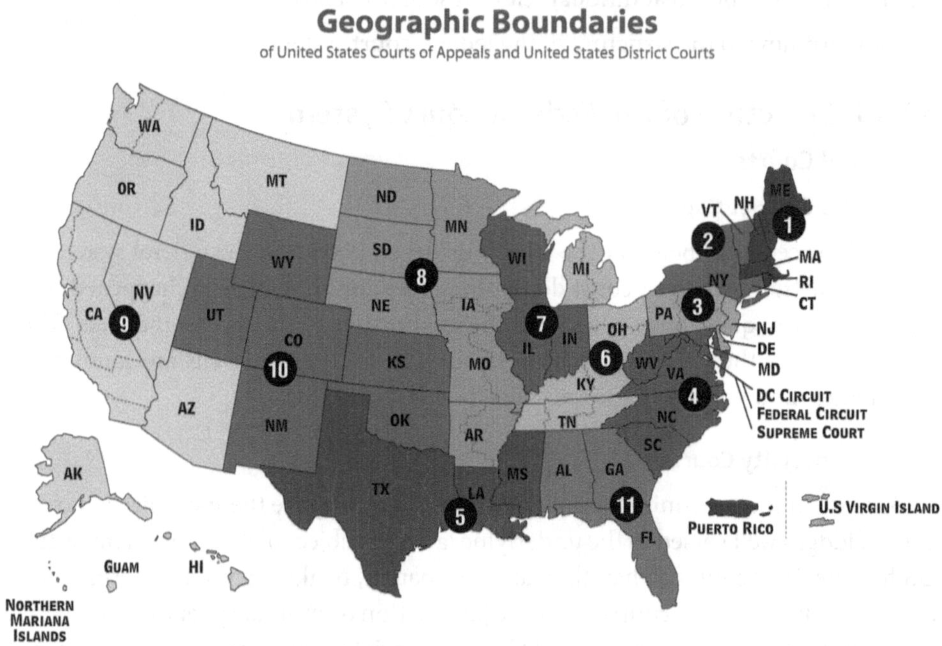

ii. US Court of Appeals for the Federal Circuit

The US Court of Appeals for the Federal Circuit was created in 1982 by the Federal Courts Improvement Act of 1982. It is the only appellate court that handles patent law appeals.[51] Its jurisdiction is determined not by geography but by subject matter. It also handles appeals from the US Court of Federal Claims, and from certain agencies and specific tribunals including, for example, the US Court of Appeals for Veteran Claims, the US International Trade Commission, the US Court of International Trade, and Boards of Contract appeals for contract disputes involving the government.

c. The Supreme Court

The ultimate federal appeals court is the Supreme Court of the United States. It is comprised of nine justices appointed for life. Justices are nominated by the president and must be confirmed by the Senate by a three-fifths vote. Many more cases are brought before the Court each year than they have time to handle; the Court typically hears between 100 and 150 cases per year of the approximately 8,000 review requests it receives. A request to have a case heard by the Supreme Court is known as a ***writ of certiorari***. Four of the nine justices must agree to hear a case for it to be placed on the calendar, or docket. The Supreme Court also has the authority to hear

51. Federal Courts Improvement Act of 1982, 96 Stat. 25, https://www.govinfo.gov/content/pkg/STATUTE-96/pdf/STATUTE-96-Pg25.pdf.

emergency cases. In 2020, for example, the Court declined to overturn an order by the Eleventh Circuit regarding voting rights in Florida that was brought as an emergency appeal in order to clarify the rights of voters in advance of the November 2020 elections.[52]

The Supreme Court considers cases on appeal that involve matters of federal law, with particular emphasis on constitutional law. Its rulings are binding on all lower courts. The Court often considers cases arising from a **circuit split**, involving a difference of opinion among the circuits regarding a particular question of law. The Court is also the **court of original jurisdiction** in certain limited matters, such as cases involving ambassadors and those in which a state is a party.[53]

A 2020 Supreme Court ruling provides an example of a case resolving a circuit split. Title VII of the Civil Rights Act prohibits employment discrimination on the basis of sex.[54] The Eleventh Circuit ruled that this section does not include sexual orientation, whereas the Second and Sixth circuits reached the opposite conclusion.[55] In *Bostock v. Clayton County*, Supreme Court Justice Gorsuch, writing for the majority, concluded that "An employer violates Title VII when it intentionally fires an individual employee based in part on sex."[56] He further stated that "An individual's homosexuality or transgender status is not relevant to employment decisions. That's because it is impossible to discriminate against a person for being homosexual or transgender without discriminating against that individual based on sex."[57]

Supreme Court decisions can have a profound impact on American life. In a 2018 study of the impact of a 2013 Supreme Court ruling regarding application of the Voting Rights Act, researchers at the Harvard Kennedy School showed that the federal oversight provided under the Voting Rights Act increased minority voter turnout by as much as 30 percent, gains that persisted for more than 40 years and continued through 2012, the last presidential election under federal oversight protections. In the 2016 presidential election, the first national election following the 2013 Su-

---

52. *Bonnie Raysor et al. v. Ron DeSantis in His Official Capacity as Governor of Florida, et al.*, Application to Vacate the Eleventh Circuit's Stay of the Order Issued by the United States District Court for the Northern District of Florida, https://www.scotusblog.com/case-files/cases/raysor-v-desantis/. A. Liptak, *Supreme Court Allows Restrictions on Voting by Ex-Felons,* New York Times (July 16, 2020), https://www.nytimes.com/2020/07/16/us/supreme-court-felons-voting-florida.html.

53. Note that matters of jurisdiction can be complex, and a full discussion is beyond the scope of this work.

54. 78 Stat. 255, 42 U.S.C. § 2000e–2(a)(1), https://www.eeoc.gov/statutes/title-vii-civil-rights-act-1964.

55. *Bostock v. Clayton County, Altitude Express v. Zarda and Moore, Harris Funeral Homes v. EEOC*, 590 U.S. ___ (2020), https://www.oyez.org/cases/2019/17-1618.

56. *Bostock v. Clayton County, Altitude Express v. Zarda and Moore, Harris Funeral Homes v. EEOC*, 590 U.S. ___ (2020), https://www.oyez.org/cases/2019/17-1618.

57. *Bostock v. Clayton County, Altitude Express v. Zarda and Moore, Harris Funeral Homes v. EEOC*, 590 U.S. ___ (2020), https://www.oyez.org/cases/2019/17-1618.

preme Court ruling, counties that were freed from federal oversight saw minority voter turnout drop more sharply than it had in decades.[58]

FIGURE 2.3 Federal Court Levels

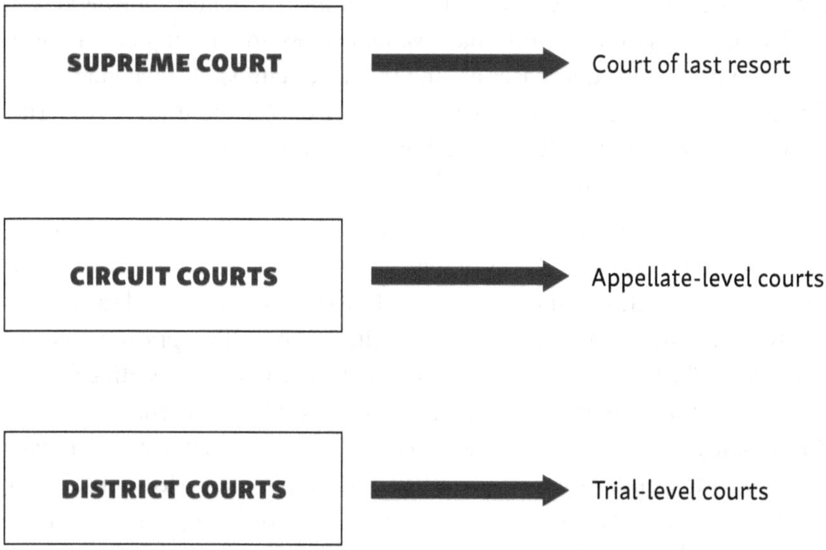

§ 2.3.2 Jurisdiction of Federal Courts

Another important concept in understanding the law is **jurisdiction**—identifying which court has authority to hear a particular case. This is determined by the subject matter of the case, the parties to the dispute, and the property in question. As mentioned, specialty courts like bankruptcy courts are the federal courts charged with hearing exclusively bankruptcy matters. Apart from these courts of limited jurisdiction, federal courts address questions of federal law and matters involving residents of two different states.[59] Questions of federal law include constitutional questions and interpretation of federal statutes and regulations. Federal courts will also hear cases involving another country, cases between two or more states, admiralty cases, and cases in which the US is a party.[60] Other cases are handled at the state court level, discussed in § 2.4.

58. D. Ang, *Do 40-Year-Old Facts Still Matter? Long-Run Effects of Federal Oversight under the Voting Rights Act*, HKS Faculty Research Working Paper Series RWP18-033 (October 2018), https://www.hks.harvard.edu/publications/do-40-year-old-facts-still-matter-long-run-effects-federal-oversight-under-voting.

59. Questions of federal law involve subject matter jurisdiction, where cases between residents of different states involve diversity jurisdiction.

60. For more on this subject, see Federal Judicial Center, https://www.fjc.gov/history/courts/jurisdiction-federal-courts.

We now turn from consideration of federal governmental structure and function and continue our study of the law with an examination of Article IV that addresses state governments.

EXERCISES

1. If a party chooses to appeal a US district court ruling in Nevada, what is the name of the court where the appeal is brought?
2. What types of matters are brought in federal court?
3. Name two types of specialty courts and describe the rationale behind their creation.
4. Explain the concept of *stare decisis.*

§2.4 The States

Article VI, Section 2: "This Constitution, and the Laws of the United States which shall be made in Pursuance thereof; and all Treaties made, or which shall be made, under the Authority of the United States, shall be the supreme Law of the Land; and the Judges in every State shall be bound thereby, any Thing in the Constitution or Laws of any State to the Contrary notwithstanding."[61]

Under our constitutional system laws are made in both state and federal legislatures and case law is drawn from courts at state and federal levels. As this section describes, just who should craft each law and which laws govern when there is a conflict is a matter of some complexity and debate. We begin with the concept of federalism and the Tenth Amendment.

§2.4.1 Federalism

Tenth Amendment: "The powers not delegated to the United States by the Constitution, nor prohibited by it to the states, are reserved to the states respectively, or to the people."[62]

Federalism is defined by Merriam-Webster as "the distribution of power in an organization (such as a government) between a central authority and the constituent" and "support or advocacy of this principle."[63] In application, for our purposes, it refers to the balance of power and authority between the federal and state governments. Recall our discussion of the enumerated powers of the federal government in § 2.1.2.

---

61. US Constitution (1787, 1992), https://www.archives.gov/founding-docs/constitution.
62. US Constitution (1787, 1992), https://www.archives.gov/founding-docs/constitution.
63. https://www.merriam-webster.com/dictionary/federalism.

"The Tenth Amendment's simple language... emphasizes that the inclusion of a bill of rights does not change the fundamental character of the national government. It remains a government of limited and enumerated powers, so that the first question involving an exercise of federal power is not whether it violates someone's rights, but whether it exceeds the national government's enumerated powers."[64]

Keep the concept of federalism in mind as we turn to the structure and function of state governments in § 2.4.3 and explore how state laws and rulings intersect with those of the federal government in § 2.4.4.

§ 2.4.2 State Constitutions

Like the federal government, each state adopts its own constitution that provides the framework for its governmental structure and function. In general, state constitutions are more detailed and lengthier than the US Constitution and are amended more frequently. Most have a structure similar to that of the US Constitution, with a preamble, articles, and amendments. The state constitution is the governing law of the state, subordinate only to the US Constitution.

§ 2.4.3 Structure of State Governments

a. Legislative

State legislatures are generally structured like the federal government, with a bicameral legislature comprised of a house of representatives and a senate. Nebraska is the exception, with a unicameral legislature. In general, state legislative bodies function much like Congress, with bills assigned to committee for development and presentation to the floor for a vote. In states with a bicameral structure, both houses must enact a bill before it is presented to the governor to be signed into law.

Some situations may fall under both federal and state law, and employers must be aware of both.[65] For example, the federal government has established rules regarding child labor under the Fair Labor Standards Act.[66] All states have child labor laws as well. According to the US Department of Labor, "When federal and state standards

---

64. G. Lawson & R. Shapiro, *The 10th Amendment, Common Interpretation*, National Constitution Center, https://constitutioncenter.org/the-constitution/amendments/amendment-x/interpretations/129. The National Constitution Center is a nonpartisan organization whose stated mission is to serve as America's leading platform for constitutional education and debate, fulfilling our congressional charter "to disseminate information about the United States Constitution on a nonpartisan basis in order to increase awareness and understanding of the Constitution among the American people."

65. Some circumstances, such as new construction, may also be subject to municipal codes that are beyond the scope of this work.

66. Fair Labor Standards Act, 29 U.S.C. 201, et seq., https://uscode.house.gov/view.xhtml?path=/prelim@title29/chapter8&edition=prelim.

are different, the rules that provide the most protection to youth workers will apply. Employers must comply with both federal law and applicable state laws."[67]

Pause for Reflection Sam Hunter is a vice president of operations at a meat packing plant in Colorado. He gets a call from a good friend asking for a job for his nephew Bud, who is fifteen. "He could do whatever you need him to do. He's a good kid but has really been struggling since his dad died and they lost the farm. He has seen plenty of hogs slaughtered so he can handle being on the floor." Sam has never hired a fifteen-year-old worker but knows he (or his human resources manager) will have to investigate what restrictions might be imposed by the child labor laws. "Pete, I'll have to get back to you on that to see what we can do."

Sam learns that federal law prohibits youth workers from working more than three hours per day on a school day or eight hours a day on non-school days. In addition, federal law limits youth workers from working in certain hazardous occupations, including slaughtering animals; it does permit them to perform meat packaging. He learns that Colorado has child labor laws that are more restrictive and prohibit "Slaughter of livestock and rendering and packaging of meat."[68] Sam calls Pete and says, "You know, Pete, I don't think I am going to be able to use Bud on the floor at all, but I think we have an office position he could fill." Is this permissible?

b. Executive

The executive branch within a state government is led by the governor, an elected official. She is charged with implementing and enforcing state law. She signs bills sent to her from the legislature into law (or vetoes them, in some situations, subject to a supermajority override, as in the US Congress). As the president is commander in chief of the military, the governor also has authority over the state's militia. The governor has the power to issue executive orders for the state. An example would be the actions of state governors in establishing quarantine rules for their states during the coronavirus pandemic. Other state elected officials who perform executive functions under the direction of the governor include the lieutenant governor, the secretary of state, the attorney general, and various other commissioners.

As in the federal government, many of the administrative functions of state governments are accomplished through state agencies. There is tremendous variability in "the scale and structure of the bureaucratic networks of functionally specialized agencies that the fifty US state governments have formed to implement their varied responsibilities," according to a 2018 analysis of state agency websites.[69] In their anal-

---

67. US Dept. of Labor, Workers Under 18, https://www.dol.gov/general/topic/hiring/workersunder18.

68. Colorado Dept. of Labor and Employment, Colorado Youth Law, referring to the Colorado Youth Employment Opportunity Act, C.R.S. 8-12-101 et. seq., specifically C.R.S. 8-12-110 (2)(g).

69. S. Kosack, M. Coscia, E. Smith, K. Albrecht, A. László Barabási, & R. Hausmann, *Functional Structures of US State Governments*, 115 Proceedings of the National Academy of Sciences 46 (Nov. 2018), 11748–53, https://www.pnas.org/doi/abs/10.1073/pnas.1803228115.

ysis of 47,631 websites, the authors found that the variability was most strongly linked with state economic structures, and that "[v]oters' recent ideological preferences about the proper roles and extent of government are not significantly associated with the scale and structure of their state governments as reflected online."[70] State agencies are broad ranging, addressing such diverse areas as taxation, public safety, education, transportation, tourism, and labor, to name a few.

Functions of a state agency are variable as well. Consider, for example, a state professional licensing agency—this organization may collect licensure fees and review applicants for licensure to ensure compliance with state requirements. Specialty boards, such as the board of medicine (often appointed by the governor), may establish regulations (under authority delegated by the legislature) to set specific guidelines within their area of expertise. An example would be enacting criteria for continuing education requirements, a quasi-legislative function. The board might also be asked to conduct hearings for licensed individuals charged with violating established regulations, acting in a quasi-judicial capacity.

c. Judicial

State courts are structured much like federal courts with trial level courts, at least one court of appeal and a court of last resort, often called the Supreme Court.

FIGURE 2.4 Comparison of Federal and State Court Structures

Federal Courts		State Courts (Ohio)
SUPREME COURT	Court of last resort	**SUPREME COURT**
CIRCUIT COURTS	Appellate-level courts	**COURTS OF APPEALS**
DISTRICT COURTS	Trial-level courts	**TRIAL COURTS**

70. S. Kosack, M. Coscia, E. Smith, K. Albrecht, A. László Barabási, & R. Hausmann, *Functional Structures of US State Governments*, 115 Proceedings of the National Academy of Sciences 46 (Nov. 2018), 11748–53, https://www.pnas.org/doi/abs/10.1073/pnas.1803228115.

State trial-level courts have a variety of names that can be confusing to the legal scholar, such as district court, trial court, or circuit court. Some jurisdictions also have specialty trial courts, such as a family court or small claims court. In New York the entire nomenclature differs: the trial court is the Supreme Court, the appellate court is the Supreme Court, Appellate Division, and the highest-level court is the Court of Appeals, but the overall structure remains the same. See Figure 4 for an illustration of the state court system in Ohio. Ohio trial courts include the courts of common pleas (with specialty subdivisions), municipal and county courts, and the court of claims, all of which feed into the court of appeals.

Cases at the appellate level are often heard by a panel of judges. Like federal appeals courts, they consider questions of law; questions of fact are handled at the trial court level. The state's highest-level court is the supreme court; like the US Supreme Court, it handles appeals from the appellate-level court(s).

Functionally, state courts hear all matters not heard by federal courts (see § 2.3.2). They hear the vast majority of cases in the judicial system in the US. Like federal courts, courts are bound by the rulings of law issued by the court(s) above them.

§ 2.4.4 Supremacy Clause

Article VI, Section 2: "This Constitution, and the Laws of the United States which shall be made in Pursuance thereof; and all Treaties made, or which shall be made, under the Authority of the United States, shall be the supreme Law of the Land; and the Judges in every State shall be bound thereby, any Thing in the Constitution or Laws of any State to the Contrary notwithstanding."[71]

Section 2 of Article VI of the US Constitution is known as the Supremacy Clause. It establishes the Constitution as the supreme law of the land and is the foundation for federal preemption doctrine. Preemption means that where federal and state laws conflict, the federal law will preempt state law.

Pause for Reflection Think about Sam Hunter's employment decision under the federal and state child labor laws introduced in § 2.4.3. Suppose that rather than enacting the more restrictive provision regarding packaging of meat currently found under state law, the Colorado legislature had tried to enact a law that allowed youth workers to perform slaughtering functions. Would this exceed state authority under the Supremacy Clause? Similarly, if a Colorado state court judge interpreted the law to permit youth workers to work four hours on a school day during the busiest time of year, would that ruling run afoul of the Supremacy Clause?

71. US Constitution (1787, 1992), https://www.archives.gov/founding-docs/constitution.

In summary, this chapter provides an overview of the constitutional structure and function of the legislative, executive, and judicial branches of the federal government. We summarize how laws are made. In addition, we describe the divisions of state government as compared to the federal government and considered sources of legal authority. We introduce the concept of checks and balances between the branches of government and the interplay between state and federal law. Let's turn now to reading and analyzing the law.

EXERCISES

1. Explain federalism and the respective roles of state and federal governments.
2. What is the structure of state court systems?
3. List three possible functions of a state agency.
4. Describe the importance of the Supremacy Clause.

CHAPTER THREE

Reading, Briefing, and Understanding Case Law

Scott Turow, then a beginning law student and now a successful novelist, compared legal case reading to "something like stirring concrete with my eyelashes."[1]

§ 3.1 Why Learn to Read Legal Cases?

Learning to read legal cases is helpful for several reasons:

- It sharpens your legal vocabulary.
- It demonstrates the art of legal analysis.
- It is a fundamental skill necessary to succeed as you move forward in your legal studies.

As Scott Turow affirms, reading legal cases is not easy. Our goal in this chapter is to make case reading easier. Though we can't change the concrete, we can provide a better stirring tool. We do this by adjusting novice case readers' expectations (§ 3.2), providing case reading strategies (§ 3.3), demonstrating the general case structure (§ 3.3.1), and teaching the art of briefing cases (§ 3.5).

§ 3.2 Adjusting Your Expectations for This Challenging Task

The legal and academic literature supports Turow's claim about the difficult task of learning to read legal cases. Many articles describe the stress and frustration of first-year law students trying to read their first legal cases.[2] Our own experience

1. P. Dewitz, *Reading Law: Three Suggestions for Legal Education*, 27 U. Tol. L. Rev. (1996), 657, 661, quoting from Scott Turow's novel One L: The Turbulent True Story of a First Year at Harvard Law School (1978).

2. See L. M. Christensen, *The Psychology Behind Case Briefing: A Powerful Cognitive Schema*, 29 Campbell L. Rev. 5 (2006); see also R. J. Aldisert, M. Rasch, & M. P. Bartlett, *Opinion Writing and Opinion Readers*, 31 Cardozo L. Rev. 1 (2009); R. J. Aldisert, Opinion Writing (2011); P. Dewitz, *Reading Law: Three Suggestions for Legal Education*, 27 U. Tol. L. Rev. (1996), 657; L. M.

supports this claim. As our students endeavored to read their first case, we would first identify, define, and discuss new legal terms. Even with that, so much of the writing was unfamiliar and tough to parse. The structure of the case was foreign, and the court's conclusions were difficult to understand. We cautioned students to be patient with themselves, explaining that after reading many cases it would get easier. We knew there had to be a better way. And there is.

Several studies found that adjusting student expectations lessened their discontent with the process.[3] Armed with this information, we adjusted our students' expectations (and we hope to do the same for you):

- First, proceed with patience.
- When you first read a legal case, it is almost like reading something in a different language. You wouldn't expect to read five pages in French if you were not fluent in French. Try not to expect reading a case to be much easier than that at first.
- New legal terms and phrases will need definition and careful study. Learning many new terms at once is time consuming. Expect that this will take time.
- As Professor Dewitz points out in *Reading Law: Three Suggestions for Legal Education*, many say that it is the law school struggle that leads to good lawyering. The research shows that this is false.[4] We know that learning requires hard work and dedication, but we don't espouse this struggle theory.

Finally, again, proceed with patience.

§3.3 Strategies for Reading Legal Cases

A helpful approach to reading legal cases is presented in Judge Ruggero J. Aldisert's book OPINION WRITING.[5] Judge Aldisert sat on the federal appellate bench for fifty years and authored thousands of opinions. The American Bar Association honored him as the first to receive the Distinguished Appellate Jurist Award.[6] He also

---

Christensen, *The Paradox of Legal Expertise: A Study of Experts and Novices Reading the Law*, 2008 BYU EDUC. & L. J. 53 (2008).

3. See L. M. Christensen, *The Psychology Behind Case Briefing: A Powerful Cognitive Schema*, 29 CAMPBELL L. REV. 5 (2006); see also R. J. Aldisert, M. Rasch, & M. P. Bartlett, *Opinion Writing and Opinion Readers*, 31 CARDOZO L. REV. 1 (2009); R. J. Aldisert, OPINION WRITING (2011); P. Dewitz, *Reading Law: Three Suggestions for Legal Education*, 27 U. TOL. L. REV. (1996), 657; L. M. Christensen, *The Paradox of Legal Expertise: A Study of Experts and Novices Reading the Law*, 2008 BYU EDUC. & L. J. 53 (2008).

4. P. Dewitz, *Reading Law: Three Suggestions for Legal Education*, 27 U. TOL. L. REV. (1996), 657, 672.

5. R. J. Aldisert, OPINION WRITING (2011).

6. R. J. Aldisert, OPINION WRITING (2011).

received the Golden Pen Award from the Legal Writing Institute.[7] OPINION WRITING has "justly been recognized as an invaluable guide for judges everywhere."[8]

Why, you may ask, do we include such detail about Judge Aldisert? Vetting your sources is critical in scholarship, and, of course, in thinking generally. To make lucid decisions, you must begin with good information from reliable sources. Judge Aldisert is an excellent source regarding legal opinions, and his book explains how a legal case is constructed. He also later authored an article in which he said that studying how an opinion is written helps in learning to read legal cases.[9] We agree.

§3.3.1 Legal Case Structure

Examining how a case is structured, and understanding its basic parts, will assist you in reading and understanding legal cases. It is important, therefore, to discover the parts of a legal opinion.

OPINION WRITING provides that all well-written legal cases should have five basic parts[10]:

- Introduction/Orientation paragraph
- Issues presented
- Statement of facts
- Discussion of the law
- Conclusion

As you read a case, you should look for these sections. They will not, however, always be easy to identify. In fact, not all cases will have the orientation/introduction section (as you will note in the *Palsgraf* case). Every case, however should have the issue, facts, discussion, and conclusion.

Unfortunately, not all judges are good writers. Some judges will help you in your quest to read cases, and others will make it more challenging. Some judges will state the issue directly: the issue presented is.... It may be a challenge to find the issue in other cases. Don't get discouraged; remember to adjust your expectations. Look for these sections, knowing it will take time for you to recognize them readily.

Identifying the case's structure and keeping it in mind as you skim or read the case will expedite your learning. In addition, research shows that each new "genre we read requires the use of special knowledge plus the tools or strategies to use that

---

7. R. J. Aldisert, OPINION WRITING (2011).

8. Recommendation on the cover the Judge Aldisert's book by Judge Christina Snyder, US District Court Judge for Central District of California. R. J. Aldisert, OPINION WRITING (2011).

9. R. J. Aldisert, M. Rasch, & M. P. Bartlett, *Opinion Writing and Opinion Readers*, 31 CARDOZO L. REV. 1 (2009).

10. R. J. Aldisert, OPINION WRITING (2011). See Note 5, at 57–61.

knowledge."[11] A case structure is one of those tools. Another is your frame of reference, or your legal knowledge base.

§3.3.2 Your Current Legal Knowledge

"Reading comprehension is based on decoding ability, but requires three additional important types of knowledge—domain knowledge, text structure knowledge, and strategic knowledge."[12] Professor Dewitz explains these three types of knowledge as follows:

- Domain—Current knowledge on a particular subject
- Text structure—How the text is organized
- Strategic—"Intentional, flexible, and self-evaluative" strategies.[13]

In reading about a familiar subject, these strategies are often unconscious.[14]

Domain Knowledge: Lack of familiarity with the subject matter, lack of domain knowledge, makes reading legal cases difficult. When you begin your legal studies your familiarity with legal terms and ideas may be slight. Increasing your legal vocabulary will help.

You must approach reading a case the way you would any subject with which you are not familiar. If you are a novice astronomer beginning to read about the galaxy and space exploration, you would likely find many unfamiliar terms. As you continue to study, you will become more familiar with the language and more comfortable reading. The same is true with the law. Define terms. Consider writing the definitions in your own words after you look them up. Increasing your legal vocabulary with improve your ability to understand legal cases.

The case brief exercises after each case in this chapter will help you see how legal terms are used as you compare your case brief to those drafted by the authors and the attorneys at Lexis. The more cases you read and brief, the better your legal domain knowledge will be.

Before we move on to the next section, note that in addition to domain knowledge, reading comprehension requires text structure and flexible, strategic reading. You recall the discussion of case structure in §3.3.1, and you see that Professor Dewitz agrees. We now introduce a third author who concurs that flexible, strategic reading is fundamental to improving case reading skills.

---

11. P. Dewitz, *Reading Law: Three Suggestions for Legal Education*, 27 U. Tol. L. Rev. (1996), 657.
12. P. Dewitz, *Reading Law: Three Suggestions for Legal Education*, 27 U. Tol. L. Rev. (1996), 657.
13. P. Dewitz, *Reading Law: Three Suggestions for Legal Education*, 27 U. Tol. L. Rev. (1996), 657, 659.
14. P. Dewitz, *Reading Law: Three Suggestions for Legal Education*, 27 U. Tol. L. Rev. (1996), 657.

§3.3.3 Flexible Reading (Skimming)

Professor Leah Christensen studied the strategies used by judges and lawyers when reading legal cases.[15] She compared the way law students read judicial opinions as novices to how judges and lawyers read cases as experts. She found their case reading approaches quite different. Her study highlighted the advanced techniques employed by the expert readers. She suggests that these techniques can be shared with novice readers to enhance and even accelerate their case reading skills. Her strategy recommendations include the following:

1. "Read with a purpose."
2. "Use background knowledge to situate the case."
3. "Establish the context of the case before beginning to read."
4. "Evaluate the case and have an opinion about the outcome."
5. "Read flexibly; skim and skip when appropriate."[16]

Notice that Professor Dewitz also highlighted (2) background knowledge and (5) reading flexibly and skimming when appropriate. Judge Aldisert would agree with (1) reading with a purpose and (3) establishing context for the case. We focus here on skimming techniques.

"[E]xpert readers... read flexibly and efficiently, varying both the order of their reading and the time allotted to different sections."[17] Novice readers tend to read a case straight through, not necessarily attributing more importance to one part over another.[18] As you begin to read cases, skim the case first. As you learn which parts are most important, feel free to move around as your read. Perhaps focus on the conclusion first, and then find the issue. Read through the facts, and then dig into the court's reasoning. Over time, you will find your own approach. As you are learning, though, try to be flexible.

§3.3.4 Best Practices for Reading Cases

Based on the study by Christensen and the work by Berger,[19] the work of Aldisert, and the input from Dewitz, we recommend the following approach to reading cases:

---

15. L. M. Christensen, *The Paradox of Legal Expertise: A Study of Experts and Novices Reading the Law*, 2008 BYU Educ. & L. J. 53 (2008).

16. L. M. Christensen, *The Paradox of Legal Expertise: A Study of Experts and Novices Reading the Law*, 2008 BYU Educ. & L. J. 53 (2008).

17. L. M. Christensen, *The Paradox of Legal Expertise: A Study of Experts and Novices Reading the Law*, 2008 BYU Educ. & L. J. 53 (2008), 82, citing L. L. Berger, *Applying New Rhetoric to Legal Discourse: The Ebb and Flow of Reader and Writer Text and Context*, 49 J. Legal Educ. (1999), 155, 164.

18. L. M. Christensen, *The Paradox of Legal Expertise: A Study of Experts and Novices Reading the Law*, 2008 BYU Educ. & L. J. 53 (2008), 84.

19. L. M. Christensen, *The Paradox of Legal Expertise: A Study of Experts and Novices Reading the Law*, 2008 BYU Educ. & L. J. 53 (2008). See Note 17 at 82–85.

- If a commercial summary and headnotes are available, read them first (see these explained in § 3.6.1).
- Note the name of the parties, the date of the case, and the court.
- If the judge wrote an overview/introduction, read that.
- Skim the case.
    - Are there headings? If not, can you identify the structure?
    - What happened in the court below?
    - What is the court's holding?
    - Skim the facts.
    - Find the issue.
- Jump to the court's reasoning.
- Go back to sections you think are most important and reread.
- Write a case brief.

Focusing on case organizational structure, learning how to brief cases, improving your domain knowledge, and learning to read flexibly and skim cases for key parts of the case will help as you work toward expert case reading skills. We will return to these strategies when we read the cases in § 3.7.

§ 3.4 The Case Brief

A case brief is a way to break down a case to help you analyze and understand it. Case briefs can take different forms. When you first begin briefing cases, you should do them in some detail. In addition to the basics listed below, a detailed case brief may include the citation, case objectives, the parties' arguments, and concurring and/or dissenting opinions. Once you become familiar with legal cases, you will find your own method to break the case down and analyze it. There are a variety of approaches. It is all about carefully reading and understanding the case. You will eventually determine what works best for you.[20]

A case brief generally contains the following parts:

- **Facts:** The parties to a legal case set forth their version of what has happened to bring them to court. The facts are set forth at the trial level.
- **Prior Proceedings:** A determination from a judicial authority that occurred prior and is directly related to the instant case.
- **Issue:** The legal question that the court must answer.
- **Holding:** The court's answer to the legal question (the issue) before the court.

---

20. Note that your professor may have preferences regarding case brief formatting.

- **Reasoning:** Whereas a holding tells "what" the court decided, the reasoning tells "how" and "why" the court decided the way it did. The court sets forth the rationale that led to its conclusion (holding/decision). This often involves synthesizing prior precedential cases and statutes and regulations that together provide the rules that govern the facts in the case. The judge then applies the rule of law to the facts of the case before her.

§3.5 The Parts/Sections of a Legal Case

Though you will encounter some variation, most cases have the following parts:

- citation
- caption
- docket number
- deciding court
- date of decision
- procedural posture
- case summary/overview
- headnotes
- attorneys' names
- judge authoring the opinion
- the opinion
- any concurring or dissenting opinions

Below we define each section. We then highlight these sections in the case you are going to read: *White City Shopping Ctr., LP v. PR Rests., LLC*. You will note the attorneys' names (9) are missing. This is very unusual; you will almost always see the attorneys' names listed.

1. **Citation:** A citation tells the reader how to find the case. The books in which cases are published are called reporters. A case is often published in more than one reporter. A case may be found, for example, in a state reporter, a regional reporter, and additional reporters; they are printed by different entities. The general format of a citation is XXX Reporter YYY. XXX represents the volume of the reporter. YYY represents the page number on which the case starts. You could walk into a law library and go to the correct volume of a reporter, find the right page, and you would find your case. Currently, most of this research is done with online programs. The citations, however, still use the aforementioned format and the same reporter system.

2. **Caption:** The names of the parties in a case are found in the caption. Generally, the caption contains the full names of all the parties. You can discern from the caption which party is the plaintiff (brings the case) and which is the defendant (opposes the case). If the case is on appeal, you can tell which party is the **appellant** (brings the appeal) and which is the **appellee** (opposes the appeal).
3. **Docket number:** The docket number is the identification number assigned to a case. Every document of a case is logged with that number.
4. **Deciding Court:** This is the court that made the decision about the case.
5. **Date of Decision:** This is the date that the case was decided.

Case Summary: The case summary is a heading that generally includes the procedural posture (6) and the overview (7).

6. **Procedural Posture:** The procedural posture tells you the procedural steps that occurred to bring the case before this court.
7. **Overview:** The publisher writes the overview. This is not part of the case. Though you should not rely on it as it is not part of the case itself, it can be very helpful in giving you an idea about the case before you read the entire case.
8. **Headnotes:** The headnotes delineate the points of law discussed in the case. Like the case summary, the headnotes are written by the publisher (here Lexis) to help the reader understand the case. They can, therefore, be helpful in doing further research. You will notice that the headnotes are numbered. Those numbers lead you to the place that discusses that point of law. The "key numbers" in front of each head note can lead you to another set of books called digests. Digests are research tools that were used extensively when all research was done in books rather than online.
9. **Attorneys' Names:** The attorneys representing the parties in a case are usually listed before the opinion.
10. **Judge Authoring the Opinion:** At the trial court level there is one judge and that judge is the author of the opinion. At the appellate level there are generally an odd number of judges; that avoids a tie in the voting. When there are several judges, one judge is usually chosen to write the opinion. You will note that in this case the author is listed as *Per Curiam*. This Latin term means "by the court." It is somewhat controversial as many believe the public should be able to know where different justices stand on important issues.
11. **Opinion:** The word "opinion" signals that you are now reading the case itself. This is written by the judge (often with the help of her or his clerks). Unlike the parts mentioned above, which are written by the publisher, the opinion comes from the court.

12. **Any Concurring or Dissenting Opinions:** If one or more of the judges disagrees with the opinion, he or she can write a dissenting opinion. Remember, though, that this is not the law. The majority opinion is the law. Legal discussion in the dissent is referred to as **dicta.** "Dicta" is "Latin for "remark," a comment by a judge in a decision or ruling that is not required to reach the decision, but may state a related legal principle as the judge understands it."[21] While it may be cited in legal argument, it does not have the full force of a precedent A concurring opinion is written when a judge agrees with the holding of the majority opinion, but for different reasons. The judge sets forth these reasons in a concurring opinion.

§3.6 Reading Legal Cases (Two Examples)

We begin with a short and relatively easy case. You will notice that before the opinion itself, there is extensive material. To understand the origin of this extra material, let's take a minute to explain the different publishing routes for court cases. The government publishes cases in **reporters**. As mentioned above, you could go into a legal library and, if they have reporters, you could find any published opinion. These reporters include the opinion and the citation, the docket number, the name of the deciding court, the date of decision, and any concurring or dissenting opinions (labeled as parts 1–5 and 12 in §3.5 above).

In addition to government reporters, commercial companies like Westlaw and LexisNexis publish cases. Included with the basics delineated above, these companies employ lawyers who write case summaries. These summaries are a great way to "situate the case" and "establish context," as Professor Christensen suggests.

Almost no trial court-level cases are published. Can you guess why? Remember the definition of precedent. The case must be from the same jurisdiction, with similar facts, *from a higher court*. Because trial court cases are cases of first impression, they are not a "higher" court.

§3.6.1 Reading *White City Shopping Ctr., LP v. PR Rests., LLC*

You may have read about this case in the paper. The Superior Court of Massachusetts found that a taco is not a sandwich. We chose this case because it is relatively short, contains familiar subject matter (sandwiches), and the structure is almost identical to Judge Aldisert's framework. Judge Locke, who wrote the opinion, also provides headings in the body of the opinion. This will help you see the structure.

Below, you will see some legal terms from the case. We define them for you here to expand your "domain knowledge" (§3.2.2). Reviewing new terminology before

21. https://dictionary.law.com/Default.aspx?typed=dictum&type=1.

you read a case will help you read through the case with more ease. In addition, again, you always want to read the summary whenever provided.

Examine the headnotes before you read the case. As stated above, they highlight the points of law discussed in the case. The lawyers from Lexis pull them directly from the case.[22] You should never, however, quote from the headnotes; always quote directly from the case.

Carefully read the headnotes. They likely contain unfamiliar vocabulary, but reviewing them prior to reading the case will add to your strategic approach. This case has four headnotes: two regarding contracts and two regarding civil procedure (the rules that courts must follow when hearing cases).

Let's look at one of the civil procedure headnotes together. It provides in part: "A preliminary injunction is warranted only when the moving party establishes both a likelihood of success on the merits of the claim, and a substantial risk of irreparable harm in the absence of an injunction." Reading this headnote focuses you. You know to be alert for a further explanation on these two points: likelihood of success on the merits, and risk of irreparable harm. You can see how helpful headnotes can be in focusing the reader.

A final note: You will notice below that Lexis includes "core terms." These are simply the words most often repeated in the case—in that order. You can see that by scanning these terms, you may get a feel for the case.

KEY LEGAL TERMS

The terms with an asterisk below are taken directly from the uscourts.gov/glossary

Plaintiff: "A person or business that files a formal complaint with the court."

Defendant: "An individual (or business) against whom a lawsuit is filed. In a civil case, the person or organization against whom the plaintiff brings suit; in a criminal case, the person accused of the crime."

Counterclaim: "A claim brought against an opposing party after the original claim was brought. Often it is the defendant against the plaintiff. (In the *White City* case below, defendant PR brought a counterclaim against plaintiff White City.)"

Declaratory judgment: "A judge's statement about someone's rights. For example, a plaintiff may seek a declaratory judgment that a particular statute, as written, violates some constitutional right."

Injunction: "A court order preventing one or more named parties from taking some action. A preliminary injunction often is issued to allow fact-finding, so a judge can determine whether a permanent injunction is justified."

Intervenor: A person or business who is not a party to a suit, but who has an interest in the outcome.

---

22. Previously, the headnotes were written in the Lexis lawyers' own words. Now they are direct quotes from the case. This may not be the case for all commercial printers.

Now, just before you read the case, recall the case reading strategies provided in § 3.3.4:

- If a commercial summary and headnotes are available, read them first (see these explained in § 3.5).
- Note the name of the parties, the date of the case, and the court.
- If the judge wrote an overview/introduction, read that.
- Skim the case.
  - Are there headings? If not, can you find the structure?
  - What happened in the court below?
  - What is the court's holding?
  - Skim the facts.
  - Find the issue.
- Jump to the court's reasoning.
- Go back to sections you think are most important and reread.
- Write a case brief.

With the search for structure in mind, with relevant legal definitions reviewed, with the summary digested, and with the headnotes examined, you are ready to read the case.

Note: In Massachusetts, the trial court is called "Superior Court." This is not the norm, nor is it the norm to print trial court cases in a reporter.

Neutral — "Neutral" is the Shepards signal—covered below

As of: January 10, 2024 11:47 PM Z

White City Shopping Ctr., LP v. PR Rests., LLC — Caption (2)

Superior Court of Massachusetts, At Worcester — Deciding Court (4)

October 30, 2006, Decided ; October 31, 2006, Filed — Date of Decision (5)

Docket Number: 2006-196313 — Docket Number (3)

Reporter

2006 Mass. Super. LEXIS 544 *; 21 Mass. L. Rep. 565 — Citation (1)

White City Shopping Center, LP v. PR Restaurants, LLC dba Bread Panera

Core Terms

Lease, restaurant, sandwiches, quesadillas, burritos, parties, tacos, injunction, food, likelihood of success, irreparable harm, products, merits, space, preliminary injunction

Case Summary

(6) Procedural Posture

Plaintiff shopping center filed a declaratory judgment action against defendant sandwich restaurant, seeking a declaration that it had not breached a commercial lease when it entered into a lease with intervenor Mexican-style restaurant. Defendant sought a preliminary injunction that sought to enjoin the center from taking any action that would violate the exclusive provision of defendant's commercial lease with the center.

(7) Overview

The restaurant's lease included a clause that prohibited the center from leasing commercial space to other restaurants that sold "sandwiches" as the restaurant did. The center filed its action after a dispute arose over the center's lease of space to intervenor. Since the execution of the lease, intervenor had expended significant sums on planning costs and was obligated to spend additional sums for the construction of a restaurant. The court denied the request for a preliminary injunction. Defendant's lease did not define "sandwiches," and defendant failed to show that the term included the burritos, tacos, and quesadillas intervernor would sell. Such items did not fall within the common definition of sandwiches. Thus, defendant could not establish a likelihood that it would be successful in barring the center from leasing space to intervenor. Defendant also failed to show that its profitability would disappear if intervenor opened a restaurant, and thus, it failed to show irreparable harm. Finally, the harm to the center outweighed any harm to defendant because the center had expended considerable time and money to plan and develop intervenor's restaurant.

Outcome

Defendant's motion for a preliminary injunction was denied.

LexisNexis® Headnotes (8)

Civil Procedure > . . . > Injunctions > Grounds for Injunctions > General Overview

Civil Procedure > Remedies > Injunctions > Preliminary & Temporary Injunctions

HN1 Injunctions, Grounds for Injunctions

A preliminary injunction is warranted only when the moving party establishes both a likelihood of success on the merits of the claim, and a substantial risk of irreparable harm in the absence of an injunction. Once these factors are established, a court must balance them against the harm that an injunction will inflict on the opposing party, and must also consider the impact on the public interest.

Contracts Law > Contract Interpretation > General Overview

HN2 Contracts Law, Contract Interpretation

The interpretation of a contract is question of law for a court. A contract is construed to be given reasonable effect to each of its provisions. The object of the court is to construe the contract as a whole in a reasonable and practical way, consistent with its language, background and purpose. The starting point must be the actual words chosen by the parties to express their agreement.

Contracts Law > Contract Interpretation > General Overview

HN3 Contracts Law, Contract Interpretation

If the words of a contract are plain and free from ambiguity, they must be construed in accordance with their ordinary and usual sense.

Civil Procedure > . . . > Injunctions > Grounds for Injunctions > Irreparable Harm

HN4 Grounds for Injunctions, Irreparable Harm

Irreparable harm occurs when a loss of rights cannot be remedied even though the party seeking an injunction prevails after a full hearing on the merits. Economic loss alone, however, does not usually rise to the level of irreparable harm which a party must establish to obtain a preliminary injunction.

Judges: Jeffrey A. Locke, Justice of the Superior Court. Judge (10)

Opinion by: Jeffrey A. Locke

(11) This is the beginning of the court's opinion

Opinion

MEMORANDUM OF DECISION AND ORDER ON DEFENDANT'S MOTION FOR PRELIMINARY INJUNCTION

INTRODUCTION

Plaintiff White City Shopping Center, LP ("White City") brought this declaratory judgment action against defendant PR Restaurants, LLC ("PR") seeking a declaration that it is not in breach of its commercial lease with PR. PR counterclaimed against White City for breach of contract, breach of implied covenant of good faith and fair dealing, and violation of G.L.c. 93A. PR now moves for a preliminary injunction, seeking to enjoin White City, its partners, employees or agents, from taking any action which would violate the exclusive use provision of its commercial lease with White City. Such actions include White City taking any action that would permit Chair 5 Restaurants, ("Chair 5"), the intervening party, from operating a Qdoba restaurant at the White City Shopping Center ("Shopping Center"). For the following reasons, the defendant's motion is *DENIED.*

BACKGROUND

Defendant, PR, is a Massachusetts limited liability company that operates 22 Panera Bread ("Panera") restaurants in the New England area. Panera is a cafe-style restaurant chain that sells sandwiches, coffee, and soup. Mitchell J. Roberts is the manager of PR. PR is a tenant under a commercial lease for approximately 4,469 square feet of retail space in the Shopping Center located on Route 9, in Shrewsbury. White City, a limited partnership, is the landlord of the Shopping Center. Chair 5, the intervening party, is a Delaware limited liability company and franchisee of Qdoba, a Mexican-style restaurant chain that sells burritos, quesadillas, and tacos. Both Panera and Qdoba compete in the same "fast-casual" restaurant market.

On March 14, 2001, White City entered into a ten-year lease ("the Lease") with PR for retail space to operate a Panera restaurant in the Shopping Center. Lease negotiations lasted several months partly because of PR's request to include an exclusivity clause in the Lease. PR authored the clause which underwent three revisions prior to the Lease's execution. The exclusivity clause that both parties initially agreed to restricted White City from entering into new leases with businesses that primarily sell sandwiches. In its first iteration, Section 4.07 of the Lease states, in relevant part:

> Landlord *agrees not* to enter into a lease, occupancy agreement or license affecting space in the Shopping Center or consent to an amendment to an existing lease permitting use... for a bakery or restaurant reasonably expected to have annual sales of *sandwiches* greater than ten percent (10%) of its total sales or primarily for the sale of high quality coffees or teas, such as, but not limited to, Starbucks, Tea-Luxe, Pete's Coffee and Tea, and Finagle a Bagle... The foregoing *shall not* apply to (i) the use of the existing, vacant free-standing building

> in the Shopping Center for a Dunkin Donuts-type business, or for a business serving near-Eastern food and related products, (ii) restaurants primarily for sit-down table service, (iii) a Jewish delicatessen or (iv) a KFC restaurant operating in a new building following the demolition of the existing, freestanding building. No new building shall violate the no-build provision of this Lease.

Lease § 4.07 (emphasis supplied).

The Lease contained no definition of "sandwiches" or "near-Eastern" food. During lease negotiations, PR and White City did not discuss the definition of "sandwiches" or the type of food products they intended the term to cover. Furthermore, the parties never indicated, specified, or agreed that the term "sandwiches" included tacos, burritos, and quesadillas.

Following the Lease's execution in March, the parties amended the exclusivity clause to include additional restrictions. On December 30, 2005, Section 4.07 of the Lease was amended, as follows:

> The foregoing restriction shall also apply (without limitation) to a Dunkin Donuts location and to a Jewish-style delicatessen within the Shopping Center, but shall not apply to (i) use of the existing, freestanding building in the Shopping Center partially occupied by Strawberries and recently expanded for a business serving near-eastern food and related products, (ii) restaurants for primarily for sit down table service or (iii) a Papa Gino's restaurant (provided the same continues to operate with substantially the same categories of menu items as now apply to its stores and franchisees generally).

Lease § 4.07.

Sometime after the amendment, PR learned that White City had entered into discussions with Chair 5 to lease commercial space. Chair 5 planned to develop and construct a Qdoba restaurant in the same Shopping Center as Panera. After learning of the parties' plans, PR had its attorney contact White City to express concern and seek an assurance that White City would not enter into a lease with Chair 5. PR believed that White City's leasing of space to Chair 5 violated Section 4.07 of the Lease. Specifically, PR believed, and later asserted that tacos, burritos, and quesadillas fell within meaning of "sandwiches" and therefore, White City was prohibited from leasing to Chair 5 under the Lease. White City refused to provide the requested assurance when PR's attorney contacted it about the pending Chair 5 lease. On or around August 22, 2006, White City executed a lease with Chair 5 for 2,100 square feet of retail space in the Shopping Center. On September 28, 2006, White City filed an action against PR, seeking a declaratory judgment that it did not breach its lease with PR.

Since the execution of the Chair 5 lease, Chair 5 has spent over $ 85,000 in planning costs, and it is further contractually obligated to spend over $ 300,000 for the construction of a Qdoba restaurant in the Shopping Center. According to Chair 5, it has yet to schedule an opening date for its restaurant.

DISCUSSION

Under the well-established test of *Packaging Industries Group v. Cheney*, 380 Mass. 609, 617, 405 N.E.2d 106 (1980), HN1 a preliminary injunction is warranted only when the moving party establishes both a likelihood of success on the merits of the claim, and a substantial risk of irreparable harm in the absence of an injunction. Once these factors are established, the Court must balance them against the harm that an injunction will inflict on the opposing party, and must also consider the impact on the public interest. See *T&D Video, Inc. v. City of Revere*, 423 Mass. 577, 580, 670 N.E.2d 162 (1996).

A. Likelihood of Success on the Merits

To demonstrate a likelihood of success on the merits, PR must establish as a reasonable interpretation that the Mexican-style food products which Qdoba sells fall within the Lease's restrictions. Absent an explicit and broad definition of "sandwiches" in the Lease itself, PR has not shown a likelihood of success to establish a right to injunctive relief under relevant contract principles.

HN2 The interpretation of a contract is question of law for the court. *Sarvis v. Cooper*, 40 Mass.App.Ct. 471, 475, 665 N.E.2d 119 (1996). A contract is construed to be given reasonable effect to each of its provisions. *Id.* "The object of the court is to construe the contract as a whole in a reasonable and practical way, consistent with its language, background and purpose." *USM Corp. v. Arthur D. Little Systems, Inc.*, 28 Mass. App. Ct. 108, 116, 546 N.E.2d 888 (1989). The starting point must be the actual words chosen by the parties to express their agreement. *Id.* HN3 If the words of the contract are plain and free from ambiguity, they must be construed in accordance with their ordinary and usual sense. See *Ober v. National Casualty Co.*, 318 Mass. 27, 30, 60 N.E.2d 90 (1945).

Given that the term "sandwiches" is not ambiguous and the Lease does not provide a definition of it, this court applies the ordinary meaning of the word. New Webster Third International Dictionary describes a "sandwich" as "two thin pieces of bread, usually buttered, with a thin layer (as of meat, cheese, or savory mixture) spread between them." Merriam-Webster, 2002. Under this definition and as dictated by common sense, this court finds that the term "sandwich" is not commonly understood to include burritos, tacos, and quesadillas, which are typically made with a single tortilla and stuffed with a choice filling of meat, rice, and beans. As such, there is no viable legal basis for barring White City from leasing to Chair 5. Further, PR has not proffered any evidence that the parties intended the term "sandwiches" to include burritos, tacos, and quesadillas. As the drafter of the exclusivity clause, PR did not include a definition of "sandwiches" in the lease nor communicate clearly to White City during lease negotiations that it intended to treat burritos, tacos, quesadillas, and sandwiches the same. Another factor weighing against PR's favor is that it was aware that Mexican-style restaurants near the Shopping Center existed which sold burritos, tacos, and quesadillas prior to the execution of the Lease yet, PR made no attempt to define, discuss, and clarify the parties' understanding of the term "sandwiches." Accordingly, based on the record before the court, PR has not shown a likelihood of success on the merits.

B. Irreparable Harm

HN4 Irreparable harm occurs when a loss of rights cannot be remedied even though the party seeking an injunction prevails after a full hearing on the merits. *Planned Parenthood League of Massachusetts, Inc. v. Operation Rescue*, 406 Mass. 701, 710, 550 N.E.2d 1361 (1990). Economic loss alone, however, does not usually rise to the level of irreparable harm which a party must establish to obtain a preliminary injunction. See *Hull Mun. Lighting Plant v. Mass. Mun. Wholesale Elec.*, 399 Mass. 640, 643, 506 N.E.2d 140 (1987).

Here, PR has alleged irreparable harm on the basis that money damages will be difficult to quantify. However, this allegation is unsupported by any data showing that the profitability of Panera will disappear once Qdoba opens. Absent a showing by PR that Panera's survival is dependent upon enjoining the opening of Qdoba and where both parties sell distinct and different food products, preliminary injunctive relief is inappropriate.

C. Balance of the Harms

This court further finds that the potential harm to the plaintiffs is outweighed by the harm to the defendant where plaintiffs have expended considerable time and money to plan and develop a Qdoba restaurant at the Shopping Center, in light of the fact that this court finds that White City did not breach its lease with PR. Even though PR vigorously argues for a broad definition of "sandwiches" under Section 4.07 to include food products sold by Qdoba, this argument does not change the fact that burritos, quesadillas, and tacos are not commonly understood to mean "sandwiches." Because PR failed to use more specific language or definitions for "sandwiches" in the Lease, it is bound to the language and the common meaning attributable to "sandwiches" that the parties agreed upon when the Lease was drafted.

Having heard the parties and reviewing their filings, this court is not convinced that defendant, PR, has carried its burden in showing a likelihood of success on the merits; that it will suffer irreparable harm if the injunctive relief sought is not granted; or that its harm, without the injunction, outweighs any harm to plaintiffs from being enjoined in the operation of its restaurant.

ORDER

For the foregoing reasons stated, it is hereby *ORDERED* that the Defendant's motion for preliminary injunction be *DENIED*.

Jeffrey A. Locke

Justice of the Superior Court

DATE: October 30, 2006

§ 3.6.2 Writing a Case Brief for *White City Shopping Center*

After you have read the case through once, read it again. On the second read, try to create a case brief. Do this without looking at the example below. Spend twenty to thirty minutes on this exercise; it is time well spent. As you work on case briefing, you are beginning the process of legal analysis. You are thinking about the parts of the case and how they relate and blend. This short exercise will help you learn to read legal cases. "Although a case brief serves as an organizational tool, it also serves as a way to help students think critically and creatively about the law."[23]

EXERCISE Write a case brief for *White City Shopping Center*.

For your first case brief, write only about half or three-quarters of a page. List the parts of the case brief on the left side of the page. Keep this first attempt short. Use simple sentences in your own words. The legal terminology will come later. Fill in the parts of the case briefs using the tips below:

Facts: Write the facts using non-legal terminology as if you were telling your friend this story.

Procedural Posture: Remember that cases at the trial court level like this one are not usually published. The procedural posture tells what happened in the court below. Here, there was no court below, so no procedural posture.

Issue: What is the legal question in this case? What were the facts and legal questions presented to the court? Consider this for the "whether clause": Whether the sandwich restaurant can (fill in the blank) from signing a lease with the Mexican restaurant that (fill in the bank).

Holding: The holding is the answer to the legal question. First answer the issue question with yes or no. Then write the holding mirroring the language in the issue statement you wrote. Here is an example to get you started: No, the sandwich restaurant cannot (fill in the blank).

Reasoning: This will be the longest part. Why did the court answer the legal question this way? In the future you will want to include some of the rules and cases the court relied on. For this first attempt, just put it in your own words. Keep these things in mind as you write the reasoning. Did the lease define "sandwich"? What are the two things the sandwich company needs to do in order to obtain a preliminary injunction (remember the headnotes)? Write a sentence or two on each of these points and explain what the court determined.

Remember that a case brief is a learning tool. It helps focus you on the relevant parts of a case. Compare your case brief with the one we wrote below. We included legal terminology so that you can compare this to your plain language case brief. Your case brief likely tells the same story. The only difference is the legal terminolo-

23. L. M. Christensen, *The Psychology Behind Case Briefing: A Powerful Cognitive Schema*, 29 Campbell L. Rev. 5 (2006), 13.

gy. Spend a little time comparing the two case briefs; note where the legal terms fit in. (We use some shorthand and incomplete sentences. This is common in a case brief. It is a personal tool.)

> **Facts:** On March 14, 2001, plaintiff White City Shopping Center signed a retail lease with defendant PR, a Panera restaurant, for PR to run its restaurant in the shopping center. The lease went through several iterations regarding PR's exclusive rights clause. The final lease stated that White City could not rent to another business that primarily sold sandwiches. The exclusivity clause was amended again in 2005 to exclude Dunkin Donuts and a Jewish deli. After the amendment, White City began negotiations with a Mexican restaurant (Intervenor). August 22, 2006, White City executed a lease with the Mexican restaurant. After PR complained to White City, White City requested a declaratory judgment from the court confirming that it did not breach the lease. Defendant PR asks the court to enjoin Plaintiff White City from entering into the lease with the Intervenor Mexican Restaurant. PR contends that tacos, burritos, etc. are sandwiches in violation of the exclusivity clause.
>
> **Procedural Posture:** None. Trial court case. (Note that the Lexis attorneys include one in the intro to the case. More commonly the procedural posture states what happened in the court below.)
>
> **Issue:** Should the court grant a preliminary injunction to defendant, PR Rests., to stop plaintiff, White City Shopping Center from signing a commercial lease with a Mexican restaurant? (Note that the case was brought by plaintiff seeking a declaratory judgment.)
>
> **Holding:** No. The Court denied defendant's counterclaim for a preliminary injunction to stop plaintiff from leasing to a Mexican restaurant.
>
> **Reasoning:** Two requirements for a preliminary injunction: (1) likelihood of success on the merits, and (2)irreparable harm. *Packing Industries.* The factual issue before the court is whether tacos are sandwiches. Using a dictionary definition (two pieces of bread, buttered, layer of meat, cheese, etc.), court said tacos not sandwiches. PR can't win on merits. Irreparable harm: PR could not demonstrate money damages (or future damages). In balancing the harm to each party, court found that harm to PR was not greater than harm to plaintiff had already spent considerable money preparing the Mexican restaurant. Court denied PR's motion for preliminary injunction.

Finally, we provide a case brief written by the attorneys at LexisNexis. Not all cases have Lexis case briefs. Significant legal cases are most likely to have them (they also respond to repeated requests for case briefs from readers). We provide this additional case brief to show that case briefs can be written with slightly different parts and styles. Think about note-taking in college. Your notes would be different from your classmates even though you were listening to the same lecture. One is not right or wrong; the same is true of case briefs. A case brief should serve you.

LEXIS CASE BRIEF *White City Shopping Ctr., LP v. PR Rests., LLC*

Rule:

The interpretation of a contract is question of law for a court. A contract is construed to be given reasonable effect to each of its provisions. The object of the court is to construe the contract as a whole in a reasonable and practical way, consistent with its language, background, and purpose. The starting point must be the actual words chosen by the parties to express their agreement.

Facts:

Plaintiff shopping center filed a declaratory judgment action against defendant sandwich restaurant, seeking a declaration that it had not breached a commercial lease when it entered into a lease with intervenor Mexican-style restaurant. The contract included a clause that prohibited the center from leasing commercial space to other restaurants that sold "sandwiches" as the restaurant did. Defendant sought a preliminary injunction that sought to enjoin the center from taking any action that would violate the exclusive provision of defendant's commercial lease with the center.

Issue:

Did the defendant sandwich restaurant show sufficient basis to enjoin the plaintiff shopping center from leasing the property to intervenor Mexican-style restaurant?

Answer:

No.

Conclusion:

The court denied defendant's motion for preliminary injunction. The court noted that the defendant's lease did not define "sandwiches" and defendant failed to show that the term included the burritos, tacos, and quesadillas intervenor would sell. Thus, defendant could not establish likelihood that it would be successful in barring the center from leasing space to intervenor. Defendant also failed to show that its profitability would disappear if intervenor opened a restaurant, and thus, it failed to show irreparable harm. Finally, the harm to the center outweighed any harm to defendant because the center had expended considerable time and money to plan and develop intervenor's restaurant.

Now that you have some understanding of the case and how it was put together, let's discuss.

§3.6.3 Discussion of *White City Shopping Center*

Did you agree with the result? Is a taco a sandwich? What did you think of the judge's rationale? You will learn in Chapter Four about textualism. Judge Locke employed this method in using a dictionary definition to define sandwich. Not everyone would agree with that approach.

Two iconic judges, for example, can't agree on the definition of a sandwich. Justice Scalia, former Supreme Court justice, agrees with the *White City Shopping Ctr.* decision. As a devout textualist, he agrees with Judge Locke's use of a dictionary to define sandwich. On the other hand, Judge Richard Posner, former chief justice of the Seventh Circuit, had this to say in refuting Justice Scalia:

> "As is often the case, the court got the definition wrong," Posner writes. "A sandwich does not have to have two slices of bread; it can have more than two (a club sandwich) and it can have just one (an open-faced sandwich). The slices of bread do not have to be thin, and the layer between them does not have to be thin either. The slices do not have to be slices of bread: a hamburger is regarded as a sandwich, and also a hot dog—and some people regard tacos and burritos as sandwiches, and a quesadilla is even more sandwich-like. Dictionaries are mazes in which judges are soon lost. A dictionary-centered textualism is hopeless."[24]

Judge Aldisert tells us "[a]n opinion is defined as a reasoned elaboration, publicly stated, that justifies a conclusion or decision."[25] Did this opinion meet that standard?

Finally, if you disagree with an opinion, it doesn't necessarily mean you lack sound reasoning. Decisions are to be based on law, not opinion. You notice, however, that as the same case moves from trial court to appellate court to supreme court, the holding may reverse more than once. The law is anything but static; it can also be unpredictable.

You have successfully read your first case and written your first case brief. You reviewed two additional case briefs and compared them to each other and to the one you wrote. You are now ready to read your second case.

Again, just before you read this case, review the case reading strategies provided in § 3.3.4:

- If a commercial summary and headnotes are available, read them first (see these explained in § 3.5).
- Note the name of the parties, the date of the case, and the court.
- If the judge wrote an overview/introduction, read that.
- Skim the case.
    - Are there headings? If not, can you find the structure?
    - What happened in the court below?
    - What is the court's holding?
    - Skim the facts.
    - Find the issue.

---

24. D. C. Weiss, *Textual Originalism and the Great Sandwich Debate: Posner Reviews Scalia*, ABA Journal (2012, August 30).

25. R. J. Aldisert, M. Rasch, & M. P. Bartlett, *Opinion Writing and Opinion Readers*, 31 Cardozo L. Rev. 1 (2009), 57.

- Jump to the court's reasoning.
- Go back to sections you think are most important and reread.
- Write a case brief.

§3.6.4 Reading *Palsgraf v. Long Island Railroad*

We now discuss the most famous tort case taught to first-year law students across the country: *Palsgraf v. Long Island Railroad.*[26] *Palsgraf* helped develop tort law by introducing the concept of foreseeability. **A tort is a civil wrong that causes harm to another**. The tort of negligence has four elements: duty, breach, causation, and damages. *Palsgraf* tells us that the harm caused must be foreseeable, and the **tortfeasor (person who commits a tort)** must owe a duty to the injured party. As you will see in the case below, the court found that the railroad employee who set off the incident that caused injury to Mrs. Palsgraf could not have foreseen the injury she sustained. Further, the railroad employee did not owe a duty to Mrs. Palsgraf.

Though *Palsgraf* was decided almost one hundred years ago, it is still good law and heavily cited today in both cases and law review articles. In fact, as of January 1, 2024, *Palsgraf* had been cited in 2,334 cases; it was cited more than 35 times in 2023.[27] We mention this so that you can see that regardless of how old a case is, if it has not been overruled, it is still the law (here, it remains the law in New York).

This raises the concept of **Shepards citations.** Shepards is a product of Lexis that all lawyers use to determine whether a case or statute is still good law. Shepards is a tool that lists all the cases that cite to the case in question. It further highlights the treatment of those cases. By Shepardizing a case, you can determine whether a case has been overruled. You can see the importance of checking for the status of a case. You don't want to rely on a case that is no longer good law. Shepards is a critically important tool in conducting legal research.

Back to *Palsgraf.* The case was written by Judge Cordozo who, like Judge Aldisert, is regarded as one of the best writers on the court. As you notice his writing style, though, you will also notice that he did not include headings in the opinion. This will make it a bit more challenging to read than *White City Shopping Center*, which had clear headings. You may not have access to commercial research tools like Lexis and Westlaw, so we include this case without headings, headnotes, or a summary. We want you to be prepared if you read a case without these features. We include suggestions for how best to approach such a case.

Recall the basic structure of a legal case from Opinion Writing:[28]

---

26. 248 NY 239 (1928).
27. Information from Lexis website by Shepardizing the *Palsgraf* case.
28. R. J. Aldisert, Opinion Writing (2011).

- Opening/Orientation narrative
- Issues presented
- Statement of facts
- Discussion of the law
- Conclusion

You will see that *Palsgraf* does not appear to have a separate opening/orientation. All cases must have facts, issue, discussion, and conclusion. We have found that the opening is a matter of a judge's individual style. Note how we highlighted the parts of *Palsgraf* below.

As mentioned above, we are presenting *Palsgraf* to you as you would find it without the commercial publishing features. How do you proceed without headnotes and a case summary? In this case we recommend that you read through the case first without trying to get any in-depth understanding. During this first quick read-through, we recommend the following:

1. Legal Terms: Note any unfamiliar vocabulary and look them up.
2. Structure: During your read-through, try to make note of the facts.
   i. Scanning a paragraph, you should be able to see where the judge is telling the story.
   ii. Where you see lots of case citations, you can assume you are in the discussion section.
   iii. The issue is a bit trickier. First find the conclusion. What did the court decide in the end? Once you have the conclusion, you can often see the issue. Look at the issue and conclusion in the case briefs below (after you write yours). Can you see how the conclusion answers the issue statement?
3. Notice how the facts in *Palsgraf* are not all in the same place (unlike *White City* in which the sections were neatly separated). Though the basic parts should be in every case, each judge's style and organization will vary.

The parts are highlighted in the case below. Before you focus on the individual parts, though, read through the entire case. The dissenting opinion, which is longer than the court's opinion, has been removed. Then, go back and look at the highlighted sections. Would you have been able to identify these sections? There is no one perfect answer here, but you should agree with these section markings generally.

On the next page, you will see some legal terms from the case. Again, we define them for you here to expand your "domain knowledge." (Review section 3.2.2). As you will recall, reviewing and defining terminology before you do a careful read of the case will enhance your understanding.

KEY LEGAL TERMS

Appellant: The party who brings the case on appeal seeking reversal of a lower court's holding.

Respondent: The party who won in the court below and is now brought to court on appeal by the appellant.

Civil court: A civil court deals with private, non-criminal cases. These cases are usually between people or organizations. Criminal courts handle crimes that are committed against society such as assault, rape, murder, etc. One of the parties of a criminal case is usually the state.

Cause of action: A cause of action means a party has the elements of a case required to bring a case before the court.

Negligence: Negligence is the "failure to exercise the care toward others which a reasonable or prudent person would do in the circumstances, or taking action which such a reasonable person would not."[29]

Precedent: Remember that a precedent case is mandatory authority that must be followed by a lower court in the same jurisdiction under the same facts. *Stare decisis* is the doctrine declaring that precedent must be followed.

Tort: A tort is a wrongdoing that is redressed through the civil courts.

Tortfeasor: A person who commits a tort.

EXERCISE Review §3.5, the parts of a legal case. Label the parts of the case below. Again, this case does not have a summary or headnotes. Label the other ten parts of this case.

Note the different format of this New York case. Many cases are printed in two columns; here, New York printed this case in a single column. Also of note are the different names of the New York state courts. This case is from the court of last resort in New York. New York court structure is the same as other states: trial court, appellate court, and the court of last resort (in other jurisdictions called the supreme court). New York names its courts differently than most other states. Here are the names of the New York State courts:

Trial court is called Supreme Court of New York

Court of appeals is called Supreme Court of New York Appellate Division

Court of last resort (or supreme court) is called Court of Appeals of New York

Can you see how this might be confusing? *Palsgraf v. Long Island Railroad* was heard by New York's highest court. Here is that case:

29. https://dictionary.law.com/Default.aspx?typed=negligence&type=1.

Helen Palsgraf, Respondent,
v.
The Long Island Railroad Company, Appellant.

Court of Appeals of New York
Argued February 24, 1928
Decided May 29, 1928

248 NY 339

OPINION OF THE COURT

CARDOZO, Ch. J.

Plaintiff was standing on a platform of defendant's railroad after buying a ticket to go to Rockaway Beach. A train stopped at the station, bound for another place. Two men ran forward to catch it. One of the men reached the platform of the car without mishap, though the train was already moving. The other man, carrying a package, jumped aboard the car, but seemed unsteady as if about to fall. A guard on the car, who had held the door open, reached forward to help him in, and another guard on the platform pushed him from behind. In this act, the package was dislodged, and fell upon the rails. It was a package of small size, about fifteen inches long, and was covered by a newspaper. In fact it contained fireworks, but there was nothing in its appearance to give notice of its contents. The fireworks when they fell exploded. The shock of the explosion threw down some scales at the other end of the platform, many feet away. The scales struck the plaintiff, causing injuries for which she sues.

Facts

Issue

The conduct of the defendant's guard, if a wrong in its relation to the holder of the package, was not a wrong in its relation to the plaintiff, standing far away. Relatively to her it was not negligence at all. Nothing in the situation gave notice that the falling package had in it the potency of peril to persons thus removed. Negligence is not actionable unless it involves the invasion of a legally protected interest, the violation of a right. "Proof of negligence in the air, so to speak, will not do" (Pollock, Torts [11th ed.], p. 455; Martin v. Herzog, 228 N.Y. 164, 170; cf. Salmond, Torts [6th ed.], p. 24). "Negligence is the absence of care, according to the circumstances" (WILLES, J., in Vaughan v. Taff Vale Ry. Co., 5 H. & N. 679, 688; 1 Beven, Negligence [4th ed.], 7; Paul v. Consol. Fireworks Co., 212 N.Y. 117; Adams v. Bullock, 227 N.Y. 208, 211; Parrott v. Wells-Fargo Co., 15 Wall. [U.S.] 524). The plaintiff as she stood upon the platform of the station might claim to be protected against intentional invasion of her bodily security. Such invasion is not charged. She might claim to be protected

Conclusion

Discussion of the law *(continues on p. 62)*

against unintentional invasion by conduct involving in the thought of reasonable men an unreasonable hazard that such invasion would ensue. These, from the point of view of the law, were the bounds of her immunity, with perhaps some rare exceptions, survivals for the most part of ancient forms of liability, where conduct is held to be at the peril of the actor (Sullivan v. Dunham, 161 N.Y. 290). If no hazard was apparent to the eye of ordinary vigilance, an act innocent and harmless, at least to outward seeming, with reference to her, did not take to itself the quality of a tort because it happened to be a wrong, though apparently not one involving the risk of bodily insecurity, with reference to some one else. "In every instance, before negligence can be predicated of a given act, back of the act must be sought and found a duty to the individual complaining, the observance of which would have averted or avoided the injury" (McSHERRY, C. J., in W. Va. Central R. Co. v. State, 96 Md. 652, 666; cf. Norfolk & Western Ry. Co. v. Wood, 99 Va. 156, 158, 159; Hughes v. Boston & Maine R. R. Co., 71 N.H. 279, 284; U. S. Express Co. v. Everest, 72 Kan. 517; Emry v. Roanoke Nav. Co., 111 N.C. 94, 95; Vaughan v. Transit Dev. Co., 222 N.Y. 79; Losee v. Clute, 51 N.Y. 494; DiCaprio v. N. Y. C. R. R. Co., 231 N.Y. 94; 1 Shearman & Redfield on Negligence, § 8, and cases cited; Cooley on Torts [3d ed.], p. 1411; Jaggard on Torts, vol. 2, p. 826; Wharton, Negligence, § 24; Bohlen, Studies in the Law of Torts, p. 601). "The ideas of negligence and duty are strictly correlative" (BOWEN, L. J., in Thomas v. Quartermaine, 18 Q.B.D. 685, 694). The plaintiff sues in her own right for a wrong personal to her, and not as the vicarious beneficiary of a breach of duty to another.

Discussion of the law *(continued from p. 61)*

Conclusion

A different conclusion will involve us, and swiftly too, in a maze of contradictions. A guard stumbles over a package which has been left upon a platform. It seems to be a bundle of newspapers. It turns out to be a can of dynamite. To the eye of ordinary vigilance, the bundle is abandoned waste, which may be kicked or trod on with impunity. Is a passenger at the other end of the platform protected by the law against the unsuspected hazard concealed beneath the waste? If not, is the result to be any different, so far as the distant passenger is concerned, when the guard stumbles over a valise which a truckman or a porter has left upon the walk? The passenger far away, if the victim of a wrong at all, has a cause of action, not derivative, but original and primary. His claim to be protected against invasion of his bodily security is neither greater nor less because the act resulting in the invasion is a wrong to another far removed. In this case, the rights that are said to have been violated, the interests said to have been invaded, are not

Policy Reasoning

even of the same order. The man was not injured in his person nor even put in danger. The purpose of the act, as well as its effect, was to make his person safe. If there was a wrong to him at all, which may very well be doubted, it was a wrong to a property interest only, the safety of his package. Out of this wrong to property, which threatened injury to nothing else, there has passed, we are told, to the plaintiff by derivation or succession a right of action for the invasion of an interest of another order, the right to bodily security. The diversity of interests emphasizes the futility of the effort to build the plaintiff's right upon the basis of a wrong to some one else. The gain is one of emphasis, for a like result would follow if the interests were the same. Even then, the orbit of the danger as disclosed to the eye of reasonable vigilance would be the orbit of the duty. One who jostles one's neighbor in a crowd does not invade the rights of others standing at the outer fringe when the unintended contact casts a bomb upon the ground. The wrongdoer as to them is the man who carries the bomb, not the one who explodes it without suspicion of the danger. Life will have to be made over, and human nature transformed, before prevision so extravagant can be accepted as the norm of conduct, the customary standard to which behavior must conform.

Policy Reasoning *(continued)*

The argument for the plaintiff is built upon the shifting meanings of such words as "wrong" and "wrongful," and shares their instability. What the plaintiff must show is "a wrong" to herself, i. e., a violation of her own right, and not merely a wrong to some one else, nor conduct "wrongful" because unsocial, but not "a wrong" to any one. We are told that one who drives at reckless speed through a crowded city street is guilty of a negligent act and, therefore, of a wrongful one irrespective of the consequences. Negligent the act is, and wrongful in the sense that it is unsocial, but wrongful and unsocial in relation to other travelers, only because the eye of vigilance perceives the risk of damage. If the same act were to be committed on a speedway or a race course, it would lose its wrongful quality. The risk reasonably to be perceived defines the duty to be obeyed, and risk imports relation; it is risk to another or to others within the range of apprehension (Seavey, Negligence, Subjective or Objective, 41 H. L. Rv. 6; Boronkay v. Robinson & Carpenter, 247 N.Y. 365). This does not mean, of course, that one who launches a destructive force is always relieved of liability if the force, though known to be destructive, pursues an unexpected path. "It was not necessary that the defendant should have had notice of the particular method in which an accident would occur, if the possibility of an accident was clear to the

Issue

Discussion of the Law *(continues on pp. 64–65)*

ordinarily prudent eye" (Munsey v. Webb, 231 U.S. 150, 156; Condran v. Park & Tilford, 213 N.Y. 341, 345; Robert v. U. S. E. F. Corp., 240 N.Y. 474, 477). Some acts, such as shooting, are so imminently dangerous to any one who may come within reach of the missile, however unexpectedly, as to impose a duty of prevision not far from that of an insurer. Even today, and much oftener in earlier stages of the law, one acts sometimes at one's peril (Jeremiah Smith, Tort and Absolute Liability, 30 H. L. Rv. 328; Street, Foundations of Legal Liability, vol. 1, pp. 77, 78). Under this head, it may be, fall certain cases of what is known as transferred intent, an act willfully dangerous to A resulting by misadventure in injury to B (Talmage v. Smith, 101 Mich. 370, 374). These cases aside, wrong is defined in terms of the natural or probable, at least when unintentional (Parrot v. Wells-Fargo Co. [The Nitro-Glycerine Case], 15 Wall. [U.S.] 524). The range of reasonable apprehension is at times a question for the court, and at times, if varying inferences are possible, a question for the jury. Here, by concession, there was nothing in the situation to suggest to the most cautious mind that the parcel wrapped in newspaper would spread wreckage through the station. If the guard had thrown it down knowingly and willfully, he would not have threatened the plaintiff's safety, so far as appearances could warn him. His conduct would not have involved, even then, an unreasonable probability of invasion of her bodily security. Liability can be no greater where the act is inadvertent.

Discussion of the Law *(continued from p. 63)*

Negligence, like risk, is thus a term of relation. Negligence in the abstract, apart from things related, is surely not a tort, if indeed it is understandable at all (BOWEN, L. J., in Thomas v. Quartermaine, 18 Q.B.D. 685, 694). Negligence is not a tort unless it results in the commission of a wrong, and the commission of a wrong imports the violation of a right, in this case, we are told, the right to be protected against interference with one's bodily security. But bodily security is protected, not against all forms of interference or aggression, but only against some. One who seeks redress at law does not make out a cause of action by showing without more that there has been damage to his person. If the harm was not willful, he must show that the act as to him had possibilities of danger so many and apparent as to entitle him to be protected against the doing of it though the harm was unintended. Affront to personality is still the keynote of the wrong. Confirmation of this view will be found in the history and development of the action on the case. Negligence as a basis of civil liability was unknown to mediaeval law (8 Holdsworth, History of English

Law, p. 449; Street, Foundations of Legal Liability, vol. 1, pp. 189, 190). For damage to the person, the sole remedy was trespass, and trespass did not lie in the absence of aggression, and that direct and personal (Holdsworth, op. cit. p. 453; Street, op. cit. vol. 3, pp. 258, 260, vol. 1, pp. 71, 74). Liability for other damage, as where a servant without orders from the master does or omits something to the damage of another, is a plant of later growth (Holdsworth, op. cit. 450, 457; Wigmore, Responsibility for Tortious Acts, vol. 3, Essays in Anglo-American Legal History, 520, 523, 526, 533). When it emerged out of the legal soil, it was thought of as a variant of trespass, an offshoot of the parent stock. This appears in the form of action, which was known as trespass on the case (Holdsworth, op. cit. p. 449; cf. Scott v. Shepard, 2 Wm. Black. 892; Green, Rationale of Proximate Cause, p. 19). The victim does not sue derivatively, or by right of subrogation, to vindicate an interest invaded in the person of another. Thus to view his cause of action is to ignore the fundamental difference between tort and crime (Holland, Jurisprudence [12th ed.], p. 328). He sues for breach of a duty owing to himself.

Discussion of the Law *(continued)*

The law of causation, remote or proximate, is thus foreign to the case before us. The question of liability is always anterior to the question of the measure of the consequences that go with liability. If there is no tort to be redressed, there is no occasion to consider what damage might be recovered if there were a finding of a tort. We may assume, without deciding, that negligence, not at large or in the abstract, but in relation to the plaintiff, would entail liability for any and all consequences, however novel or extraordinary (Bird v. St. Paul F. & M. Ins. Co., 224 N.Y. 47, 54; Ehrgott v. Mayor, etc., of N.Y., 96 N.Y. 264; Smith v. London & S. W. Ry. Co., L. R. 6 C.P. 14; 1 Beven, Negligence, 106; Street, op. cit. vol. 1, p. 90; Green, Rationale of Proximate Cause, pp. 88, 118; cf. Matter of Polemis, L. R. 1921, 3 K.B. 560; 44 Law Quarterly Review, 142). There is room for argument that a distinction is to be drawn according to the diversity of interests invaded by the act, as where conduct negligent in that it threatens an insignificant invasion of an interest in property results in an unforseeable invasion of an interest of another order, as, e. g., one of bodily security. Perhaps other distinctions may be necessary. We do not go into the question now. The consequences to be followed must first be rooted in a wrong. The judgment of the Appellate Division and that of the Trial Term should be reversed, and the complaint dismissed, with costs in all courts.

Conclusion

ANDREWS, J. (dissenting).

Did you notice something different in these sections? We included a policy section. This is actually part of the discussion. Rather than Judge Cordozo simply explaining how he followed precedent in reaching this decision, he also included policy as part of the discussion. You will see this in many cases, but not all. Because Judge Cordozo was actually introducing a new legal concept here, he explained why this was important not only for the parties in this case but also for society.

You may have also found this case more difficult to read because the issue was not clearly delineated and the parts of the case skipped around. Most cases will have the parts a bit more clearly delineated.

§3.6.5 Writing a Case Brief for *Palsgraf v. Long Island Railroad*

Just as you did in *White City*, read this case through once. Then, read it again (and here, because there are no headings, you actually skimmed the case before these two more careful readings). On the second careful read, try to create a case brief. Again, do this without looking at the example case briefs below. Spend about twenty to thirty minutes on this exercise. Again, as you work on case briefing, you are beginning the process of legal analysis. You are thinking about the parts of the case and how they relate and blend together. Do this exercise before you move ahead. This short exercise will help you begin the process of legal analysis as you continue to read future cases.

EXERCISE For your second case brief, again, list the parts of a case brief on the left side of the page: Facts, Procedural Posture, Issue, Holding, and Reasoning. **This time, try to include some legal terms**. Your case brief will likely not have as much legal terminology as the two below. Remember to be patient with yourself and have reasonable expectations. Continue to use simple sentences. Again, this learning exercise will provide most benefit if you refrain from looking at the two examples below until you are finished. Here are tips for writing the case brief:

Facts: Write the facts. This time try to include some legal terminology. The fact section will not generally include citations to other cases. This is where you are telling the story of what happened to the parties.

Procedural Posture: Unlike *White City*, *Palsgraf* was heard at both the trial court and appellate court before it arrived here at the court of last resort. Include this information and what happened at the lower courts.

Issue: What is the legal question in this case? What is the question the court is addressing here? Look at the holding and see if you can find the issue from the holding. It is important for you to try to write out these parts of the case brief in your own words.

Holding: The holding is the answer to the legal question. First answer the issue question with yes or no. Then write the holding mirroring the language in the issue statement you wrote.

Reasoning: This will be the longest part. Why did the court answer the legal question this way? In the future you will want to include some of the rules and cases the court relied on. For this first attempt, just put it in your own words. Keep these questions in mind as you write the reasoning: How does the court define negligence? What does the court say about duty? Did the railroad guards owe a duty to Palsgraf? What does the expression "Negligence in the air" mean? Write a sentence or two on each of these points and explain what the court determined.

Now read through the case brief that we wrote and the one drafted by Lexis. Compare your case brief to each of the other two. Also compare the case brief we wrote with the case brief Lexis wrote. Different language might be used, but it is just a matter of style and focus. Remember that these are learning tools for the individuals writing them. Time you spend comparing your case brief will be instrumental in moving you toward expanded "domain knowledge." Focus especially on the legal terms used in the two case briefs provided. If the definitions are not in this chapter or the glossary, be sure you look them up and write them down. Your legal literacy is improving.

AUTHORS' CASE BRIEF *Palsgraf v. Long Island Railroad*

Facts

The plaintiff, Helen Palsgraf, was standing on the railroad platform of Long Island Railroad. A train, not the one she was waiting for, stopped at the station. The train started to depart and a passenger successfully jumped aboard the train while it was moving. A second passenger, carrying a package, also attempted to board the moving train and it looked like he was about to fall. A guard employee of the Long Island Railroad reached for his hand to help him aboard. A second guard pushed the man from behind. During this time the package he was carrying fell. The package contained fireworks, which exploded when it hit the tracks. The explosion caused some scales located on the platform near Helen Palsgraf to strike her. She sued the railroad for damages.

Procedural Posture

This case is brought on appeal from the Supreme Court Appellate Division (in New York, this is the appellate court) that confirmed the judgment of the Supreme Court (in New York, this is the trial court) that found in favor of plaintiff Palsgraf.

Issue

Whether the railroad guards were negligent, and owed a duty to Palsgraf and were therefore liable for Palsgraf's injuries?

Holding

No. The guards did not owe a duty to Palsgraf and could not have foreseen the injuries she sustained.

Reasoning

The guards did not owe a duty to Palsgraf. If they owed a duty to anyone it would be the passenger who they assisted while attempting to jump aboard the train; perhaps they would be liable for the loss of his package. The guards acted, however, in concern for the boarding passenger's safety. The court found that the guards could not have foreseen the injury to Palsgraf based on their actions helping the boarding passenger. Negligence cannot "occur in the air." Citing Pollock on Torts, 11th edition. For negligence to be found, one must find a duty. Citing *W. Va. Central R. Co. v. State*. "The ideas of negligence and duty are strictly correlative." Citing *Thomas v. Quartermaine*. Judge Cordozo explained that not only did the guards not owe a duty to Palsgraf, but no ordinary person could foresee that the actions taken by the guards could have injured Palsgraf. Judge Cordozo also included an extensive policy argument providing hypotheticals regarding how the law would develop in an unacceptable manner should the finding be for Palsgraf.

LEXIS CASE BRIEF *Palsgraf v. Long Island Rail Road*

Rule:

If no hazard is apparent to the eye of ordinary vigilance, an act innocent and harmless, at least to outward seeming, with reference to a plaintiff, does not take to itself the quality of a tort because it happened to be a wrong, though apparently not one involving the risk of bodily insecurity, with reference to someone else. In every instance, before negligence can be predicated of a given act, back of the act must be sought and found a duty to the individual complaining, the observance of which would have averted or avoided the injury. The ideas of negligence and duty are strictly correlative.

Facts:

Plaintiff ticket-holding passenger Helen Palsgraf was standing on a platform of defendant Long Island Railroad Company. A man carrying a package jumped aboard the car of a moving train at a nearby platform. A guard in the car reached to help him in, and a guard on the platform pushed the man from behind. The package was dislodged, fell onto the rails, and exploded. The shock of the explosion caused a scales to fall onto plaintiff passenger, who filed this lawsuit for injuries due to defendant's alleged negligence. The trial term court (the Supreme Court) entered a verdict for plaintiff. In 1927, the Supreme Court, Appellate Division affirmed the judgment in favor of plaintiff. These two lower courts held that the negligent acts of the railroad's employees caused the package that contained explosives to be thrown under the train where they exploded. Defendant railroad sought appeal to the Court of Appeals of New York.

(*Procedural note: In the New York state court system, the Supreme Court is the trial level. The Supreme Court of New York, Appellate Division hears cases on first appeal. The highest court is the Court of Appeals of New York—this is the court for the instant decision.*)

Issue:

In an action for injuries sustained during an explosion when a package was dropped on a nearby rail, was defendant railroad liable for negligence due to its guards' conduct in pushing the man carrying the package?

Answer:

No

Conclusion:

In 1928, the Court of Appeals of New York reversed the judgments of the appellate division and the trial term of the Supreme Court. Ruling in favor of defendant railroad, the Court dismissed plaintiff passenger's complaint. The Court found that the conduct of the railroad's guards was not a wrong or negligence in relation to plaintiff, standing far away. There was nothing in the situation to suggest to the most cautious mind that the parcel wrapped in newspaper would spread wreckage through the station. The Court explained that negligence is not actionable unless it involves the invasion of a legally protected interest—the violation of a right, which in this case was claimed to be the right to be protected against interference with one's bodily security. Bodily security is not protected against all forms of interference or aggression, but only against some. Negligence is the absence of care, according to the circumstances. The Court concluded that there was no negligence because defendant railroad could not have reasonably foreseen that its employees' conduct would have resulted in injury to plaintiff Palsgraf. The Court noted that the plaintiff had sued in her own right for a wrong personal to her, and not as the vicarious beneficiary of a breach of duty to another.

---

§3.6.6 Discussion of *Palsgraf*

Did you find this case more difficult to read because of the lack of headings? Did you agree with the judge's conclusion? Did you agree with the judge's policy argument? As a society, do you agree that blaming an individual for unforeseen injuries would be unfair?

Finally, we did not include the dissent from this case, which, as we mentioned, was longer than the opinion. We mention the dissent here to demonstrate the important concepts of **mandatory and persuasive authority**.[30]

A case from a higher court, in the same jurisdiction, with the same facts must be followed; it is mandatory authority. The case sets precedent. Judge Cordozo's ruling in *Palsgraf* must be followed by the lower courts in the state of New York.

What about the dissent in this case by Judge Andrews? A dissent is not precedent. It is not the law and does not need to be followed. Courts may choose to follow it, though; this is persuasive authority. It is interesting to note that several state courts in other jurisdictions did choose to adopt the perspective of Judge Andrews's dissent regarding foreseeability. (To review these concepts further, see § 2.3).

§3.7 Conclusion

Case law is primary law. Just like the Constitution, statutes, and regulations, it is the law itself. Learning to read cases is an important skill for an individual studying the US legal system. To hone this skill, we presented several case reading techniques to assist you:

Adjust your expectations.

Find the structure of the opinion.

---

30. Please see the glossary for a detailed explanation of primary, secondary, mandatory, and persuasive authority.

Grow your current legal knowledge base and write out definitions.

Write case briefs to aid in your case understanding.

Precedent and *stare decisis* are important concepts in understanding where case law fits into our legal system (review § 2.3 and key terms above). We must also grasp the concepts of mandatory and persuasive authority. Continuing to build your legal vocabulary will make reading future cases much easier. As you continue to use the strategies provided, you will become more proficient at reading cases. Studying how a case is written and identifying its structure will help in understanding legal analysis. We cover legal analysis in some depth in Chapter Seven.

EXERCISES

1. What are the parts of a well-written legal opinion?
2. Name at least three strategies to assist you in reading cases.
3. What is precedent and why is it important?
4. How can adjusting your expectations when reading cases help decrease frustration?
5. What are headnotes?
6. Define plaintiff, defendant, appellant, and appellee.

CHAPTER FOUR

Statutory Analysis

We do not inquire what the legislature meant; we ask only what the statute means.

—Justice Oliver Wendell Holmes (1841–1935)[1]

There is no surer way to misread any document than to read it literally.... As nearly as we can, we must put ourselves in the place of those who uttered the words, and try to divine how they would have dealt with the unforeseen situation; and, although their words are by far the most decisive of what they would have done, they are by no means final.

—Justice Billings Learned Hand (1872–1961)[2]

§4.1 Background

As the above quotes suggest, even judges disagree about how to interpret statutes. This chapter offers some strategies and practices to help begin to analyze statutes. Statutes outline the rules that grant rights, forbid conduct, and bestow authority for individuals, federal agencies, and courts to obey.[3] Justice Oliver Wendell Holmes Jr. commented in *McBoyle v. United States* that although an individual may not "consider the text of the law before he murders or steals, it is reasonable that a fair warning should be given to the world in language that the common world will understand, of what the law intends to do if a certain line is passed."[4] Given the multiple

1. Quoted in Antonin Scalia and Bryan A. Garner, READING LAW: THE INTERPRETATION OF LEGAL TEXTS (2012), 29. Original source is Oliver Wendell Holmes, *The Theory of Legal Interpretation*, 12 HARVARD LAW REVIEW (1899), 417, 419.

2. Quoted in James D. Zirin, SUPREMELY PARTISAN: HOW RAW POLITICS TIPS THE SCALES IN THE UNITED STATES SUPREME COURT, 233. Original source is *Giuseppi. v. Walling*, 144 F.2d 608, 624 (2nd Cir. 1944).

3. E. C. Zoldan, *The Conversation Canon*, 110 KENTUCKY L. J. (2022), 38.

4. Quoted in D. S. Louk, *The Audiences of Statutes*, 105 CORNELL L. REV. (2020), 167. Original source is *McBoyle v. United States*, 283 U.S. 25 (1931).

purposes and the difficulty of crafting understandable yet precise language in a statute, where do lawmakers begin? Legislators have a manual for drafting statutes in the U.S. House of Representatives that states "IDENTIFY THE AUDIENCE. Decide who is supposed to get the message."[5] The terminology and structure of a statute should be written so the intended audience will understand it.[6]

A statute written in today's complex world can easily be hundreds of pages long with multiple interrelated sections each written by different individuals; it is no wonder statutes can be vague and ambiguous with inconsistencies and mistakes making the meaning of some parts difficult to interpret.[7] Oftentimes, statutes are based on multiple compromises from unfinished decisions about specific legal issues leading to intentionally vague language, instead of clarity essential to reader understanding.[8] For example, the Supreme Court has commented that the Affordable Care Act, which is over 1,000 pages long, "contains more than a few examples of inartful drafting" and "does not reflect the type of care and deliberation that one might expect of such significant legislation."[9]

Vagueness can be improved by legislators paying more attention to drafting straightforward and clear language; however, when statutes are ambiguous, the courts have the job of interpreting the statute.[10] A survey of forty-two federal appellate judges was conducted on how they interpreted ambiguous statutes.[11] While some judges responded that they wanted more guidance on interpreting statutes; others requested to "just write better statutes! That's the problem. They are so poorly drafted, and we as lower courts are stuck trying to figure out what Congress intended."[12]

§4.2 Statutory Interpretation

Students of the law must also be able to read and interpret statutes, which is a learned skill. Let's examine the Why, When, and How of statutory interpretation.

Why? So why is this an important skill to master?

To stay current: Staying abreast of current industry trends reflected in law and regulations is vital, especially in heavily regulated areas like health care.

---

5. D. S. Louk, *The Audiences of Statutes*, 105 Cornell L. Rev. (2020), 140.
6. D. S. Louk, *The Audiences of Statutes*, 105 Cornell L. Rev. (2020), 140.
7. R. H. Fallon, *The Statutory Interpretation Muddle*, 114 Nw. U. L. Rev. (2019), 317.
8. D. S. Louk, *The Audiences of Statutes*, 105 Cornell L. Rev. (2020), 153.
9. R. H. Fallon, *The Statutory Interpretation Muddle*, 114 Nw. U. L. Rev. (2019), 324.
10. D. S. Louk, *The Audiences of Statutes*, 105 Cornell L. Rev. (2020), 157.
11. A. R. Gluck & E. A. Posner, *Statutory Interpretation on the Bench: A Survey of Forty-Two Judges on the Federal Courts of Appeals*, 131 Harvard Law Review (2018), 1300.
12. A. R. Gluck & E. A. Posner, *Statutory Interpretation on the Bench: A Survey of Forty-Two Judges on the Federal Courts of Appeals*, 131 Harvard Law Review (2018), 1347.

To communicate: Once you review a statute, you may need to relay your findings to others in your organization. You do not want everyone responsible for hospital billing to read a five-page regulation and the accompanying seventy-seven pages of commentary appearing in the Federal Register regarding hospital price transparency.[13] You will need to understand, condense, and synthesize the ideas so that they can be applied to your organization.

To predict: You may be called on to anticipate how a given statute or regulation is likely to impact your organization.

To plan: If you learn that a major piece of legislation is expected this term that will address electronic medical records, you may not want to sign the contract for a new software system just yet until you ensure that it will be compliant with all new requirements, both statutory and regulatory.

To influence: You may want to advocate for adoption, rejection, or modification of statutes and regulations, both pending and adopted.

When? You may need to interpret legislation at multiple points in the passage of its life cycle, including the inception, during committee and floor debate, prior to executive signature, and beyond.

How? So how do we approach reading legislation? It is helpful to look at how judges interpret the language and meaning of statutes. Judges tend to use one of two major theoretical approaches to statutory interpretation.

§ 4.3 Theories of Statutory Interpretation

Justice Scalia has shared his disappointment that there is not an agreed-on statutory interpretation theory.[14] Two major theories have emerged for courts to interpret statutes, referred to as textualism and purposivism.[15]

§ 4.3.1 Textualism

Textualism has been called "ordinary meaning" jurisprudence and asserts that judges are restricted primarily to analysis of the text alone, giving each word its typical meaning in regular usage. This approach is often associated with the former Justice Scalia. The main tenets of textualism include: "(1) that a statute is a command

---

13. Medicare and Medicaid Programs: CY 2020 Hospital Outpatient PPS Policy Changes and Payment Rates and Ambulatory Surgical Center Payment System Policy Changes and Payment Rates. Price Transparency Requirements for Hospitals To Make Standard Charges Public, Final Rule, 45 CFR Subchapter E, Federal Register, Vol. 84, No. 229, Wednesday, November 27, 2019, Rules and Regulations, 65524–606.

14. R. H. Fallon, *The Statutory Interpretation Muddle*, 114 Nw. U. L. Rev. (2019), 270.

15. A. R. Moncrieff, *Statutory Realism: The Jurisprudential Ambivalence of Interpretive Theory*, 72 Rutgers U. L. Rev. (2019), 39.

from the legislature, (2) the meaning and legitimacy of which are discernible from the legislative enactment itself, and (3) are alterable only by legislative amendment."[16]

Textualists think that the text in statutes are commands, and that individuals and courts should adhere to these rules no matter what the consequences are, even if it generates a poor result or the outcome defeats the legislation's purpose.[17] Textualists believe that any change of a statute's meaning to deal with real-world concerns must be amended formally by Congress, not the courts.[18] However, in a survey of federal appellate judges about their real-world practices of statutory interpretation, none of the forty-two judges identified themselves as textualists without some qualification, admitting to using some decision tools, such as legislative history and canons of construction.[19]

An example of textualism is found in *Smith v. United States* where Smith was arrested on drug charges after offering to trade an automatic weapon for cocaine to an undercover agent.[20] The court literally applied Title 18 U.S.C. § 924(c)(I), to find Smith guilty of enhanced drug penalties since he, "during and in relation to... [a] drug trafficking crime[,] uses... a firearm."[21] The dissent argued that the language "uses a firearm'" should not apply with these facts since the defendant was exchanging the gun for cocaine and not using it as a weapon.[22]

§ 4.3.2 Purposivism

Another approach to interpret statutes is called **purposivism**, which focuses on addressing the issue that the legislature was trying to fix when it wrote the statute.[23] Purposivists believe that using extrinsic interpretive sources, like legislative history and canons, is appropriate when the statute does not include sufficient information.[24] Purposivists recognize that statutes can become outdated and thus require courts to consider new information "to preserve the statute's operational meaning (its desirable real-world consequences) even if that approach sacrifices or ignores the semantic meaning of the statutory text."[25]

---

16. A. R. Moncrieff, *Statutory Realism: The Jurisprudential Ambivalence of Interpretive Theory*, 72 Rutgers U. L. Rev. (2019), 127.

17. A. R. Moncrieff, *Statutory Realism: The Jurisprudential Ambivalence of Interpretive Theory*, 72 Rutgers U. L. Rev. (2019), 42–43, 83, 111.

18. A. R. Moncrieff, *Statutory Realism: The Jurisprudential Ambivalence of Interpretive Theory*, 72 Rutgers U. L. Rev. (2019), 127.

19. A. R. Gluck & E. A. Posner, *Statutory Interpretation on the Bench: A Survey of Forty-Two Judges on the Federal Courts of Appeals*, 131 Harvard Law Review (2018), 1310.

20. R. H. Fallon, *The Statutory Interpretation Muddle*, 114 Nw. U. L. Rev. (2019), 277.

21. R. H. Fallon, *The Statutory Interpretation Muddle*, 114 Nw. U. L. Rev. (2019), 321.

22. R. H. Fallon, *The Statutory Interpretation Muddle*, 114 Nw. U. L. Rev. (2019), 277.

23. V. C. Brannon, *Statutory Interpretation: Theories, Tools, and Trends*, Congressional Research Service (2023, March 10), 12, https://crsreports.congress.gov/product/pdf/R/R45153.

24. D. S. Louk, *The Audiences of Statutes*, 105 Cornell L. Rev. (2020), 138, 193. 224.

25. A. R. Moncrieff, *Statutory Realism: The Jurisprudential Ambivalence of Interpretive Theory*, 72 Rutgers U. L. Rev. (2019), 87.

Purposivists argue that as new situations arise that the lawmakers did not address specifically, the judge must interpret the statute as the legislators would have intended. She may read the legislative history, including committee reports if available, to try to learn what the legislators intended at the time of enactment. She might examine how the agency charged with implementing the law has interpreted similar laws. She may look to additional documentation, for example, using the Federalist papers in constitutional interpretation. She might consider the work of authoritative legal scholars. She will certainly look to the opinions of other cases in the same and overseeing jurisdictions, and she may look to the opinions of courts in other jurisdictions for reference. Finally, she might argue for or against the law based on policy considerations. Purposivists expect judges to take a holistic approach to understand the reason for the policy and uphold its aim, in spite of the statutory language.[26] In other words, "the letter of the law ought to yield to the spirit of the law whenever the two conflict."[27]

The purposivism approach is exemplified in *King v. Burwell*.[28] The language of the Affordable Care Act (ACA) stipulates that individuals are eligible for tax subsidies if they purchased insurance on "an Exchange established by the State."[29] The issue was whether tax subsidies were available to individuals who bought insurance from federal exchanges.[30] Chief Justice Roberts reasoned that "[i]f we give the phrase "the State that established the Exchange' its most natural meaning," then other sections of the ACA would become nonfunctional, so he surmised that the statute required an interpretation in the context of the broader ACA goals to provide health insurance.[31] The court found that the tax subsidies should be permitted for individuals who purchased insurance from the federal exchange when their state failed to implement an exchange.[32] Chief Justice Roberts stated: "Congress passed the Affordable Care Act to improve health insurance markets, not to destroy them.... If at all possible, we must interpret the Act in a way that is consistent with the former and avoids the latter."[33] The dissenting judges stated that "when the [ACA] says 'Exchange established by the State', it does not mean 'Exchange established by the State or the Federal Government.'"[34] Additionally, Justice Scalia argued that "[i]t is entire-

26. A. R. Moncrieff, *Statutory Realism: The Jurisprudential Ambivalence of Interpretive Theory*, 72 RUTGERS U. L. REV. (2019), 82.

27. A. R. Moncrieff, *Statutory Realism: The Jurisprudential Ambivalence of Interpretive Theory*, 72 RUTGERS U. L. REV. (2019), 82.

28. *King v. Burwell*, 576 U.S. 473 (2015).

29. Section 1311 of the Patient Protection and Affordable Care Act [i.e., 42 U.S.C. § 18031]. 26 U.S.C. §§ 36B(b)–(c).

30. M. Seidenfeld, *Textualism's Theoretical Bankruptcy and Its Implications for Statutory Interpretation*, 100 B. U. L. REV. (2020), 1846.

31. R. H. Fallon, *The Statutory Interpretation Muddle*, 114 NW. U. L. REV. (2019), 324.

32. R. H. Fallon, *The Statutory Interpretation Muddle*, 114 NW. U. L. REV. (2019), 324.

33. R. H. Fallon, *The Statutory Interpretation Muddle*, 114 NW. U. L. REV. (2019), 324.

34. R. H. Fallon, *The Statutory Interpretation Muddle*, 114 NW. U. L. REV. (2019), 324.

ly plausible that tax credits were restricted to state Exchanges deliberately—for example, in order to encourage States to establish their own Exchanges."[35]

Another case example of purposivism that demonstrates how the court interpreted the language of a statute to uphold its intent is found in *Ziccarelli v. Dart.*[36] The pertinent section of the Family and Medical Leave Act (FMLA) is U.S.C. § 2615(a)(I) that disallows employers from "interfer[ing] with, restrain[ing], or deny[ing] the exercise of or the attempt to exercise any right provided under [the FMLA] by their employees."[37] The facts include the employer saying to Ziccarelli "you've taken serious amounts of FMLA.... Don't take any more FMLA. If you do so, you will be disciplined."[38] Thereafter, Ziccarelli did not request FMLA and retired in a few weeks.[39] The relevant required element to bring an FMLA claim is § 2615(a)(I)(v) in which the plaintiff must show they "were denied FMLA benefits to which they were entitled."[40] The court held that the statute did not require an actual denial of FMLA leave and that the employer's statements to Ziccarelli interfered with his taking FMLA.[41] Here, the court's reasoning is that the employer's interference equates to denying Ziccarelli his FMLA rights and meeting the statutory requirement for his claim.[42]

§ 4.4 Getting Started

Your work may require you to interpret a statute, so where should you begin? Oftentimes, a statute will have elements like a preamble, definitions, headings, marginal notes, and other operative and enforcement provisions.

---

35. R. H. Fallon, *The Statutory Interpretation Muddle*, 114 Nw. U. L. Rev. (2019), 325.

36. *Ziccarelli v. Dart,* United States Court of Appeals for the Seventh Circuit, 35 F.4th 1079 (2022).

37. Ziccarelli v. Dart: *Seventh Circuit Entrenches Conduct Categories for FMLA Interference Claims*, 136 Harv. L. Rev. (March 2023), 1477.

38. Ziccarelli v. Dart: *Seventh Circuit Entrenches Conduct Categories for FMLA Interference Claims*, 136 Harv. L. Rev. (March 2023), 1477.

39. Ziccarelli v. Dart: *Seventh Circuit Entrenches Conduct Categories for FMLA Interference Claims*, 136 Harv. L. Rev. (March 2023), 1477.

40. Ziccarelli v. Dart: *Seventh Circuit Entrenches Conduct Categories for FMLA Interference Claims*, 136 Harv. L. Rev. (March 2023), 1478.

41. Ziccarelli v. Dart: *Seventh Circuit Entrenches Conduct Categories for FMLA Interference Claims*, 136 Harv. L. Rev. (March 2023), 1479.

42. Ziccarelli v. Dart: *Seventh Circuit Entrenches Conduct Categories for FMLA Interference Claims*, 136 Harv. L. Rev. (March 2023), 1480.

§4.4.1 Careful Reading

First, you must have a thorough understanding of the legal issue(s) related to your organization's goals and the associated facts to identify the pertinent statute to analyze, making sure that the identified statute has not been repealed or amended.[43] A typical approach to interpreting a statute is to assume that the language is its usual meaning given its context.[44] Then carefully read the statute and realize that your initial understanding of the statute may be one of several possible interpretations, and that you may later have a very different interpretation as you continue the analysis.[45]

Pause for Reflection Reading of statutes and regulations requires very careful reading, down to the articles and punctuation.

Consider this scenario: Tim takes his boat out to Black Walnut State Park for some fishing. The state regulation regarding recreational boats states:

"Boats must be registered annually with the state. Boat owners must demonstrate compliance with this license requirement by

1-displaying the state-issued sticker on the boat;

2-displaying the license registration number on the boat; or

3-carrying on their person a copy of the license at all times when operating the boat.

Boat owners may be fined up to $300.00 for non-compliance."

As Tim gets ready to put the boat in the water, he notices that the sticker has fallen off. He checks his tackle box and finds his license.

Questions:

1. Should he go out? Why or why not?
2. What is the key language in determining an answer?

If you said that Tim can go out, you are correct; Tim is compliant because he has his license. The key language is the word "or" requiring that only one of the three requirements must be met to be compliant.

Tim goes back to Black Walnut State Park in January, anxious to try out his new snowmobile. As he finishes his ride, he is surprised to find the park ranger waiting for him beside his snowmobile trailer. The ranger points to a sign at the trailhead displaying a new local ordinance:

---

43. S. Kumar & T. Beech, *A Guide to Reading, Interpreting and Applying Statutes*, Georgetown Law (2017), 1–2, https://www.law.georgetown.edu/wp-content/uploads/2018/12/A-Guide-to-Reading-Interpreting-and-Applying-Statutes-1.pdf.

44. D. S. Louk, *The Audiences of Statutes*, 105 CORNELL L. REV. (2020), 173.

45. S. Kumar & T. Beech, *A Guide to Reading, Interpreting and Applying Statutes*, Georgetown Law (2017), 1–2, https://www.law.georgetown.edu/wp-content/uploads/2018/12/A-Guide-to-Reading-Interpreting-and-Applying-Statutes-1.pdf.

"No motorized recreational vehicles permitted on trails, including but not limited to ATVs, motorcycles, mopeds, motorized bicycles and motorized scooters."

Tom says, "But sir, it doesn't say anything about snowmobiles."

Questions:

1. Is he correct? Why or why not?
2. What is the key language?

Tim is incorrect because a snowmobile is a motorized recreational vehicle. No type of recreational motorized vehicle is permitted on the trails. The key language is "including but not limited to."

§4.4.2 Cross-References

The Supreme Court has advised that "Statutory construction ... is a holistic endeavor. A provision that may seem ambiguous in isolation is often clarified by the remainder of the statutory scheme."[46] Often a reader needs to understand the background law in a particular area to make sense of a statute. Many statutes also cross-reference other statutes. Additionally, statutes frequently refer to other provisions within the legislation.

Consider, for example, a law enacted by the state of Tennessee requiring employers to report to the Department of Health a health care practitioner who refuses or fails a drug test. To understand the applicability of provision (b), a reader must determine which health care practitioners are covered under the act by referring to provision (a).

> (a) As used in this section ... "Healthcare practitioner" or "practitioner" means any person required to be licensed, permitted, certified, or authorized: (A) Under this title by a board or committee under the division of health-related boards specified in section 68-1-101(a)(8), who has humans for patients; or (B) Under title 68, chapter 24 ...; or (C) Under title 68, chapter 140.
>
> (b) A healthcare practitioner violates the practitioner's practice act by refusing to submit to a drug test or testing positive for any drug on any government or private sector preemployment or employer-ordered confirmed drug test for an employer when the practitioner does not have a lawful prescription for using the drug or a valid medical reason for using the drug.[47]

46. V. C. Brannon, *Statutory Interpretation: Theories, Tools, and Trends*, Congressional Research Service (2023, March 10), 25, https://crsreports.congress.gov/product/pdf/R/R45153.

47. T.C.A. 63-1-126 (a)–(b).

§4.4.3 Date of Enactment

A reader must note the date a statute was enacted to determine its applicability in each case. Also note the dates of any amendments. These dates are often found in small type at the bottom of subsections.

§4.4.4 Modification of Prior Statutes

Please note that sometimes an act accomplishes its purposes by making changes to preexisting law.

You will find that sometimes the words in a statute are clear and straightforward, but oftentimes there is some ambiguity that needs to be analyzed. Then you may use extrinsic tools, like canons, legislative history, and past statutory implementation.[48]

§4.5 Canons

Canons are "guiding principles for interpreting statutes."[49] They provide methods that courts use to resolve challenging interpretation questions.[50] Courts use substantive or "policy" canons, which are presumptions to interpret statutes for specific audiences.[51] Additionally, there are semantic or "linguistic" canons, which are presumptions to interpret statutory words and phrases.[52] In a survey of forty-two federal court judges, they all acknowledged using the canons and categorized them into four groupings.[53] The first was canons as "tools of persuasion" to bolster arguments to persuade colleagues.[54] The second was canons as "useful decision tools" in determining case holdings.[55] The third was some canons are "actual rules" requiring mandatory use, like the rule of lenity for courts to find in

48. V. C. Brannon, *Statutory Interpretation: Theories, Tools, and Trends*, Congressional Research Service (2023, March 10), 20, https://crsreports.congress.gov/product/pdf/R/R45153.

49. V. C. Brannon, *Statutory Interpretation: Theories, Tools, and Trends*, Congressional Research Service (2023, March 10), 27, https://crsreports.congress.gov/product/pdf/R/R45153.

50. M. Foerster, *Canons of Construction: What Is Their Role, If Any, in Modern Jurisprudence?* (2022), https://www.americanbar.org/groups/judicial/publications/appellate_issues/2022/winter/canons-of-construction/.

51. A. R. Gluck & E. A. Posner, *Statutory Interpretation on the Bench: A Survey of Forty-Two Judges on the Federal Courts of Appeals*, 131 Harvard Law Review (2018), 1330.

52. A. R. Gluck & E. A. Posner, *Statutory Interpretation on the Bench: A Survey of Forty-Two Judges on the Federal Courts of Appeals*, 131 Harvard Law Review (2018), 1330.

53. A. R. Gluck & E. A. Posner, *Statutory Interpretation on the Bench: A Survey of Forty-Two Judges on the Federal Courts of Appeals*, 131 Harvard Law Review (2018), 1329–32.

54. A. R. Gluck & E. A. Posner, *Statutory Interpretation on the Bench: A Survey of Forty-Two Judges on the Federal Courts of Appeals*, 131 Harvard Law Review (2018), 1330.

55. A. R. Gluck & E. A. Posner, *Statutory Interpretation on the Bench: A Survey of Forty-Two Judges on the Federal Courts of Appeals*, 131 Harvard Law Review (2018), 1330–31.

favor of defendants for ambiguous statutes.[56] The fourth was canons can make judicial opinions seem more legitimate.[57] Some examples of canons used to interpret ambiguous statues follow.[58]

SEMANTIC CANONS[59]

Artificial person: use of the word person includes a corporation.

Omissions: matters not mentioned in a statute should be considered to be deliberately omitted.

Gender: typically references to male and men are construed to include female and women and vice versa.

Number: the singular usually includes the plural.

General/specific: where two laws conflict, the more detailed law governs.

Headings: preface, titles, and headings may also be looked to for intent but are not determinative.

Consistent uses: identical words in different sections of a statute are considered to have the same definition.

Validity: an interpretation that upholds a statute outweighs an interpretation that would invalidate it.

Rule against surplusage[60]: no part of a statute should be considered irrelevant.

Whole text canon: statutes should be read as a whole for continuity; statutory phrases should not be interpreted out of context.

SUBSTANTIVE CANONS[61]

Constitutional avoidance: "[W]here an otherwise acceptable construction of a statute would raise serious constitutional problems, the Court will construe the

---

56. A. R. Gluck & E. A. Posner, *Statutory Interpretation on the Bench: A Survey of Forty-Two Judges on the Federal Courts of Appeals*, 131 Harvard Law Review (2018), 1331–32.

57. A. R. Gluck & E. A. Posner, *Statutory Interpretation on the Bench: A Survey of Forty-Two Judges on the Federal Courts of Appeals*, 131 Harvard Law Review (2018), 1332.

58. List drawn from a longer list from V. C. Brannon, *Statutory Interpretation: Theories, Tools, and Trends*, Congressional Research Service (2023, March 10), Appendix 51–62, https://crsreports.congress.gov/product/pdf/R/R45153.

59. List drawn from a longer list from V. C. Brannon, *Statutory Interpretation: Theories, Tools, and Trends*, Congressional Research Service (2023, March 10), Appendix 51–57, https://crsreports.congress.gov/product/pdf/R/R45153.

60. Surplusage in legal terms is extraneous, irrelevant material.

61. List drawn from a longer list from V. C. Brannon, *Statutory Interpretation: Theories, Tools, and Trends*, Congressional Research Service (2023, March 10), Appendix 57–62, https://crsreports.congress.gov/product/pdf/R/R45153.

statute to avoid such problems unless such construction is plainly contrary to the intent of Congress."[62]

Federalism: courts require an unambiguous statement of congressional intent if an interpretation would intrude on state sovereignty.

In Pari Materia: multiple statutes addressing a subject should be read to provide consistency.

Narrow exception: exceptions to longstanding policy are generally construed narrowly.

Rule of lenity: courts should find in favor of defendants for ambiguous statutes.

§4.6 Legislative History

Legislative history comprises all the documents created by Congress during the introduction and debate of a bill and is often referenced by courts to interpret statutes.[63] Similarly, you may find reviewing the legislative history useful to interpret ambiguous statutes. However, please note that legislative history can be manipulated by legislators or committee staff working on the bill.[64] Chief Justice Roberts noted that "all legislative history is not created equal," with Chief Judge Katzmann recommending prioritizing committee reports with less weight on statements made from the legislature or chamber floor by non-sponsor legislators.[65] Various types of legislative documents can be found in the link in the footnote.[66]

§4.7 Past Statutory Interpretation

Administrative agencies frequently have issued regulations that can explain how to interpret and apply a statute; these are found in the Code of Federal Regulations (CFR).[67] Additionally, it may be helpful for you to review prior cases applying the same statute to see how courts have interpreted and implemented a particular statute

---

62. *Edward J. DeBartolo Corp. v. Florida Gulf Coast Building & Construction Trades Council*, 485 U.S. 568, 575 (1988).

63. *United States Legislative History: What is Legislative History?* University at Buffalo (2022, August 25), https://research.lib.buffalo.edu/us-legislative-history.

64. M. Seidenfeld, *Textualism's Theoretical Bankruptcy and Its Implications for Statutory Interpretation*, 100 B. U. L. Rev. (2020), 1852.

65. S. Kumar & T. Beech, *A Guide to Reading, Interpreting and Applying Statutes*, Georgetown Law (2017), 9, https://www.law.georgetown.edu/wp-content/uploads/2018/12/A-Guide-to-Reading-Interpreting-and-Applying-Statutes-1.pdf.

66. *United States Legislative History: What is Legislative History?* University at Buffalo (2022, August 25), https://research.lib.buffalo.edu/us-legislative-history.

67. S. Kumar & T. Beech, *A Guide to Reading, Interpreting and Applying Statutes*, Georgetown Law (2017), 6, https://www.law.georgetown.edu/wp-content/uploads/2018/12/A-Guide-to-Reading-Interpreting-and-Applying-Statutes-1.pdf.

that you are analyzing.[68] For example, sometimes judges adhere to the purposivism approach and do not follow the statutory text if it impedes the intent of the statute as exemplified in *King v. Burwell* (576 U.S. 483 (2015)) and *Ziccarelli v. Dart* (United States Court of Appeals for the Seventh Circuit 35 F.4th 1079 (2022)).

In summary, analyzing and interpreting a statute can be tricky. Be extra careful when reading and interpreting language in statutes, which is critical to understanding the statute's intent. You can assume the ordinary or the typical meaning of the statute's language given its context. You may draw on time-honored rules or canons of construction. These include semantic canons and substantive canons. You could read the legislative history to try to learn what the legislators intended at time of enactment. You might examine how the federal agency charged with implementing the statute or how past court decisions have interpreted the statute. Using these methods and tools can assist you in analyzing and interpreting statutes in your work to meet your organization's goals.

EXERCISES

1. What is the statutory interpretation theory that focuses on addressing the issue that the legislature was trying to fix when it wrote the statute?
2. What are three reasons why students of the law need to interpret statutes?
3. List four things to do or review when preparing to interpret a statute.
4. What is the canon that states courts should find in favor of defendants for ambiguous statutes?
5. What legislative history documents should be prioritized when interpreting a statute?

---

68. S. Kumar & T. Beech, *A Guide to Reading, Interpreting and Applying Statutes*, Georgetown Law (2017), 5–6, https://www.law.georgetown.edu/wp-content/uploads/2018/12/A-Guide-to-Reading-Interpreting-and-Applying-Statutes-1.pdf.

CHAPTER FIVE

Administrative Agencies

§5.1 An Era of Regulation

"We live in an era of regulation, but our jurisprudence has fallen behind. Despite the central place that regulations occupy in our law, their interpretation has garnered little focused consideration."[1] These words of Professor Kevin M. Stack that introduced this book bear repeating.

An understanding of regulations, also known as rules, is important to understanding the legal landscape. Please review the structure and basic information about agencies found under the executive branch in § 2.2.2. In this chapter, we take a deeper dive and examine the proliferation of agencies, how Congress and agencies interact, and where the courts fit into the picture. Then, we demonstrate how to find proposed rules and regulations and submit comments. Hopefully, you will feel inspired to write comments on the proposed rules that affect you and your organization.

§5.2 How Did We Get Here? A Brief History of Administrative / Regulatory Law

"Power tends to corrupt, and absolute power corrupts absolutely."[2] Having escaped the tyranny of King George, and with a concern about the corruptibility of power, the drafters of our Constitution strove to decentralize power in their new government. The people were to have sovereign power.

This power to the people is established in Article I, Section 1 of the U.S. Constitution: "All legislative Powers herein granted shall be vested in a Congress of the United States, which shall consist of a Senate and House of Representatives."[3] "We the people" have the voting power to elect those in Congress who write our laws. We can also voice our concerns to legislators and comment on proposed or current legislation. Most important, though, is our voting power. In this way, the people control the laws that govern them.

---

1. K. M. Stack, *First Principles for Interpreting Regulations*, THE REGULATORY REVIEW (2013, February 11) (quote in paragraph one).

2. Lord Baron Acton (1834–1902). This particular version is attributed to Lord Acton, though several others expressed the same idea.

3. U.S. Constitution, Article I, Section 1.

What power, though, do "we the people" have over governmental agencies? We do not elect agency employees and we cannot vote them out. As the number of agencies grows, the discussion surrounding agency authority ensues.[4] Some find the proliferation of agencies out of control and note that it is difficult to even find consensus on the number of agencies. Currently, the Federal Register lists 439.[5]

To get an idea of the vastness and complexity of just one agency, let's look at the Department of Transportation (DOT). In 2023, the DOT had more than 55,000 employees. We do not vote for the secretary of transportation; that is an appointed position. Similarly, we do not have voting rights to choose any of those 55,000-plus employees.

Also, under the DOT are several subagencies:

U.S. Department of Transportation Office of the Secretary (OST)

National Highway Traffic Safety Administration (NHTSA)

Federal Aviation Administration (FAA)

Office of Inspector General (OIG)

Federal Highway Administration (FHWA)

Pipeline and Hazardous Materials Safety Administration (PHMSA)

Federal Motor Carrier Safety Administration (FMCSA)

Federal Railroad Administration (FRA)

Great Lakes St. Lawrence Seaway Development Corporation (GLS)

Federal Transit Administration (FTA)

Maritime Administration (MARAD)

Thus, much controversy surrounds the proliferation of agencies and the powers that they wield. As you recall from § 2.2.2, agencies have been granted the authority to make laws from the enabling act that Congress includes in the statute that delegates the power to the agency. Agencies have lawmaking powers (also known as quasi-legislative), and they can render judgments (also known as quasi-judicial). But there is really nothing "quasi" about it; just think of the power of the Internal Revenue Service (IRS).

As the world has become more complex, however, is it reasonable to expect Congress to write all the laws that affect our daily lives? With that, two conflicting ideas come to mind:

1. How can congresspeople address these very complex issues? Do they have the expertise to address, for example, airline safety, food and drug safety,

---

4. See, e.g., S. Sullivan, *Powers, But How Much Power? Game Theory and the Nondelegation Principle*, 104 Va. L. Rev. (2018), 1229.

5. https://www.federalregister.gov/agencies

or safeguards in the banking industry? Isn't it necessary to have experts address these complicated, technical issues?

2. But then, without our voting power, do "we the people" have any input about these regulations that govern us?

As you recall from § 2.2.2.b.iii (Informal Rulemaking), the Administrative Procedures Act requires that all rules be published in the Federal Register and allows time for the public to comment on the rules before they become law. In this way we can exert some influence on newly proposed rules. We will discuss how to submit comments in § 5.4 and § 5.5.

§5.3 Agency Authority

An understanding of agency authority is important to us not only as employees but also as citizens. Though agency authority has always been a topic of debate, in the past several years the debate has escalated. We have an example in recent history that highlights both the importance of and the controversy surrounding agency authority: the Centers for Disease Control and Prevention ("CDC") and the COVID pandemic.

During the COVID pandemic, the CDC issued several public health emergency orders: The CDC ordered a mask mandate, refused migrants at the border, and placed a moratorium on evictions.[6] We see the extent of the controversy as the courts got involved. A Florida court struck down the CDC's mask mandate.[7] The Supreme Court struck down the CDC's eviction moratorium.[8] The turning away of migrants at the border, which was supported by both Republican and Democratic administrations, was referred to as Title 42. This order ended in May 2023 as the president ended the COVID national emergency.[9]

Let's look more closely at one of these orders: the CDC moratorium on evictions.[10] Prior to the pandemic, there was an affordable housing crisis.[11] The pandemic intensified this crisis; and consequently many individuals were having trouble paying their rent; they were being evicted.[12] The CDC's moratorium stopped landlords from evicting tenants.

6. Khalik, F. & Parmet, W.E. (2023). *Judicial Review of Public Health Powers Since the Start of the Covid-19 Pandemic: Trends and Implications.* Am J Public Health 113 (3) 280-287.

7. *Health Freedom Def. Fund, Inc. v. Biden*, 572 F. Supp. 3d 1257 (2021).

8. *Ala. Ass'n of Realtors v. HHS*, 141 S. Ct. 2485 (2021).

9. https://www.dhs.gov/news/2023/01/05/dhs-continues-prepare-end-title-42-announces-new-border-enforcement-measures-and.

10. https://nlihc.org/sites/default/files/gap/Gap-Report_2023.pdf.

11. https://nlihc.org/sites/default/files/gap/Gap-Report_2023.pdf, 9.

12. https://nlihc.org/sites/default/files/gap/Gap-Report_2023.pdf, 24.

The CDC contended that the enabling clause of the Public Health Act of 1944 section 261 provided authority.[13] Those opposing this authority claimed that this 1944 statute focused on isolation and quarantine to avoid the spread of deadly diseases; they claimed this had nothing to do with evicting renters. The CDC offered that the evictions made it difficult for people to properly isolate during the pandemic, but those in opposition said that the eviction moratorium far outstripped the language and intention of the enabling statute.[14]

That enabling statute provides that the surgeon general may take certain actions prescribed in the enabling statute to prevent the spread of disease.[15] In addition, the surgeon general may take "other measures, as in his judgment may be necessary."[16] As agencies were reorganized, this power eventually shifted from the surgeon general to Health and Human Services[17] and one of its agencies, the CDC.

In finding that the CDC overstepped its authority, the Supreme Court stated that "[t]he CDC has imposed a nationwide moratorium on evictions in reliance on a decades-old statute that authorizes it to implement measures like fumigation and pest extermination. It strains credulity to believe that this statute grants the CDC the sweeping authority that it asserts."[18] So, we can see that the Supreme Court may block an agency's actions if the action exceeds the scope of its legislative delegation.

The questioning of an agency's authority was not lost on the public. During the COVID pandemic, many news organizations covered the controversy centering on whether the CDC overstepped its authority in issuing these emergency public health orders in the first place. A glance at the titles footnoted here provides a sampling of how prevalent this issue was in the news.[19]

---

13. *Ala. Ass'n of Realtors v. HHS*, 141 S. Ct. 2485, 2487 (2021).

14. *Ala. Ass'n of Realtors v. HHS*, 141 S. Ct. 2485, 2488 (2021).

15. 42 U.S.C. § 264(a)(b). Regulations to control communicable diseases

(a) Promulgation and enforcement by Surgeon General. The Surgeon General, with the approval of the Administrator [Secretary], is authorized to make and enforce such regulations as in his judgment are necessary to prevent the introduction, transmission, or spread of communicable diseases from foreign countries into the States or possessions, or from one State or possession into any other State or possession. For purposes of carrying out and enforcing such regulations, the Surgeon General may provide for such inspection, fumigation, disinfection, sanitation, pest extermination, destruction of animals or articles found to be so infected or contaminated as to be sources of dangerous infection to human beings, and other measures, as in his judgment may be necessary.

(b) Apprehension, detention, or conditional release of individuals. Regulations prescribed under this section shall not provide for the apprehension, detention, or conditional release of individuals except for the purpose of preventing the introduction, transmission, or spread of such communicable diseases as may be specified from time to time in Executive orders of the President upon the recommendation of the Secretary, in consultation with the Surgeon General.

16. 42 U.S.C. § 264(a)(b).

17. The Department of Health, Education, and Welfare (HEW) was created in 1953. It became the Department of Health and Human Services (HHS) in 1980.

18. *Ala. Ass'n of Realtors v. HHS*, 141 S. Ct. 2485 (2021).

19. U.S.-Mexico Border: Thousands of Migrants Expelled under Coronavirus Powers, BBC (April 10, 2020); CDC Officials Objected to Order Turning Away Migrants at Border, WALL STREET JOURNAL (October 3, 2020)]; C.D.C. Confirms It Will Lift Public Health Order Restricting Immi-

We can see from the response of the courts, then, that agency authority can be challenged. To discover how agency authority developed, though, we need to take a step back.

§5.3.1 The Non-Delegation Doctrine

A word about our coverage of this subject before we continue: We understand that this is a complex topic, and it may seem that we are going a bit too far down the rabbit hole. This information, however, will allow you to follow the Supreme Court's decisions on this important topic and have enough background to form your own opinion. Do you support delegation or agree with the non-delegation camp?

Article I, Section 1 of the Constitution vests lawmaking in a bicameral Congress. This is often referred to as the vesting clause.[20] Based on a strict construction of the vesting clause, a doctrine emerged claiming that legislative power could not be delegated: the **non-delegation doctrine.** This doctrine asserts that the legislative branch, under Article I, Section 1, cannot cede its legislative power to another branch.

The delegation/non-delegation question has been a contentious debate for years. The crux of the controversy is that some believe that the proliferation of agencies has, in essence, created a fourth branch of government. This fourth branch can make and enforce laws, which some consider contrary to Article I, Section 1. Those on the other side find that it is impossible for Congress to enact all the laws for a society that has become so technologically advanced and complex.

> For much of the nineteenth and early twentieth centuries, the nondelegation doctrine served as a robust check on governmental expansion. Then, during the New Deal revolution, the Supreme Court reined in the doctrine, thereby paving the way for the rise of the modern administrative state.[21]

So, over the years, the courts have addressed the non-delegation doctrine and worked to modify and constrain the power of Congress to delegate power to agencies. One example was the development of the **intelligible principle.** Established in a 1928 Supreme Court case,[22] the intelligible principle confirms that Congress may only delegate authority to another branch of government if it sets forth "a legal framework to constrain the authority of the delegee, such as an administrative agency."[23]

---

gration, New York Times (April 1, 2022); Battle over CDC's Powers Goes Far beyond Travel Mask Mandate, NPR (April 21, 2022); What Is Title 42, Why Is It Ending and What's Happening Now at the Border? CNN (May 11, 2023).

20. The Founders set forth three vesting clauses in the Constitution: vesting legislation in a bicameral Congress, executive power in the president, and judicial power in the Supreme Court (and any inferior courts established by Congress).

21. K. Whittington & J. Uliano, *The Myth of the Nondelegation Doctrine*, 165 U. Pa. L. Rev. (2017), 379.

22. *J. W. Hampton Jr. & Co. v. United States*, 276 U.S. 394 (1928).

23. https://www.law.cornell.edu/constitution-conan/article-1/section-1/origin-of-the-intelligible-principle-standard

In *J. W. Hampton Jr. & Company v. United States*,[24] the Supreme Court held that Congress did not violate the nondelegation clause when it allowed the executive branch to levy a tariff higher than the amount stated in the Tariff Act of 1922. The issue was whether this violated the non-delegation doctrine. The Court found that it did not. In reaching its conclusion, the Court explained that as long as Congress set forth clear guidelines and limits in delegating authority to other branches, it did not violate Article I, Section 1 of the Constitution. This is now referred to as the intelligible principle. The Court stated that "[i]f Congress shall lay down by legislative act an intelligible principle to which the person or body authorized to fix such rates is directed to conform, such legislative action is not a forbidden delegation of legislative power."[25]

This provides the gist of what you need to know about the non-delegation doctrine. If you are interested in knowing more, however, see the excerpted text below. You may find that the controversy is best understood by reading quotes from various scholars on the issue.

Yale law professor William N. Eskridge Jr. supports the delegation argument under the Article I, Section 1 Delegation Doctrine. As mentioned above, this is referred to as the vesting clause, as the Constitution vests legislative power in Congress.

The Vesting Clause text is ambiguous, even read in light of the Constitution's structure.[26] One might read Article I, Section 1 to prohibit Congress from delegating the power to adopt rules having the effect of law (a broad reading of "legislative Powers") or the power to pass statutes (a narrower reading). But one also might read the Vesting Clause to give Congress the supreme authority to make law, including the discretion to delegate lawmaking authority to other officials.

Neomi Rao, federal judge for the Court of Appeals in D.C., strongly supports the non-delegation doctrine. Judge Rao contends "that the non-delegation principle has stubbornly persisted precisely because of its centrality to a republican form of government." She highlights the Constitution drafters' clear intent on a representative legislature.[27]

> The non-delegation principle serves as an important textual and structural limit on the federal government. Congress has limited and enumerated powers that confine the overall scope and power of the federal government to better preserve individual liberty. The non-delegation principle reinforces these limits. If widescale delegation is permissible, executive agencies have discretion to increase the reach of the federal government without going through the difficult process of bicameralism and presentment. Moreover, non-delegation reinforces separation of powers. Open-ended delegation allows lawmaking to be combined with law execution (and adjudication) in executive agencies in a manner that raises questions about political accountability, constitutional limits, and due process.... [T]he Executive power does not include the power to make the law.

---

24. *J. W. Hampton Jr. & Co. v. United States*, 276 U.S. 394 (1928).

25. *J. W. Hampton Jr. & Co. v. United States*, 276 U.S. 394, 409 (1928).

26. See T. Merrill, *Rethinking Article I, Section 1: From Nondelegation to Exclusive Delegation*, 104 Colum. L. Rev. (2004), 2097, 2114–39.

27. See G. Lawson, *Delegation and Original Meaning*, 88 Va. L. Rev. (2002), 327, 332.

Supreme Court Justice Antonin Scalia provides the following perspective in his dissenting opinion in the case of *Mistretta v. United States* (1989):

> I think the Court errs, in other words, not so much because it mistakes the degree of commingling, but because it fails to recognize that this case is not about commingling, but about the creation of a new Branch altogether, a sort of junior varsity Congress. It may well be that in some circumstances such a Branch would be desirable; perhaps the agency before us here will prove to be so. But there are many desirable dispositions that do not accord with the constitutional structure we live under. And in the long run the improvisation of a constitutional structure on the basis of currently perceived utility will be disastrous.[28]

Finally, the government website that provides analysis and interpretation of the U.S. Constitution explains the non-delegation doctrine this way:

> The nondelegation doctrine, however, does not require complete separation of the three branches of government, and its continuing strength is the question of much debate. In its nondelegation jurisprudence, the Supreme Court has recognized the need and importance of coordination among the three branches of government so long as one branch does not encroach on the constitutional field of another branch. The nondelegation doctrine seeks to distinguish the constitutional delegations of power to other branches of government that may be necessary for governmental coordination from unconstitutional grants of legislative power that may violate separation of powers principles.[29]

---

§5.3.2 The *Chevron* Deference

As Congress has continued to delegate legislative power to agencies, the courts have continued to clarify how this is best accomplished. The U.S. Constitution provides that laws are written by Congress, enforced by the executive, and interpreted by the courts. A controversy exists, nonetheless, about who interprets regulations. In a 1984 Supreme Court case, *Chevron U.S.A., Inc. v. Natural Resources Defense Council*,[30] the Court, based on a two-part test, held that courts should defer to an agency's interpretation of the legislature's statute. In the courts, much political controversy ensued.

Chevron involved the Clean Air Act of 1977. Congress did not define an important term in the act, nor was it explained in the act's legislative history. The Supreme Court then allowed the Environmental Protection Agency (EPA) to define the term.[31] Moreover, the Court held that if a statute is ambiguous, the delegated agen-

28. 488 US 361, 427 (1989).

29. https://constitution.congress.gov/browse/essay/artI-S1-5-1/ALDE_00000014/. "In publication for over 100 years, the Constitution Annotated is a comprehensive, government-sanctioned record of the interpretations of the Constitution."

30. 467 U.S. 837 (1984).

31. The term was "stationary sources." *Chevron, U.S.A., Inc. v. NRDC, Inc.*, 467 U.S. 837 (1984).

cy's interpretation holds as long as the interpretation is reasonable.[32] This became known as the ***Chevron* deference.** It allows agencies to interpret ambiguous statutes. Under the Constitution, however, the courts interpret the law.

As of the writing of this book, the Supreme Court has indicated an interest in addressing the *Chevron* deference doctrine. On May 1, 2023, the Supreme Court granted ***certiorari*** to hear *Loper Bright Enterprises v. Raimondo, Secretary of Commerce.*[33] Many think the Court will overturn *Chevron.* As we await the outcome of that case, some believe the *Chevron* deference doctrine is already obsolete and has been replaced by the major question doctrine. ***Chevron* deference Note: The Supreme Court overturned the *Chevron* doctrine in *Loper Bright Enterprises v. Raimondo* (June 28, 2024) while this book was at press. We added detailed, updated information in the Glossary under *Chevron* Deference.**

§5.3.3 The Major Question Doctrine

The question of when Congress may delegate its legislative authority was further refined by **the major question doctrine**. This term was coined in a 1980s law journal article by then Circuit Court Judge Stephen Breyer.[34] Though not specifically named in cases until recently, several cases hesitated to allow congressional delegation to an agency when the issues involved were of substantial economic or political consequence.

The major question doctrine was named specifically and was central in Chief Justice John Roberts's opinion in the landmark case of *West Virginia v. Environmental Protection Agency* (2022). In this case, the Court held that the EPA did not have the authority to place a cap on greenhouse gas emissions. The Court asserted that "where a statute is ambiguous" as to the parameters surrounding delegation to an agency, Congress must instead provide "clear . . . authorization."[35]

Chief Justice Roberts continued:

> [I]n certain extraordinary cases, both separation of powers principles and a practical understanding of legislative intent make us "reluctant to read into ambiguous statutory text" the delegation claimed to be lurking there. Utility Air, 573 U.S., at 324. To convince us otherwise, something more than a merely plausible textual basis for the agency action is necessary. The agency instead must point to "clear congressional authorization" for the power it claims. Ibid. . . .
>
> As for the major questions doctrine, it took hold because it refers to an identifiable body of law that has developed over a series of significant cases all addressing a particular and recurring problem: agencies asserting highly

---

32. *Chevron, U.S.A., Inc. v. NRDC, Inc.*, 467 U.S. 837 (1984).

33. 2023 U.S. LEXIS 1847, *Certiorari* granted.

34. S. Johnson, *Deregulation: Too Big for One Branch, But Maybe Not for Two*, 53 Seton Hall L. Rev. (2023), 839, 894.

35. S. Johnson, *Deregulation: Too Big for One Branch, But Maybe Not for Two*, 53 Seton Hall L. Rev. (2023), 839, 894.

consequential power beyond what Congress could reasonably be understood to have granted. Scholars and jurists have recognized the common threads between those decisions. So have we. See *Utility Air*, 573 U.S., at 324 (citing *Brown & Williamson* and *MCI*); *King v. Burwell*, 576 U.S. 473, 486 (2015) (citing *Utility Air*, *Brown & Williamson*, and *Gonzales*).[36]

In her Harvard Law Review article, Professor Mila Sohoni contends that four Supreme Court cases decided in 2021, including *West Virginia v. Environmental Protection Agency*, replaced the *Chevron* deference doctrine with the major questions doctrine. Her article summarizes this transformation discussing the four cases she calls the "major questions quartet." Professor Sohoni claims that the "first crucial thing to understand about the major questions [doctrine] is what it did to administrative law."[37] She continued, "While ostensibly applying existing major questions case law, the [Supreme Court] in actuality altered the doctrine of judicial review of agency action in its method and content, in ways that will have momentous consequences."[38]

In summary, where does that leave us? As you read this text, the Supreme Court will likely already have decided the fate of *Chevron*. Agencies now provide the vast majority of our laws. This chapter has hopefully provided you with the background needed to keep abreast of agency developments. With an understanding of the complexity of agency authority, you may now choose to participate in rulemaking by following the process and perhaps even by submitting your comments.

§5.4 Researching Regulations on Regulations.gov

Back in 2003, to promote public participation in federal government rulemaking, the rulemaking program launched. As part of the program, Regulations.gov was established. Many agencies participated by making their rulemaking transparent to the public online through Regulations.gov.[39]

Though Regulations.gov was a great improvement from the public's access to the federal government's rulemaking process prior to 2003, many problems remained. Searching remained difficult until 2019. Prior to this date, the docketing of rule materials could be haphazard, and important supporting information was unavailable.[40]

In 2019, the General Services Administration launched a new and greatly improved Regulations.gov website. We can attest to the fact that the previous site was difficult to use, and the new site is much easier. Though we hesitate in a text to reference specific pages from an online source, as they change over time, we think it is

36. *West Virginia v. EPA*, 597 U.S. 697, 723 (2022)
37. Sohoni, M. (2022). The Major Questions Doctrine. *131 Harv. L. Rev. 262.*
38. Sohoni, M. (2022). The Major Questions Doctrine. *131 Harv. L. Rev. 262.*
39. https://www.fdms.gov/about-us.
40. https://www.theregreview.org/2019/05/28/coglianese-rubin-improving-regulations-gov/.

important to see examples of exactly how this works. Regardless of your employment situation, accessing regulations that apply to your industry and understanding how to submit comments can render you a changemaker as you act to improve your industry.

Over three hundred agencies currently use Regulations.gov. The Federal Register is housed there (it also remains in hard copy). At Regulations.gov you can read proposed rules and final rules, submit comments, and read comments submitted by others. Final rules are also found in the Code of Federal Regulations (CFR). See Appendix A for all the CFR titles.

The chart below shows two of the proposed rules that were (as of this writing) pending. This is one of the features on the front page of Regulations.gov. We see the date that comments are due. Let's focus on the proposed rule on the right (we will be using the Clean Water Act in the example section below). When you are on the website, you would simply click on the box on the right.

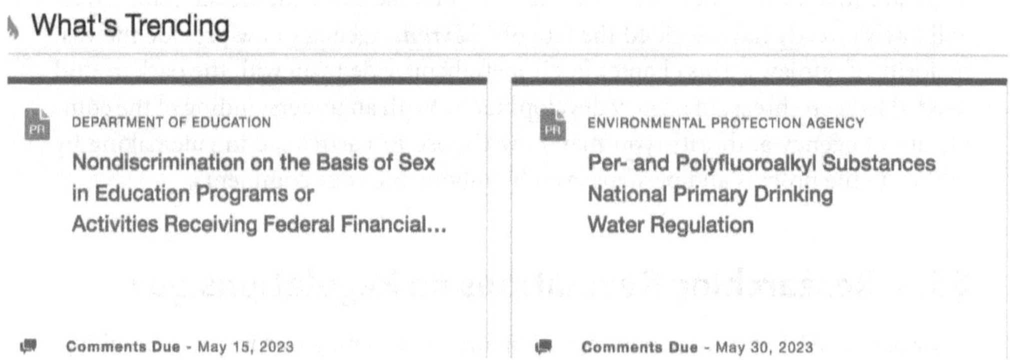

Below is the top part of the first page that comes up when you click on that box.

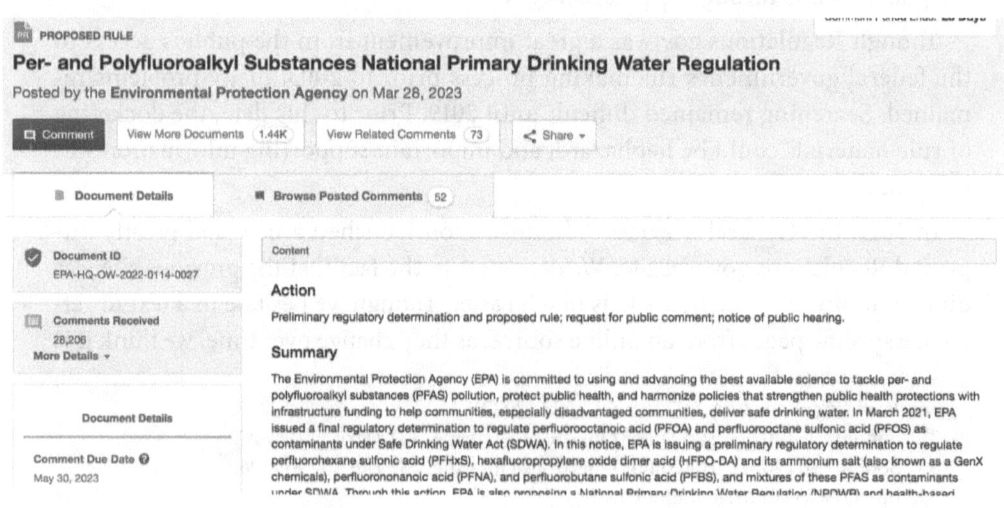

Notice the blue tab in the upper left. You click the blue comment box to submit a comment. Scrolling down a bit, you see that there are already over 28,000 comments submitted. To see comments, click on "Browse posted comments" near the top.

The balance of the proposed rule follows. The proposed rules tend to be quite long, and as you can see, they can be quite technical. In 2011 the president issued an executive order requiring that proposed rules have executive summaries that make the material easier for the public to understand.[41]

Again, the updated version of Regulations.gov is much more user friendly. You can jump on and look around, and you may be surprised at how easy it is to use. If you would like more information on how to use the site, we recommend that you explore the following:

Regulations.gov/about

Regulations.gov/FAQ

Federalregister.gov

Legal Information Institute

§5.5 Influencing Regulations

Assume that there is a proposed rule that relates to your industry, and you wish to submit a comment. You go to Regulations.gov. You can use the filters on the left: document type, when the proposed rule was posted, when comments are due, and which agency you'd like to search. You can also ask that it only show proposed rules that are currently open for comment.

Let's say that you are the company safety officer, and you follow the Occupational Safety and Health Administration (OSHA) proposed rules.

- You click on OSHA (you see there are 29,000+ entries).
- You click on "Show only documents open for comment" (there are fifteen).
- If any are relevant to your work, you can submit a comment.

With the help of the Government Office of Management and Budget, the Brookings Institute drafted an excellent document on how to draft comments: "How to Effectively Comment on Regulations."[42] The Brookings Institute explains the agency requirements regarding submitted comments:

> By law, agencies must review all public comments received and, while they can categorize similar comments (e.g. identical chain/form letters), they are

41. Executive Order 13563 of January 18, 2011.

42. https://www.brookings.edu/wp-content/uploads/2018/08/ES_20180809_RegComments.pdf.

required to respond to all comments in the preamble of their final regulation whether they accept the suggestion or not. Agencies have to explain the rationale for not incorporating a comment (e.g. out of scope, no statutory authority) or, for those comments they find persuasive, they have to explain why they have decided to incorporate the suggestion.[43]

Here are the Brookings Institute verbatim suggestions for writing an effective comment:

> **How should I structure my comment?**
>
> At the top of your comment, identify the document you are commenting on by its docket number, subject heading, federal register date and page number.
>
> In your comment, you should include:
>
> (1) an introduction where you explain why you are interested in the regulation, highlight any credentials or experience that may distinguish your comment from others, and whether you are commenting on your own behalf, on the behalf of another organization, or are endorsing or joining with another comment or commenter;
>
> (2) a background where you clearly identify the issues within the regulatory action on which you are commenting, and list your recommendations upfront. If you are commenting on a particular word or phrase, or if you are responding to specific questions or requests for data, state this clearly and provide the relevant page number, column, and paragraph citation from the federal register document;
>
> (3) analysis which lays out your detailed argument and evidence to support your recommendations;
>
> (4) a conclusion which recaps your main argument and lists your recommendations again.
>
> Your comment should also include citations for all information and research you relied on.[44]

Consider jumping on to Regulations.gov and looking around. You can enter any agency that governs your workplace. See what regulations are requesting comments. If any are relevant, consider making a comment. Input based on your unique experience may make all the difference.

43. https://www.brookings.edu/wp-content/uploads/2018/08/ES_20180809_RegComments.pdf.

44. https://www.brookings.edu/wp-content/uploads/2018/08/ES_20180809_RegComments.pdf.

§5.6 Observe the Interplay of Congress, Agencies, and the Courts

Below are a few examples of how the law develops and changes as Congress, agencies, and the courts play their part in shaping the law.

§5.6.1 Family Medical Leave Act of 1993

The Seventh Circuit Court of Appeals case *Ziccarelli v. Dart*[45] provides an excellent example of the interplay between Congress's Family Medical Leave Act and the Department of Labor's corresponding regulations. This 2022 case also addressed the *Chevron* deference doctrine and found that it did not apply in this case. Finally, the court also reviews caselaw to define terms and confirm that it is following precedent.

The Family Medical Leave Act (FMLA) "was designed 'to balance the demands of the workplace with the needs of families' while guaranteeing workers reasonable access to medical leave 'in a manner that accommodates the legitimate interests of employers.'[46] To that end, the FMLA grants eligible employees up to 12 work-weeks of unpaid leave (480 hours) per year for medical and family reasons."[47]

In this case, Salvatore Ziccarelli had been employed for twenty-seven years by the Cook County Sheriff's Office. He suffered from posttraumatic stress disorder and over the years had taken quite a bit of time off each year under the FMLA. In 2016 he phoned the FMLA manager to request additional time off under the FMLA. According to Ziccarelli he was told that he should not take additional FMLA, and if he did, he would be disciplined. The FLMA manager strongly disputed this interpretation of their conversation.[48] Ziccarelli sued claiming that his rights under the FMLA had been violated.

Other issues were raised and adjudicated in this case, but for our purposes, we focus only on the FMLA. The district court had granted summary judgment for the defendant Sheriff's Office finding that Ziccarelli's FMLA rights weren't actually denied. The Seventh Circuit Court of Appeals, however, found that the differing versions of the conversation between Ziccarelli and the FMLA manager presented a genuine issue of material fact in dispute. The court also held that an employee need not actually be denied FMLA rights to prevail if the employer has interfered with those rights. The Seventh Circuit, therefore, overturned the district court's grant of summary judgment for the defendant Sheriff's Office in favor of Ziccarelli.[49]

---

45. *Ziccarelli v. Dart*, 35 F.4th 1079 (7th Cir. 2022).
46. *Ziccarelli v. Dart*, 35 F.4th 1079, 1083 (7th Cir. 2022).
47. *Ziccarelli v. Dart*, 35 F.4th 1079, 1083 (7th Cir. 2022).
48. *Ziccarelli v. Dart*, 35 F.4th 1079, 1083 (7th Cir. 2022).
49. The defendant petitioned for *writ of certiorari* to the U.S. Supreme Court. *Certiorari* denied October 11, 2022.

Again, this case is an excellent example of the interworking of Congress, the courts, and agencies. In reaching its decision, the court relied on the specific language of the FMLA demonstrating how the court examines and interprets the language of a statute. The court also referenced the Department of Labor's regulations to support its conclusion. It noted, however, that the language of the FMLA was not ambiguous and therefore the *Chevron* deference doctrine did not apply (see § 5.3.2 to review this concept). Finally, the court highlighted several cases that addressed this issue, and concluded that although the wording varied from case to case, denial was not essential to prove interference with the FMLA.[50]

§ 5.6.2 Safe Drinking Water Act of 1974

Let's examine a crucial issue that affects all of us: clean water. Congress recognized the importance of safe drinking water and enacted the Safe Drinking Water Act in 1974 (SDWA).[51] But how is this achieved? Is it reasonable to expect our congresspeople to know which contaminants are safe in your drinking water? In the SDWA, Congress empowered the Environmental Protection Agency (EPA) to implement rules in its enabling statute.

As you learned in Chapter Two, Congress enacts a statute and provides guidelines for an agency to carry out the intent of the statute. In this case, Congress's SDWA provides permission and guidance for the EPA to promulgate rules that will provide the public with safe water.

> The Safe Drinking Water Act (SDWA) requires EPA to establish and enforce standards that public drinking water systems must follow. EPA delegates primary enforcement responsibility (also called primacy) for public water systems to states and Indian Tribes if they meet certain requirements. Approximately 150,000 public water systems provide drinking water to most Americans.[52]
>
> EPA sets legal limits on over 90 contaminants in drinking water. The legal limit for a contaminant reflects the level that protects human health and that water systems can achieve using the best available technology. EPA rules also set water-testing schedules and methods that water systems must follow. The Safe Drinking Water Act (SDWA) gives individual states the opportunity to set and enforce their own drinking water standards if the standards are at a minimum as stringent as EPA's national standards.[53]

Here we see an example of a statute, the SDWA, that includes enabling language that authorizes the EPA to create national standards to ensure safe drinking water.

---

50. *Ziccarelli v. Dart*, 35 F.4th 1079, 1086 (7th Cir. 2022).

51. 42 U.S.C. 300f.

52. https://www.epa.gov/ground-water-and-drinking-water/basic-information-about-your-drinking-water.

53. https://www.epa.gov/dwreginfo/drinking-water-regulations.

Where the legislature delegates rulemaking authority to an agency, the statute must contain language with directions to that agency. This is referred to as the enabling language. You will notice in the statute's definitions that "[t]he term 'Administrator' means the Administrator of the Environmental Protection Agency."[54] The authorization language is often addressed to the administrator.

§5.6.3 Fair Labor Standards Act

Benjamin Meyer's UNIVERSITY OF CHICAGO LAW REVIEW article presents an interesting hypothetical that highlights the interplay among the Fair Labor Standards Act (FLSA), the Department of Labor (DOL)-associated regulations, and the courts.[55] With his permission, a direct quote of his hypothetical follows.

> [C]onsider a hypothetical family restaurant owned by a sole proprietor, Mrs. Orville. The restaurant has one cook, Chris, and two servers, Sam and Steph. In a typical restaurant, Sam and Steph will be the only employees interacting with customers during meals and, thus, the only employees who receive tips. Without any sharing arrangements, these servers will simply keep the tips they receive. However, servers often share tips with one another. Servers may do this to create a team culture in the restaurant, or to minimize the risks associated with the variance in party sizes and patron generosity. These sharing arrangements are called "tip pools." Under these informal agreements, all tips are set aside as they come in, usually in a location maintained by the employer. The pooled tips are then redistributed to employees at a later time according to a set formula. This formula is usually based on the total amount of tips received and the amount of time worked by each employee. So if Sam earns \$50 in tips and Steph earns \$20 in tips while working the same number of hours, the pool of \$70 would be split evenly between them into cuts of \$35. If one server works more hours, he or she would then receive a larger portion of the pooled tips.[56]
>
> Then consider a variation on this hypothetical situation. If Sam and Steph grow fearful that Chris (the cook) will begin to shirk in the kitchen, they may decide to bring Chris into the tip pool. Their hope would be that including Chris in this pool will lead him to care more about the speed and quality of his output, as his performance will contribute to a diner's experience and the eventual size of the tip (remuneration in which he now shares). This can also alleviate the disparity in take-home pay between the servers and Chris, again creating a team atmosphere among the restaurant's workers. However, add-

54. 42 U.S.C. Chapter 6A Section300f(7).

55. B. Meyer, *Mrs. Orville Isn't Trying to Steal Tips: An FLSA Story*, 84 U. CHI. L. REV. (2017), 1971, 1972.

56. B. Meyer, *Mrs. Orville Isn't Trying to Steal Tips: An FLSA Story*, 84 U. CHI. L. REV. (2017), 1971, 1972.

> ing someone like Chris, who is not customarily tipped, is problematic under the FLSA and a recent DOL regulation. These problems become clearer when someone like Mrs. Orville, who waits tables but is also the owner of the restaurant, inserts herself into the tip pool. Should she be able to share in these tips? While she may be a coworker of the servers, her tip receipts look a bit like an employer siphoning tips away from employees. Several FLSA provisions deal with such a situation in only glancing fashion, but the DOL has addressed this issue head-on with a recent regulation. Essentially, this regulation completely prevents people like Chris and Mrs. Orville—who don't normally receive tips—from participating in the tip pool. A circuit split has emerged as to the validity of this regulation.[57]

(**A circuit split** occurs when two or more of the federal appellate circuit courts render conflicting decisions on the same issue. A circuit split is one of the important considerations of the Supreme Court when deciding whether it should hear a case.)

Remember that these hypotheticals are not included to teach you the law of a specific area such as labor law. Rather, we hope to demonstrate the complex back and forth of the government branches as the law develops. Mr. Meyer's article provides an excellent example.

Meyer explains that the law regarding tipping began with a Supreme Court case that held that tips could be considered part of the minimum wage required under the FLSA. Later, Congress amended the FLSA and codified this holding. Then, in 1974 the "DOL was delegated the broad authority 'to prescribe necessary rules, regulations, and orders' to implement the FLSA amendments of 1974."[58] This issue remains dynamic as the DOL has promulgated additional rules.

§ 5.6.4 The Americans with Disabilities Act

Let's take another look, again (also in § 2.2.2), at an example of the interplay between the roles of Congress, executive agencies, and the Department of Justice in enacting and interpreting law. In November 2019, William Beaumont Hospital in Royal Oak, Michigan, entered into a settlement agreement with the Department of Justice, U.S. attorney's office regarding the services provided to deaf patients who use American sign language as their primary form of communication. The case stemmed from allegations that William Beaumont Hospital failed to make available qualified sign language interpreters, inappropriately relied on the patient's family as interpreters, and relied on faulty remote video interpreting services. These services had con-

---

57. B. Meyer, *Mrs. Orville Isn't Trying to Steal Tips: An FLSA Story*, 84 U. Chi. L. Rev. (2017), 1971, 1972.

58. B. Meyer, *Mrs. Orville Isn't Trying to Steal Tips: An FLSA Story*, 84 U. Chi. L. Rev. (2017), 1971, 1972

nectivity issues. In addition, the patient had vision and mobility restrictions that prevented him from seeing the screen. Communication was ineffective.

The Americans with Disabilities Act of 1990 (ADA) provides for communication services to deaf individuals through auxiliary aids and services. The law states:

> Sec. 12103. Additional definitions. As used in this chapter (1) Auxiliary aids and services. The term "auxiliary aids and services" includes (A) qualified interpreters or other effective methods of making aurally delivered materials available to individuals with hearing impairments.

The law was further refined through regulations published by the Justice Department in the Federal Register that expanded on this definition to include the use of video remote interpreting services.

> (f) ***Video remote interpreting (VRI) services.*** A public accommodation that chooses to provide qualified interpreters via VRI service shall ensure that it provides-
>
> (1) Real-time, full-motion video and audio over a dedicated high-speed, wide-bandwidth video connection or wireless connection that delivers high-quality video images that do not produce lags, choppy, blurry, or grainy images, or irregular pauses in communication;
>
> (2) A sharply delineated image that is large enough to display the interpreter's face, arms, hands, and fingers, and the participating individual's face, arms, hands, and fingers, regardless of his or her body position;
>
> (3) A clear, audible transmission of voices; and
>
> (4) Adequate training to users of the technology and other involved individuals so that they may quickly and efficiently set up and operate the VRI.

We see how the regulations describe in more detail the concept that the legislators enacted. The regulatory language was expressly quoted in the Beaumont settlement agreement.

The case was brought in 2017. When brought to the appellate court, the Eleventh Circuit reversed the trial court's summary judgment for the defendant hospital, finding that plaintiffs had legal standing in this case "given... we conclude that Plaintiffs' numerous visits to Defendants' facilities and the wealth of evidence showing repeated VRI malfunctions. Plaintiffs have Article III standing to proceed with their claims for injunctive relief." As the case proceeded through the courts, the defendant hospitals again raised the issue of standing on the grounds that they had changed their policies and procedures regarding interpreters to remove the impediment to effective communication; on each of plaintiff's subsequent visits to the hospital she was granted an interpreter. On this basis the Eleventh Circuit affirmed the defendant hospitals' motion regarding standing as the case was now moot. We see the power of law to effect real change in policies and procedures that impact people's lives. Legal interpretation flows from legislation, to regulation, to the attorney general, and back and forth between the trial and appellate courts, for determination of its application to an actual fact set.

§5.7 Conclusion

Whether you believe that agencies are the best way to regulate the complex and highly technical issues of today, or that agencies have created an unauthorized fourth branch of government, agencies are ubiquitous in our society. An understanding of its workings and the knowledge to follow rule-making and have your voice heard should prove helpful in the workplace and as a citizen.

EXERCISES Government Protection or Government Overreach?

1. Does the proliferation of agencies violate Article I, Section 1 of the U.S. Constitution?
2. How would you interpret the non-delegation clause?
3. If Congress truly cannot delegate any lawmaking powers, how would they deal with complicated issues such as clean water?
4. Section 5.3.2 mentions that the Supreme Court granted *certiorari* to hear *Loper Bright Enterprises v. Raimondo, Secretary of Commerce.*[59] Search for that case to determine if the Court has ruled. Did the Court modify the *Chevron* deference doctrine? Do you agree with the Court?
5. Appendix B contains the docket for the *Loper* case. Remember from Chapter Three that a docket is the court's system for tracking all the documents filed in a given case.
   - A. Review the *Loper* docket in Appendix B. Define the term *amicus curiae* brief and the term *writ of certiorari*. Then explain what a motion is.
   - B. Notice the number of *amicus curiae* briefs. Why do you think this is so?

59. 2023 U.S. LEXIS 1847, *Certiorari* Granted.

PART II

THE IMPORTANCE OF GOOD WRITING

CHAPTER SIX

Produce Good Writing

No matter your field, role, industry, or passion, effective writing can help sharpen critical thinking and position you to thrive in your environment.

—Greg Crawford, President, Miami of Ohio University[1]

Know your why: Why should you work to produce good writing?

This chapter explains that good writing skills provide an edge in the job market. Good writing skills also improve your critical thinking, another quality employers value.

§6.1 Writing, Communication, and Human Connection

Only through communication can human life hold meaning.

—Paulo Friere[2]

Writing is an important form of communication, and communication is fundamental to human connection. Do you agree with Paulo Friere that communication provides the meaning in our lives?

Communication requires that two parties attempting to communicate find something in common. Professor Wilbur Schramm provides that "[c]ommunication comes from the Latin communis, meaning common. When we communicate, we

1. Though President Crawford's degrees are in math and physics, he says that good writing skills were a critical component of his success. He initiated and funded the Miami Writing Institute, which is free for alumni, faculty, and staff. *Miami's Roger and Joyce Howe Center for Writing Excellence (HCWE) Created the Institute to Tackle a Topic that Permeates Every Aspect of Our Professional and Personal Lives—Writing*, https://miamioh.edu/news/2022/01/become-a-more-effective-communicator-through-the-new-miami-writing-institute-a-free-program-for-miami-staff,-faculty-and-alumni.html.

2. P. Freier, *Pedagogy of the Oppressed* (30th Anniversary Edition, (2014)), 55. Paulo Freier was a Brazilian philosopher and founder of critical pedagogy.

are trying to establish a 'commonness' with someone."[3] Professor Schramm is considered the father of communication studies and was the first to introduce communication departments to colleges and universities across the United States. He was also the founder of the renowned Iowa Writer's Workshop.[4]

Professor Schramm provides the communication diagram below:

FIGURE 6.1 The writer encodes her idea, and the receiver decodes it. The critical communication piece is the intersection of the circles, which represents the field of common experience.[5]

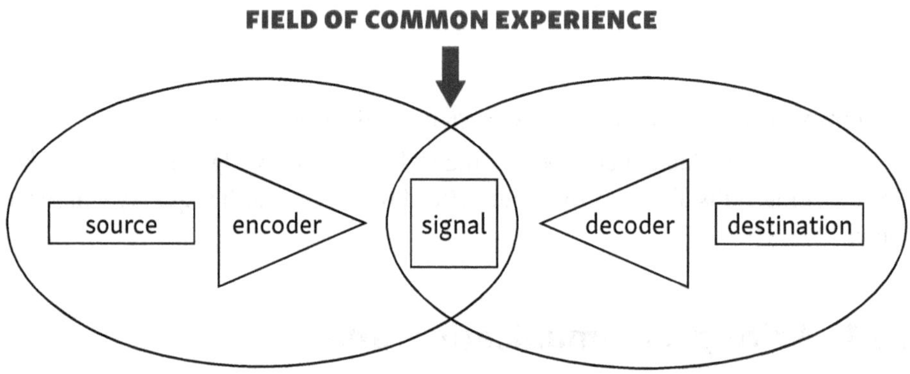

If there is no common experience (intersection of the circles), communication is hindered. It is with this commonness that effective communication occurs. Further, miscommunication can occur at several points. The writer may incorrectly encode the message (unclear writing) and/or the reader may incorrectly decode the message (misunderstanding). As a writer, then, it is important to consider the best way to encode the message. We must also consider how the reader might decode it.

A great writer, therefore, must focus on connecting with the reader. The writer must discern the specific areas of commonality with her reader. If you are a surgeon writing an article for other surgeons on total hip replacements, your word choices will be quite different than those you would use to explain a total hip replacement to one of your patients. Similarly, every writer must consider the background and experience of her readers and choose language accordingly.

The writer, therefore, takes the reader by the hand, or in this case by the sentence, and leads her thought by thought through the written piece. One mind shares her thoughts with another. Through effective communication we enhance human connection.

---

3. W. Schram (Ed.), *How Communication Works*, in THE PROCESS AND EFFECTS OF MASS COMMUNICATION (1954), 26.

4. https://writersworkshop.uiowa.edu/about/about-workshop/history.

5. W. Schram (Ed.), *How Communication Works*, in THE PROCESS AND EFFECTS OF MASS COMMUNICATION (1954), 26.

Pause for Reflection Consider the importance of commonality with your reader.

Give examples of a reader who would be easy for you to reach.

Give examples of a reader who might be difficult for you to reach.

Consider how a reader might inaccurately decode a message.

How would your writing be different in each situation?

Considering the political divisions in our country today; discuss where we might find commonness.

§6.2 Why Improve Your Writing?

§6.2.1 Businesses Seek Employees with Good Writing Skills

A search of any major business magazine (BLOOMBERG BUSINESSWEEK, ECONOMIST, FORBES, FORTUNE, HARVARD BUSINESS REVIEW, INC., and MONEY, to name a few) indicates that employers seek employees with good writing skills.[6] This may not seem like a tall order, but studies reveal that, in fact, it is.

The National Assessment of Education Progress, the accepted measure for student proficiency, reveals that only 25 percent of American high school seniors had writing skills at a proficiency level.[7] Yet the National Association of Colleges and Employers reports that 75 percent of employers seek employees with strong written communication skills.[8] This shortcoming in our educational system finds its way into the workplace, and employers lament the lack of proficient writing skills among their employees.

> Deficiencies in employees' writing skills have tangible and intangible costs. In 2004, the National Commission on Writing (NCW) published the results of a study for which it had collected cost data from 64 of 120 large American corporations that were affiliated with the Business Roundtable and that employed nearly 8 million people. According to the report, American firms may spend as much as \$3.1 billion annually to remediate their employees' writing deficiencies.[9]
>
> The intangible costs of employees' deficient writing skills are (a) image degradation for both employees and employers; (b) negative impact on productivity when employees must reread, perhaps several times, poorly written material

6. K. Moore, Study: Poor Writing Skills Are Costing Businesses Billions, INC. (2016, March 31). See also D. Parekh, Why Writing Is an Asset, FORBES (2021); B. Birchard, The Science of Strong Writing, HARVARD BUSINESS REVIEW (2021, July–August).

7. https://nces.ed.gov/nationsreportcard/pubs/main2011/2012470.aspx.

8. https://www.naceweb.org/talent-acquisition/candidate-selection/the-attributes-employers-seek-on-a-candidates-resume/.

9. Z. Quible & F. Griffin, *Are Writing Deficiencies Creating a Lost Generation of Business Writers?* 83 JOURNAL OF EDUCATION FOR BUSINESS 1 (2007), 32–36, https://doi.org/10.3200/JOEB.83.1.32-36.

to decipher the intended meaning; and (c) the outcome when an incorrect decision is made because of poorly or ineffectively written material.[10]

It appears, then, that improving your writing skills will very likely provide an edge in the workplace.

§6.2.2 Improve Your Writing to Improve Your Critical Thinking

Another important reason to improve your writing skills is to improve your critical thinking skills. "Critical thinking has been identified as a crucial general skill contributing to academic and career success in the twenty-first century."[11] Like President Greg Crawford's quote explaining that effective writing sharpens critical thinking, Pulitzer Prize-winning author David McCullough also finds that writing and thinking are closely linked: "Writing is thinking. To write well is to think clearly. That's why it's so hard."[12]

Albert Einstein is quoted as saying that "if you can't explain something to a six-year-old, you don't understand it yourself."[13] Writing can be difficult because the writer often needs to take complex material, sort through it, synthesize it, and deliver it to the reader in an easily accessible form. A highly skilled writer can take a complex topic and simplify it for a reader at any level. Working through this arduous process requires higher-order thinking, and several studies have demonstrated that improving your writing improves critical thinking.

In one such study, biology students were divided into two groups: one group had writing requirements and the other group did not. The aim was to determine whether writing did, in fact, improve critical thinking. The two groups' analytical skills were very similar at the beginning of the term. At the end of the term, the writing group improved their critical thinking skills significantly. The writing group increased from the 45th percentile to the 52nd percentile, and the nonwriting group decreased from the 42nd percentile to the 40th percentile.[14]

Another study conducted with dental students found that critical thinking skills were improved when the curriculum added reflective writing assessments.[15] Yet an-

10. Z. Quible & F. Griffin, *Are Writing Deficiencies Creating a Lost Generation of Business Writers?* 83 Journal of Education for Business 1 (2007), 32–36, https://doi.org/10.3200/JOEB.83.1.32-36.

11. A. Shaw et al., *Thinking Critically About Critical Thinking: Validating the Russian HEIghten® Critical Thinking Assessment*, 45 Studies in Higher Education 9 (2020), 1933–48.

12. https://www.ncbi.nlm.nih.gov/pmc/articles/PMC6920649/.

13. Many attribute this statement to Albert Einstein, though some deny it was he who said it.

14. I. Quitadamo & M. Kurtz, *Learning to Improve: Using Writing to Increase Critical Thinking Performance in General Education Biology*, 6 CBE-Life Sciences Education 2 (2007), 140–54.

15. J. Woldt & M. Nenad, *Reflective Writing in Dental Education to Improve Critical Thinking and Learning: A Systematic Review*, 85 J. Dent. Educ. (2021), 778–85, https://doi.org/10.1002/jdd.12561.

other study was conducted with chemistry students.[16] This study, and several others, cite a 2014 study of first-year and fourth-year college chemistry students. The students who received traditional instruction scored significantly lower on critical thinking tests than the students instructed with the Science Writing Heuristic (SWH) method. The SWH method focuses on writing. These students scored considerably higher on critical thinking tests. The researchers concluded that the SWH method, which includes writing assignments, promoted critical thinking skills.[17]

Therefore, in addition to improving job performance, saving time and money, and enhancing your brand's reputation, studies indicate that improving your writing can actually improve your thinking. How is this explained?

The Oxford Dictionary provides a useful definition of critical thinking: "The objective analysis and evaluation of an issue in order to form a judgment." Writing a piece based on research, whether it is from peer-reviewed literature or data from your workplace, requires skills that reflect this critical thinking definition. You must analyze the literature or data, evaluate it, and form a judgment (often in terms of a conclusion or thesis statement).

A look at the Watson-Glaser Critical Thinking Appraisal (W-GCTA) provides additional insight. The W-GCTA has been used by employers to evaluate candidates' critical thinking and problem-solving skills for more than eighty-five years. The test is comprised of questions in five areas[18]:

- Drawing inferences
- Recognizing assumptions
- Argument evaluation
- Deductive reasoning
- Logical interpretation

---

16. N. Hike & S. Hughes-Phelan, *Using the Science Writing Heuristic to Support NGSS-Aligned Instruction*, 97 Journal of Chemical Education 2 (2020), 358–67, DOI: 10.1021/acs.jchemed.9b00472.

17. T. Gupta, K. Burke, A. Mehta, & T. Greenbowe, *Impact of Guided-Inquiry-Based Instruction with a Writing and Reflection Emphasis on Chemistry Students' Critical Thinking Abilities*, 92 J. Chem. Educ. 1 (2014, September 9), 32–38. The SWH laboratory instruction approach has been used successfully for over a decade to engage students in laboratory activities. SWH-based instruction emphasizes knowledge construction through individual writing and reflection, and collaborative learning as a group. In the SWH approach, writing is a core component of learning. Previous studies on the SWH approach have reported effective implementation of the SWH approach leads to an improvement in overall student academic performance and content knowledge.

18. R. Bernard, D. Zhang, P. Abrami, F. Sicoly, E. Borokhovski, & M. Surkes, *Exploring the Structure of the Watson-Glaser Critical Thinking Appraisal: One Scale or Many Subscales?*, 3 Thinking Skills and Creativity 1 (2008), 15–22, https://doi.org/10.1016/j.tsc.2007.11.001.

The W-GCTA takes these question areas and includes them in a model identified with the acronym RED:

Recognize assumptions

Evaluate arguments

Draw conclusions

Using these three RED steps helps you identify bias in your own thinking. You recognize opinion versus assumption, and you recognize both versus fact.[19] Decisions based on facts are desirable, but assumptions are not bad. You just need to recognize them as such and challenge them. Many decisions in science and business, for example, may begin with data. As you analyze the data, you make assumptions. Then you challenge these assumptions. You may take action, and continue to challenge and evaluate.

A strong argument can be made that these skills are also needed to produce clear, effective writing. As you gather data at work, or you compile your research at school, you need to recognize assumptions, evaluate arguments made, and draw conclusions. That is, solving complex problems uses very similar skills used in writing on complex subjects.

Complex problem-solving skills are in high demand in the workplace, and writing is an important way to improve those skills and to deliver the results. In addition, in today's world where much of the information we receive may be biased from one direction or another, recognizing assumptions, evaluating arguments presented, and then drawing your own conclusions are critical life skills.

Pause for Reflection Recognizing scholarly, vetted sources and information you can trust is critical in producing good writing and also in making sound life decisions.

How do you evaluate facts presented in an article, in the news, or online?

How do you distinguish between facts and falsehoods?

How do you vet facts before you draw conclusions?

§6.3 Become a Great Writer

Writing, therefore, aids us in communication and improves our critical thinking skills. How, then, do we sharpen our writing skills?

Our focus in this book is on expository and persuasive writing. These skills are used most often in business and scholarship. Expository writing explains. It aims to educate the reader with facts; it is objective. Persuasive writing, on the other hand,

---

19. R. Bernard, D. Zhang, P. Abrami, F. Sicoly, E. Borokhovski, & M. Surkes, *Exploring the Structure of the Watson-Glaser Critical Thinking Appraisal: One Scale or Many Subscales?*, 3 THINKING SKILLS AND CREATIVITY 1 (2008), 15–22, https://doi.org/10.1016/j.tsc.2007.11.001.

aims to convince or influence the reader. Good persuasive writing is often backed by verifiable facts and evidence.

Expository writing may be used at work to describe a product to a customer. Human resources may use expository writing to explain a policy to a worker. A worker may employ persuasive writing to sell a product. She may write to persuade her boss that she deserves a promotion. An employee may champion the opening of another distribution center with persuasive writing. The countless business examples of expository and persuasive writing point to the importance of sharpening these skills.

This chapter is intended to explain how good expository and persuasive writers are made, not born. With hard work, everyone can be good expository and persuasive writers. Shakespeare, Tolstoy, Austen, and other creative writers may be in the born-not-made category, but writing a good essay, thesis, report, policy, or email is a learned skill. Two elements are key: an understanding of writing mechanics and the willingness to rewrite... and rewrite. If one is willing to put in the work, one can be a great writer. And all of us, whatever our current skill level, can continue to improve.

One of our favorite pieces on writing was authored by Marc H. Raibert almost forty years ago (1985). Raibert, a professor of electrical engineering and computer science at MIT who founded Boston Dynamics, tells us that "Almost all good writing starts out bad. Rather than leave it bad, the good writer rewrites and refines it until it is good, or even very good."[20] He supports the idea that anyone can produce good writing if they are willing to put in the work. Assuming that you are willing, let us begin to be great, or perhaps in your case, greater writers.

How to Begin

That blank page of paper, or perhaps the blank computer screen, awaits. How do we begin?

First, we want to avoid these two mistakes:

Waiting too long to start writing (see § 6.4.1: Brainstorming)

Starting to write too soon (see § 6.4.2: Organizing)

What is an antidote to these two mistakes? The Betty S. Flowers Paradigm.[21]

Betty S. Flowers was a professor of English at the University of Texas. She was also formerly the director of the L. B. Johnson Library and Museum. Her popular prescription for writing is a favorite among many writing teachers. Dr. Flowers recommends a useful writing blueprint in the form of a madman, an architect, a carpenter, and a judge. She stresses the importance of greeting these writing collaborators in this specific order.[22]

---

20. M. Raibert, *Good Writing* (1985), https://www.cs.cmu.edu/~pausch/Randy/Randy/raibert.htm

21. B. A. Garner, *Using the Flowers Paradigm to Write More Efficiently*, TRIAL: JOURNAL OF THE ASSOCIATION OF TRIAL LAWYERS OF AMERICA (May 1997).

22. B. A. Garner, *Using the Flowers Paradigm to Write More Efficiently*, TRIAL: JOURNAL OF THE ASSOCIATION OF TRIAL LAWYERS OF AMERICA (May 1997).

A look at the Betty S. Flowers Paradigm reveals that it is a clever way to explain what writing instructors have taught us over the years:

First, jot down your ideas. Dr. Flowers calls this the Madman; we also call it brainstorming.

Next, pull like ideas together. This is the architect, which we call organizing.

Once the initial work on organizing is finished, the carpenter steps in and tinkers with the sentence structure. This may involve wordsmithing. At this stage, however, it is more important to organize the sentences into paragraphs so that they flow logically.

Finally, the judge steps in. The judge provides the editing and rewriting.

Dr. Flowers makes it clear that the judge should not appear until this fourth step. She wisely counsels that bringing the judge in too early will make the writing process much more difficult, and much lengthier. The judge looks at writing with a critical eye. You don't want the critic peeking in on the madman. At that early brainstorming stage, the judge prevents the ideas from flowing freely.

The section below on good expository and persuasive writing will follow Dr. Flowers's blueprint set forth above.

Specifically, we will address the following writing steps:

§6.4.1 Brainstorming (The Madman)

§6.4.2 Organizing (The Architect)

§6.4.3 Writing Mechanics (The Carpenter)

§6.4.4 Editing (The Judge)

§6.4 The Writing Process

§6.4.1 Brainstorming (The Madman)

When you first begin writing, you should let your ideas flow freely. Many of us get stuck by allowing immediate evaluation and self-criticism to jump in too soon. At this stage you want to get your ideas down as quickly and unabashedly as possible. The editing and all-important rewriting will come later.

Perhaps you have a whiteboard with sticky notes, or a chalkboard, or a computer program to begin your brainstorming. If you are interested, many books and articles have been published on the art of brainstorming. Find the technique that works best for you. We find that paper and pencil work well. You can also find online brainstorming programs. Some programs have online sticky notes. The advantage of using sticky notes for your ideas (either on the computer or on a tabletop) is that you can move them around when you start to organize.

You may have conducted extensive research on your topic. Your "brainstorming" may be enhanced by this research. The research may provide background and various perspectives on the topic. This information will be included in your brainstorming list. Consider including citations to simplify your work later in the process.

As you continue in the process, you will find that some of your brainstorming ideas will need to be deleted. No problem. That is an important part of the process. When you feel you have the ideas that you will need for the piece you are writing, move on to the next step: organizing.

§6.4.2 Organizing (The Architect)

Much of good writing comes down to good organization. You may find that creating the structure of your piece is the most difficult part of the process. The time you invest in the structure, though, will make the writing process easier. It will also allow your reader to follow your thoughts in a logical manner.

Further, we contend that it is here, in the organizing step, that the process of writing and of critical thinking work back and forth, hand in glove. As you evaluate the material you have gathered, synthesize it, and put it together logically, you clarify your thinking on the topic, and you clarify your writing. This is a circular process.

The work of organizing, then, crystallizes your thinking on the topic. That is, the labor of organizing is where you find the holes in your logic, where you find that you need additional research, and where you discover the best structure for your piece. Taking adequate time to organize near the beginning of the project cuts time spent and leads to the best final product.

No matter how beautiful a wall is in your home (the sentence) or a room (the paragraph), they will not stand without strong structural framing (organization). Spend time on the structure and organization of your written piece. It will pay off.

After your uncensored ideas are transcribed, then, the architect begins to work on the structure. Organize what you have written. You may find that much of what your madman had to say is not usable; that's fine. It's all part of the process. The architect will organize what is useful and the piece will begin to take shape. How does the architect accomplish this important task?

a. Organizing Tools

Although outlining may not appeal to some writers, it is a valuable tool. Finetune your own writing process by deciding which type of outline works best for you. Below are a few different tools to help in organizing your writing.

Regardless of the organizing tool you choose, the focus will be on main ideas and sub ideas and sub-sub ideas, etc. Many methods to organize your writing are available. We have included some of our favorites here.

How does an outline help?

Good way to connect your ideas

Good way to order your ideas

Good way to determine whether you need more support and research

i. The Formal Outline

You are likely familiar with the formal outline; perhaps you used it in high school or college. The outline is generally set forth in a hierarchical order. Some use Roman numerals, capital letters, numbers, small letters, etc. to delineate the main ideas and the supporting ideas and sub-supporting ideas. This organization will help the reader follow the logic as the writer presents it.

The outline may contain words and phrases or may be written in complete sentences. Perhaps the outline will include citations of the sources. The key is to take the ideas from the madman and put like things together. Then put them into a logical progression in the outline. Outlining is an iterative process. Continue to rework your outline until it begins to flow smoothly.

As you examine your list, find a system to group ideas together. As mentioned previously, if the brainstorming is done on sticky notes, you can move the notes around (either on a tabletop or using a computer program) grouping like ideas together. You can also use color coding. Highlight categories of ideas with different colors.

As you work through this process, an idea about how to begin to structure your paper will emerge. Again, do not shortchange this process. The time spent grouping and organizing your ideas will facilitate the writing process.

Here is an example of a formal outline style.

Chapter 3 Writing

I. Writing, communication, and human connection
II. Why improve your writing?
   A. Businesses seek employees with good writing skills
   B. Improve your writing to improve your critical thinking
III. Become a great writer
   How to begin

In the process of writing this chapter, the outline was edited more than once. In the editing process certain sections were moved as they made more sense under a different heading. The original outline is a working guide; it is meant to be edited and improved throughout the writing process.

ii. The Mind Map

For those of you who prefer a visual diagram rather than columns of words, consider using a mind map. Diagramming software, which is popular in the business sector, includes mind maps. Diagrams are often used by employees to collaborate on projects. These diagrams can also be used for organizing your writing after brainstorming. Here are a few of these diagramming software programs:

Miro

Lucidchart

Visio

SmartDraw

Minitab Workspace

Figure 6.2 shows a typical mind map that can be used to outline a paper. The main idea, or thesis statement, is in the center. All boxes and lines must lead to that. A mind map like this is a good reminder that all support and details must relate to the main idea. This particular mind map scheme would work well for a persuasive piece. We created the diagram below with SmartDraw in ten minutes. Try it. You might find the organization process more fun.

FIGURE 6.2 Created using SmartDraw.

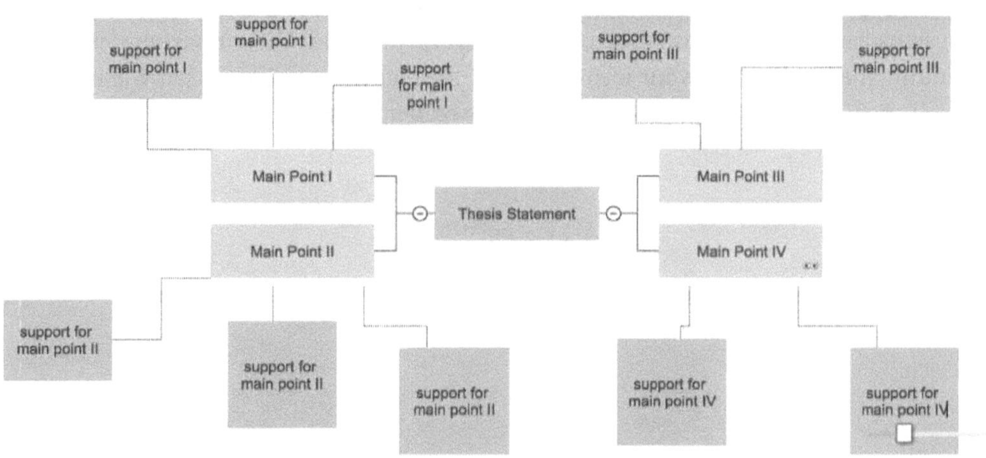

Perhaps you prefer different shapes. You can also use colors to indicate different categories and levels. You can create a bubble diagram such the one shown in Figure 6.3 in MS Word. This particular diagram would work well for an expository piece such as explaining an employment policy. You can then list the points that fall under each bubble category.

FIGURE 6.3 From www.conceptdraw.com.

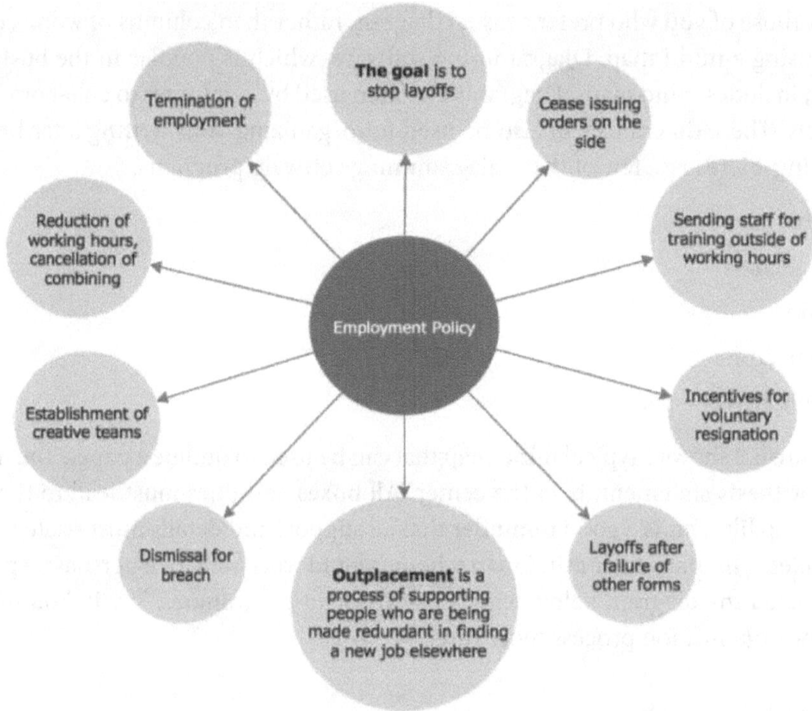

Figure 6.4 is another mind map format. As you can see, many different forms and designs can be used to assist in organizing your material. This important step of finding the hierarchy in your ideas is part of the analytical thinking that will eventually help your final paper flow logically. The reader will have an easier time following your ideas.

FIGURE 6.4 Micro (Micro's Mind Map Template).

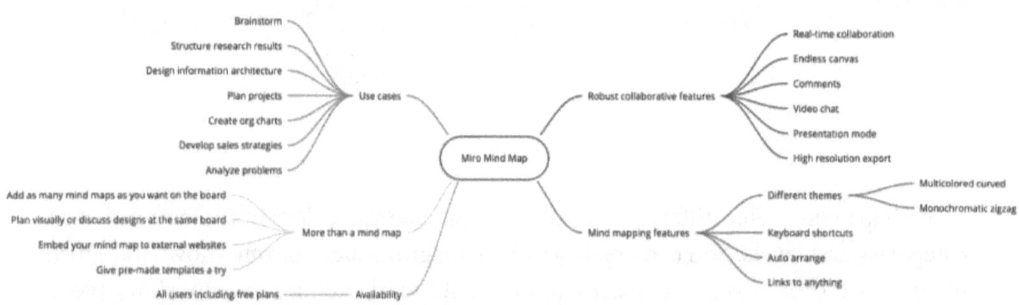

Therefore, strict rules do not apply in ordering your ideas. Writing structure depends on the content and the audience. Below are a few additional things to consider:

- When explaining how to do something, chronological order likely works best.
- When persuading, consider ordering your paper by level of importance.
  - You might prefer to start with the most important point and support it with more minor points (recommended).
  - You could also begin with more minor points that lead to the major point.

iii. The Paragraph—An Important Organizing Tool

The paragraph is fundamental to good writing. If you can write a great paragraph, you can be a great writer. Whether you are working on a five-paragraph essay, a five-page report, or a fifty-page thesis, the foundation is the same: the paragraph.

The paragraph helps organize your writing. Have you ever looked at a full page of text with no paragraphs? You likely had a deep sigh before you start reading because it is a chore. As the writer, you want your reader to continue reading with enthusiasm and avoid those deep sighs. The paragraph helps. It breaks your writing down into digestible ideas; it groups your ideas for the reader. Each paragraph carries one primary thought guiding your reader through your piece.

The key to the paragraph is the topic sentence. You may remember the topic sentence from grammar school, but perhaps you didn't realize its all-important place in the paragraph. The topic sentence is another organizational tool. It tells the reader the main idea of the paragraph. Then every sentence in that paragraph must relate to and explain that topic sentence.

In grading work from our students, we often asked them to highlight the topic sentence of each paragraph. That sentence is most often placed at the start of the paragraph, but in highlighting those topic sentences, the writer can check to see if her work flows logically. We will discuss the all-important topic sentence in more detail in § 6.4.3.b (Topic Sentences).

§ 6.4.3 Writing Mechanics (The Carpenter): The Sentence, Grammar, and Punctuation

We know that many of you may have a firm grasp of grammar and punctuation and can therefore skip to § 6.4.4 (Editing: The Judge). If you want to review or sharpen your writing mechanics, however, some basics follow.

Writing mechanics are important to clear communication. Working at the sentence level you are helping the reader understand your ideas. Writing mechanics and rules help make writing clearer, although some writing rules may be outdated. One such rule is that you should never end a sentence with a preposition. Winston Churchill had something to say about this rule: "Supposedly an editor had clumsily rearranged one of Churchill's sentences to avoid ending it in a preposition, and the Prime Minister, very proud of his style, scribbled this note in reply: 'This is the sort of English up with which I will not put.'"[23] A rule should not be followed if it makes your writing unclear or awkward. Use the rules that make your writing clearer.

Many people can't hide their eyeroll when it comes to talking about punctuation and grammar. We understand. Our approach in this section is not an all-encompassing discussion of grammar rules. On the contrary, we focus on a few things that will improve your writing immediately. For example, while there are twelve-plus comma rules, we focus on a few that will be most helpful.

Therefore, we highlighted the most common writing problems we have encountered in our combined thirty-plus years teaching writing to legal master's students and law students. In addition to addressing the most common writing errors of our students, we address the writing errors that studies show are bothersome to business professionals. Without eyeroll, then, but with eyes focused on improving our writing, let us begin.

The most common student errors (in our experience) include:

Sentence fragments

Run-on sentences

Comma misuse

Misuse of semicolons and colons

Nominalizations

Passive voice

Pronoun agreement (rules have changed with the singular "they")

Misspellings

Businesses state the following "bothersome errors" (from peer-reviewed study):

Wrong word

Run-on sentences

Fragments

Word endings

Misspellings

These business errors are found in an excellent peer-reviewed study by Gubala, Larson, and Melonçon entitled *Do Writing Errors Bother Professionals? An Analysis*

23. https://brians.wsu.edu/2016/11/14/churchill-on-prepositions/

of the Most Bothersome Errors and How the Writer's Ethos Is Affected.[24] Their 2020 study built on similar studies dating back to the 1980s. The specific questions these authors asked of business professionals included the following:

> Does error bother business professionals, and if so, which errors are most bothersome?
>
> How do errors affect a writer's ethos?
>
> Are there differences in the perception of error?
>
> How do readers perceive writers whose work include errors?[25]

The authors provide that these errors had been reported in several studies since 1981. In fact, they state that in this age of multiple technological writing aids in terms of spelling and grammar checks, the errors have "increased in levels of bothersomeness." One of the most important findings of the study is the negative perception in the workplace of writers with poor writing skills.

a. The Sentence

Use the simple **subject-verb-object** construction.

Generally, American English sentence structure is subject-verb in that order. Every sentence must have a subject and a verb. *Mary writes.* This is a complete sentence with the subject *Mary* and the verb *writes*. Often a sentence will also have a direct object. In a sentence in which the subject does something (the verb provides the action), the direct object is the result of the action. *Mary writes novels*. Here *novels* is the direct object.

Without getting too deep into the grammar weeds, if your sentences tend to ramble and thus become unclear, pare them down to the subject-verb-object construction. This is the heart of the sentence. Then add back only what you need. Finally, place the subject at the beginning of the sentence, or very near the beginning; follow the subject closely with the verb. Of course, you will not do this for every single sentence, but generally, this makes for clearer writing.

b. Topic Sentences

If you were to spend time on just one thing to improve your writing today, focus on writing good topic sentences. The topic sentence is usually the first sentence in the paragraph. It provides the main idea and tells the reader what to expect. A good topic sentence not only names the main idea of the paragraph but provides some

---

24. C. Gubala, K. Larson, & L. Meloçon, *Do Writing Errors Bother Professionals? An Analysis of the Most Bothersome Errors and How the Writer's Ethos Is Affected*, 43 Journal of Business and Technical Communication 3 (2020), 250–86, DOI: 10.1177/1050651920910205.

25. C. Gubala, K. Larson, & L. Meloçon, *Do Writing Errors Bother Professionals? An Analysis of the Most Bothersome Errors and How the Writer's Ethos Is Affected*, 43 Journal of Business and Technical Communication 3 (2020), 254, DOI: 10.1177/1050651920910205.

information. The trick to writing a good topic sentence is knowing how much information to provide.

Below are some examples of a topic sentence for a paragraph that provides information about the challenges a chief human resource officer faces with employees working from home.

If you don't provide enough information, the topic sentence is too thin and doesn't forecast what is to come. Here is a thin topic sentence:

Chief human resource officers face many challenges.

If you provide too much information, there is nothing left for the paragraph to say. Here is a topic sentence with too much detail:

Chief human resource officers face many challenges with the new work-from-home model including productivity tracking, addressing employee mental health, and enhancing the employee experience. (Note: This looks more like a thesis statement for a longer paper. A paragraph should focus on one idea; this sentence has too many ideas to lead a paragraph.)

This topic sentence seems just about right:

Chief human resource officers face many new challenges as employees move from the workplace to work at home.

The topic sentence is also critically important in maintaining your logical flow. In addition to providing a signpost about what is to come in the paragraph, the topic sentence connects the current paragraph to the previous paragraph. That is, the topic sentence often provides language that connects the current idea to the previous idea.

EXERCISE Spend some time on your topic sentences; it is a great way to improve your writing. This exercise may be one you are tempted to skip. Don't. As mentioned above, writing good topic sentences will revolutionize your writing; the time you spend practicing will pay off.

Write a topic sentence about air pollution that is too thin.

Write a topic sentence about air pollution that has too many details.

Write a topic sentence about air pollution that is just right.

Consider writing a few more triads on various topics (working from home, year-round grammar school, college students taking a gap year).

c. The Sentence Fragment

Here is an example of a sentence fragment: (incorrect) *Because I was late for the meeting.* Many people make this mistake. *I was late for the meeting* is a complete sentence. *Because I was late for the meeting* is an incomplete sentence; it is a fragment. Why?

A sentence is a complete thought. *Because I was late for the meeting* is not a complete thought. It leaves you asking, so what? Here is where things might get confusing. If your friend asked you why you were fired, you might answer, *Because I was late for the meeting.* This has become more common in conversational English. In your writing, though, it is best to avoid sentence fragments. A complete sentence has a subject and a verb and is a complete thought.

d. The Run-On Sentence (Comma Splice)

Example (incorrect): *My employer should pay for me to get a legal master's degree I would be even more proficient at my job.*

This is a run-on sentence. It is two sentences that should have a period or semicolon separating the two complete thoughts (sentences). See the correct examples below:

Example (correct): *My employer should pay for me to get a legal master's degree. I would be even more proficient at my job.*

Example (correct): *My employer should pay for me to get a legal master's degree; I would be even more proficient at my job.*

You can also write these sentences using the coordinating conjunction "and" and a comma. Example (correct): *My employer should pay for me to get a legal master's degree, and I would be even more proficient at my job.* While we are here, let's introduce the very helpful acronym FANBOYS: **F**or, **A**nd, **N**or, **B**ut, **O**r, **Y**et, and **S**o. These words are the seven coordinating conjunctions. They allow you to connect two complete sentences with a coordinating conjunction and a comma. Here are some examples:

I was up until midnight, ***but*** *I did not complete my assignment.*

You can stay up late and watch television, ***or*** *you can get to bed early.*

Each sentence contains two complete sentences joined with a comma and a coordinating conjunction. Sometimes students separate two complete thoughts with a comma only. That is called a comma splice and it is incorrect.

Example (incorrect): *My employer should pay for me to get a legal master's degree, I would be even more proficient at my job.* This is a comma splice.

e. Commas

This section provides practical comma advice. As mentioned, you will not find every rule here. Rather, we are providing some of the important rules that will improve your writing immediately. You will no longer be missing commas, nor will you be sprinkling them arbitrarily.

Without good writing mechanics, our entire meaning may change. Communication may fail. You may be familiar with the book EATS, SHOOTS AND LEAVES: THE ZERO TOLERANCE APPROACH TO PUNCTUATION by Lynne Truss.[26] The clever book cover shows a panda eating bamboo shoots and leaves from a tree and another panda walking away with a pistol in his hand. The picture highlights the clear distinction between a happy panda having lunch as he eats shoots and leaves, versus a panda walking away with a pistol as he eats, shoots, and leaves. The commas make all the difference.

Not convinced yet? Though mechanics are important in all writing, they are particularly important in legal writing. Below is a 2017 legal case that, as the judge stated in the first sentence, "For want of a comma, we have this case."[27] This dispute between a dairy company and its drivers revolved around an overtime statute that requires overtime pay when an employee works more than forty hours. The drivers were company employees who wanted the overtime pay claiming that *Exemption F* supports their position. The relevant passage follows:

> Specifically, Exemption F states that the protection of the overtime law does not apply to: The canning, processing, preserving, freezing, drying, marketing, storing, packing for shipment or distribution of: . . . The parties' dispute concerns the meaning of the words "packing for shipment or distribution." The delivery drivers contend that, in combination, these words refer to the single activity of "packing," whether the "packing" is for "shipment" or for "distribution."[28]

The court ruled in favor of the delivery drivers. The drivers clearly distributed the products. Had Exemption F included the comma, it would have included distribution, which included the drivers: packing for shipment, or distribution. Do you see that with the comma the exemption would apply to those who distribute? The dairy company now sees it; they learned an expensive grammar lesson. It cost them five million dollars.[29]

Below are some basic comma rules. They will have you punctuating correctly the great majority of the time.

Separate two complete sentences with a coordinating conjunction and a comma. We discussed this above in § 6.4.3d. Again, you can use one of these coordinating conjunctions (For, And, Nor, But, Or, Yet, and So) with a comma to separate two complete sentences. Another example: *I enjoy studying the law, and this knowledge will improve my performance at work.* These are two complete sentences joined with a comma and a coordinating conjunction.

---

26. L. Truss, EATS, SHOOTS & LEAVES: THE ZERO TOLERANCE APPROACH TO PUNCTUATION (2006).

27. *O'Connor v. Oakhurst Dairy*, 851 F.3d 69, 70 (2017).

28. *O'Connor v. Oakhurst Dairy*, 851 F.3d 69, 71 (2017).

29. https://news.bloomberglaw.com/daily-labor-report/oakhurst-dairys-5m-settlement-driven-by-grammar-rules

Separate words or phrases in a series with commas. *The American flag uses the colors red, white, and blue.* This brings up a current discussion about the Oxford comma. Previously, a series did not include a comma before the "and." So that previous sentence would read as follows: *The American flag uses the colors red, white and blue.* We now recommend the use of a comma before that final "and" (the Oxford comma). Here's why. Consider this sentence: *My favorite athletes are my brothers, Michael Jordan, and Charles Barkley.* Let's look at this sentence without the Oxford comma: *My favorite athletes are my brothers, Michael Jordan and Charles Barkley.* Written this way it would falsely indicate that Michael Jordan and Charles Barkley were my brothers. The Oxford comma was also key in the delivery driver's legal case above. Though the Associated Press and others may disagree, generally you should employ the Oxford comma.

A dependent clause at the beginning of a sentence generally needs a comma. It often begins with a word like *unless* or *until* (a subordinating conjunction). It needs a comma if the dependent clause is at the beginning of a sentence, but not if the dependent clause comes at the end of the sentence. Here are some correct examples:

Until the band stops playing, we are going to stay at the party. (needs comma)

We are going to stay at the party until the band stops playing. (no comma)

Whenever it rains outside, my dog likes to splash in the puddles. (needs comma)

My dog likes to splash in the puddles whenever it rains outside. (no comma)

Direct address or introductory word/phrase requires a comma. When you are addressing a person by name or title, you need a comma. Here are some examples:

Professor, I don't understand what you are saying.

Dad, I can't find your wrench.

Sally, please tell me what time you will be home.

Yes, I did complete my legal master's degree.

Exactly, we have only fifteen minutes to catch the train.

Multiple adjectives describing a noun need commas. When you have more than one adjective describing a noun, you need to use commas. There is no comma between the final adjective and the noun.

The exception is if the adjective and noun are so closely related that you almost see them as one. You can test this by trying to switch the adjectives. Here are some examples:

The lead actor in the play was a tall, dark-haired, handsome man.

The lead actor in the play was a handsome, tall, dark-haired man. You can switch the adjectives and the sentence works. So, you need the commas.

I love to watch the antics of a colorful, jolly circus clown. This is correct. You can see that it doesn't make sense to move the adjectives around: *I love to watch the antics of a circus, jolly, colorful clown.* This is incorrect. *Circus clown* is almost seen as one word. Therefore, as in the correct example, there is no comma after jolly. Remember that the rule is that you don't include a comma between the last adjective and the noun. Here, "circus clown" is looked at as one word (the noun).

Again, there are other comma rules. Master these five, and when you are comfortable with them, you can find the others in the Purdue Online Writing Lab or other online sources. And finally, one last rule that is often broken: Remember not to use a comma to separate two complete sentences.

f. Semicolon

The semicolon is often misused, but it has very easy rules. Many people confuse semicolons with colons. Spend just ten minutes reading about semicolons below and you will have command of this punctuation.

Semicolons are used in two ways: (1) to separate two independent clauses (also known as sentences), and (2) to separate elements in a series.

(1) To separate two independent clauses

As you know, a period usually separates two complete sentences. Why would you use a semicolon instead? If you think of a period as a complete stop and a comma as a pause, the semicolon has both. It is not a complete stop, but it is more than a pause.

You use a semicolon to separate two complete sentences when you want the reader to know that they are closely related. Perhaps the best way to see how the semicolon works is by showing three examples of how two complete ideas can be written. Read through them and see if you can discern a difference.

The ever-changing regulations that govern the banking industry make a compliance plan essential. Employee compliance training must be mandatory.

The ever-changing regulations that govern the banking industry make a compliance plan essential, and employee compliance training must be mandatory.

The ever-changing regulations that govern the banking industry make a compliance plan essential; employee compliance training must be mandatory.

All three examples provide the same information. The punctuation simply provides a nuanced difference in delivering the information. Read them again, aloud. The example with the semicolon tells the reader that mandatory compliance training is closely related to the ever-changing regulations that govern the banking industry. Note that the sentence after the semicolon begins with a small letter. It is not capitalized.

(2) To separate elements in a series

In a series that contains commas, use a semicolon to show the reader which words should be grouped together. Here are two examples:

Company ABC is opening plants in Chicago, Illinois; New York, New York; and Houston, Texas.

For the company's summer party, I plan to decorate with red, yellow, and green balloons; red, yellow, and green streamers; and red, yellow, and green stars.

You can see that it might be confusing if commas were used throughout those sentences. The semicolon helps the reader see how the words should be grouped and then separated.

g. Colon

Where the semicolon rules are straightforward, the colon rules are a bit murkier. For example, many texts would suggest a colon in the following sentence:

The end of the book was shocking: the doctor died. This is correct.

Couldn't you also use a semicolon here? Yes, these are two complete sentences that are closely related. You would use the colon here if that second sentence was more than just related; use the colon if it explains, or answers, that first statement. It can also be used, as here, to emphasize that second sentence. See ... murkier.

Use a colon after a complete sentence to provide a list referred to in the sentence.

Barry plans to take four courses this semester: biology, chemistry, calculus, and Spanish. (Correct)

Colons are also used when detailing time: *5:01pm.*

Use a colon after a greeting in a business letter: *To whom it may concern:*

If you would like to take a deeper dive into punctuation and grammar, excellent resources exist. The authors highly recommend the following:

THE ELEMENTS OF STYLE by Strunk and White

PLAIN ENGLISH FOR LAWYERS by Richard Wydick

We also recommend using Grammarly online. It has two versions, and currently one is free. We also highly recommend using the Purdue Online Writing Lab (Purdue OWL). You can find succinct rules on grammar and punctuation as well as suggestions on writing a strong thesis statement and many other writing tips.

Grasping the basic rules of grammar and punctuation will enhance your writing confidence. Whether you are writing as a scholar or a business person, writing a letter or an email, good basic writing skills reflect several good qualities including attention to detail and professionalism.

§6.4.4 Editing (The Judge)

Finally, and not one minute before, you are ready to edit. This is the all-important rewrite. You need to be sure that your grammar is correct, and you have cited everything properly. Also critical during the rewrite is to carefully reread your piece and assure that it says what you intend.

James A. Michener, the Pulitzer Prize-winning author, famously said: "I'm not a very good writer, but I'm an excellent rewriter."[30] Ernest Hemingway, one of the most well-known writers of the twentieth century, also spent much of his time rewriting. In fact "Hemingway rewrote the conclusion to A FAREWELL TO ARMS many times. Among the gems of the Hemingway Collection are the 44 pages of manuscript containing a score of different endings."[31]

In working on the rewrite, it is often helpful to ask for someone to review and comment on your piece. This can be a painful process but often improves the final product. F. Scott Fitzgerald, another celebrated author of the twentieth century, provided such reviews for Hemingway, and Hemingway for Fitzgerald.

In June 1926 Fitzgerald wrote Hemingway that "parts of THE SUN ALSO RISES are careless, and ineffectual" and proceeded to give ten pages of criticism. "But remember this is a new departure for you and that I think your stuff is great."[32]

Even many of the greatest writers, then, need another set of set of eyes on their work to make it better. Find a friend to review your work and spend most of your time on the rewrite.

Teachers are known to write feedback in the margin such as this: "unclear." Another classic is "wordy." Well, I thought it was clear and had just the right number of words when I wrote it! Upon further examination, though, how can I tell if that sentence is, in fact, wordy and/or unclear? Look at the subject-verb. That is, go back to the sentence and pull out the subject-verb.

An editing example may be helpful. This sentence may have warranted the wordy/unclear feedback:

> In order to find out if operating rooms in the United States are free from elements that may cause infection, Mary, who will be undergoing a total hip surgery in the next month, did extensive research into the statutes, regulations, and policies that regulate the air circulatory system in the operating room, and she found that the operating room air quality is carefully regulated and the orthopedic surgeons wear closed-circuit helmets that help prevent airborne germs.

---

30. https://onlineacademiccommunity.uvic.ca/gradwriters/2017/11/30/im-not-a-very-good-writer-but-im-an-excellent-rewriter-revising-and-editing-with-intention/
31. https://www.archives.gov/publications/prologue/2006/spring/hemingway.html
32. P. Grande, *Fitzgerald, Hemingway and the Sun Also Rises*, LITERARY TRAVELER (2005).

Many things are wrong with this sentence. First, it is too long. Though you don't want all of your sentences to be very short, a sentence this long, even if well written, is generally confusing. Start with the subject-verb. That's a little tough here, because this should be two or three sentences.

- Let's start with Mary as the subject. Mary is what? concerned? worried? (the verb)
- About what? Infection.

So, let's start with the subject and the verb. Compare the next sentence to the one above:

> Mary, who has an upcoming hip surgery, is worried about getting an infection in the operating room. Mary's extensive research found that the operating room air quality is carefully regulated. In addition, the orthopedic surgeons wear a closed-circuit helmet that helps prevent airborne germs.

The first example has seventy-seven words. The second example has three sentences and forty-five words. A focus on the subject and the verb helps with editing and makes your writing clearer and more concise. Try it the next time you are editing a complicated sentence.

§6.5 A Research Project—An Effective Approach

§6.5.1 Research: Annotate, Organize, Synthesize

Here we present three writing skills that we can improve with a little attention. You will find that the result is worth the effort. These skills are helpful in both academia and the workplace: annotating, organizing, and synthesizing.

An expository or persuasive piece is often supported by research. Culling through the research, taking notes, and organizing your document is time consuming. The effort you devote to this process, however, will pay off down the road. Each of these steps is important.

a. Annotate

Annotate the research material as you read. Highlight the relevant passages and put notes in the margins. Highlighting the relevant parts of the articles you have found is the first step in pulling together your research. This, of course, can be done on paper or on your computer. You can also cut and paste from an article to a document opened on your computer. You may also open folders in Word for different topics and paste the material into them. If you use this approach, be sure to put quotes around all verbatim material and include citations. You will likely reword this material as you synthesize, but you want to be aware of the words you took directly from another source.

b. Organize

Categorizing is the first step in organizing. Categorizing, in particular, will help your writing take shape. By categorizing we mean pulling like ideas together.

Home-organizing TV shows and home-organizing books are currently very popular. The organizing steps touted by home organizers are quite like the organizing steps in writing. You may already be familiar with these steps.

When organizing your closet, for example, home organizers suggest you take everything out where you can see it (like brainstorming results). When you begin the writing process, you write down all your ideas with abandon; leave nothing out. Once you have everything in front of you (after brainstorming), begin the organizing process:

HOME ORGANIZING	ORGANIZING WRITING
Remove items that are no longer used or needed	Remove ideas that don't support the main idea
Categorize—put like objects together	Categorize—put like ideas together
Contain—choose a container of some kind to place the items	Contain—put your ideas into paragraphs
Find the best place in the home to put things	Find the best order to place your ideas
Arrange the containers in the space you designated in the home	Put the paragraphs in a logical order (usually an iterative process)

c. Synthesize

Research in the Workplace or Academia

You may recall writing research papers in your past scholastic endeavors. Generally, one of the most challenging aspects of this kind of writing is finding a way to combine and present the multitude of sources.

But perhaps you are a businessperson. You have no plans to write a term paper, thesis, or dissertation in the near future. Why study the art of synthesis? Because in much business writing, as in persuasive writing, synthesis is elemental. It is combining ideas or sources to support your idea or argument.

Imagine you are a product development expert, for example. You are writing to convince your company to launch a new product. You've done the research. How do you weave it all together to make a strong, persuasive presentation? Synthesis is essential.

Or perhaps you are writing a paper using peer-reviewed research articles. How do you combine this material in a way that supports your new idea (with proper attribution, of course)? When facing reams of research, business ideas, data, or statistics, it is important to synthesize the information in a way that makes sense. Novice writers sometimes simply present ideas one after the other. This leaves the reader to make sense of it. Making sense of the material, though, is the writer's job. The writer must apply her synthesizing skills to the task.

The key to synthesizing the research or ideas for your research paper, report, policy, etc. is to look for similarities and differences in the information. Many writers try to do this without spending the necessary time categorizing this information. Synthesizing is different from organizing ideas with main ideas and sub-ideas. Synthesis involves blending the ideas in a way that the reader can understand.

One of the easiest ways to synthesize material is to use a chart. This may seem like busy work; it is anything but. Below is an example you might use to synthesize the information you found when writing a paper on the benefits of working from home.

For a given piece, you might easily have thirty-plus sources. For simplicity's sake, let's assume you have five sources on the benefits of working from home. Below is a chart that would help you categorize similarities and differences in your research. The vertical column contains the sources. The horizontal column contains the topics or ideas. The headings of the horizontal columns depend on the particular topic.

If you were trying to convince your boss, one possible draft thesis statement might focus on the benefit to the company in addition to the employee:

Working from home not only benefits employees, but studies show that employees are actually more productive when working from home. Your thesis statement will likely change as you continue with your research. Also, creating the headings from your research will help you in drafting your thesis statement.

Sources	Pros of working at home for employee	Pros of working at home for employer	Cons of working at home for employee	Cons of working at home for employer	Productivity data
Source 1					
Source 2					
Source 3					
Source 4					
Source 5					

Though the focus of the paper is on the benefits, notice that two of your headings focus on the cons of working from home. It is important to address the counterargument to your thesis or proposal and explain why the pros outweigh the cons.

As indicated above, different writers will categorize the material differently. The effort to select these headings will strengthen your coherence, your logical flow.

The number of source columns and topic columns will vary greatly from project to project. The method, though, is the same. Once you have completed the chart, the writing process will be easier. Once you have the chart, think about your section headings. Then think about your topic sentences and you are on your way. Give it a try to see how it works for you. Perhaps it is not for you. That's okay, but it is imperative to find a detailed organizational structure for your data or research.

§6.6 Original Work

Students must support their original thesis statement with scholarly research. How then, they ask, can their work be original if it is based on the ideas of other writers?

An analogy may be helpful. Think of different musical notes. Each note has its own sound. A pianist can combine these notes to make a different sound: the chord. The chord can be major or minor. By blending the notes together into chords and stringing them together into measures and phrases, a composer creates an original piece of music. Similarly, a writer blends together the research or ideas or data and with proper attribution, to the various pieces she synthesizes in her own unique way, and she creates original written work. Other analogies include different fruit blended together to become something new: a smoothie. Different kinds of fabrics can be sewn together to create a designer garment. You get the idea. The material you draw from different sources can be put together in a unique way to support your original idea.

§6.7 Some Tips to Make Good Writing Even Better

In this section we include some ideas that will make your good writing even better.

§6.7.1 Active voice

§6.7.2 Inverted pyramid

§6.7.3 Keep words close to what they modify (a.k.a. misplaced modifiers)

§6.7.4 Parallel structure

§6.7.5 Procrastination avoidance

§6.7.6 Road maps/Signposts

§6.7.7 Style–cadence

§ 6.7.8 Three C's

§ 6.7.9 The verb

§ 6.7.10 Voice

§ 6.7.11 Word choice

We will address these in alphabetical order. You can jump to an area of interest.

§ 6.7.1 Active Voice

Most of your sentences should use the active voice; it is more clear and concise (note in the three C's of good writing below, clear and concise are numbers one and two). Active voice is when the subject is doing the acting. Passive voice is when the subject is receiving the action.

As noted earlier, if you put the subject at the beginning of the sentence, it helps you remain in the active voice. Here are some examples:

Active voice: *The manager fired John.* The subject is manager who is acting.

Passive voice: *John was fired by the manager.* The subject John is receiving the action. Notice the word "by" in the passive sentence. Often that indicates that the sentence is in passive voice.

Though you want to prefer active voice, sometimes the passive voice is a better choice. Look at these examples:

Active voice: *The robber shot the mayor.*

Passive voice: *The mayor was shot by the robber.*

Here, you might want the mayor to be the focus of the sentence.

§ 6.7.2 Inverted Pyramid

Note that the inverted pyramid is wide at the top and then narrows to a point. Generally, when writing, you want to begin with broader statements and follow with details. Think about telling your friend a story. You want to set the stage before you get to the details. Starting with the details can be confusing.

Here are a few examples:

The tiny blue and green buttons accented the navy piping. In addition, the striped fabric had a breezy summer effect. The embroidered lettering finished the look. The new throw pillows I bought for our cottage went perfectly with our shabby chic couch.

Do you see that you, the reader, are wondering what these details are all about? See how much easier it is to read when you put that general statement first:

The new throw pillows I bought for the cottage went perfectly with our shabby chic couch. The tiny blue and green buttons accented the navy piping. In addition, the striped fabric had a breezy summer effect. The embroidered lettering finished the look.

§6.7.3 Keep Words Close to What They Modify (a.k.a. Misplaced Modifiers)

Words or phrases that modify a noun should be kept close together. Often a phrase is tacked onto the end of a sentence, and it should be placed earlier by the noun it modifies. Some examples will highlight the point.

Terry's wallet was found by the teacher lying on the table. Was the teacher lying on the table? When we fix this sentence, we will also put it into active voice: *The teacher found Terry's wallet lying on the table.*

John saw three pigeons on the way to the doctor's office. Were the pigeons heading to the doctor? *On the way to the doctor's office, John saw three pigeons.*

§6.7.4 Parallel Structure

Parallel structure makes your writing read more smoothly. It tends to be clearer and sound better (even in your head). You want uniformity in your word endings or phrases. Parallel structure is best learned by example.

Parallel—*Margi's favorite activities are gardening, reading, and hiking.*

Not parallel—*Margi's favorite activities are gardening, reading, and to hike.*

Parallel—*Gretta enjoys going to yoga class, going to the movies, and going to pickleball class.*

Also parallel—*Gretta enjoys going to yoga class, the movies, and pickleball class.*

Not parallel—*Gretta enjoys going to yoga class, going to the movies, and to pickleball class.*

Parallel—*Sissy attended college at University of Illinois, graduate school at Rush University, and post-graduate classes at Rice University.*

Not parallel—*Sissy attended college at University of Illinois, graduate school at Rush University and took a few post-graduate classes at Rice University.*

§6.7.5 Procrastination Avoidance

Most people experience writer's block now and then. Communication does not always flow easily. Writing is sometimes easy to procrastinate. We might want our writing to be perfect, so we hesitate to begin. Perhaps we don't enjoy writing, so we avoid it all together. This brings to mind Dorothy Parker's feelings about writing: "I hate writing, but I love having written."[33] You, like Dorothy, may not find the process easy or enjoyable. You will hopefully, though, find the end result gratifying.

To get you unstuck, remember the words of Marc Raibert: "Almost all good writing starts out bad."[34] Don't be afraid to write the bad stuff. That will get you started. You can work to make it great. (We highly recommend a quick read of this short, clever, and very helpful article by Mr. Raibert: *Good Writing*, https://www.cs.cmu.edu/~pausch/Randy/Randy/raibert.htm.)

§6.7.6 Road Maps/Signposts

Your objective in writing is to make your piece easy for your reader to understand. Roadmaps and signposts help. Just as you need signposts in reaching a destination on the road, you need to provide signposts in your written piece. Take the time to insert headings. Carefully choose your transitions to make your writing flow.

§6.7.7 Style-Cadence

Shorter sentences are often easier to follow. If you find yourself with unwieldy sentences, remove unnecessary words. That said, a string of short, choppy sentences is undesirable. As Strunk and White say, "Variety in sentence length is what's needed. All short will sound stupid. All long will sound stuffy."[35] As you are working on the final edit, notice the cadence. Change up the sentence lengths where necessary. Sometimes reading aloud helps.

Also, use paragraphing to make your piece easier for the reader. As mentioned previously, the paragraph helps organize your thoughts for the reader to easily digest. Finally, be careful to avoid full-page paragraphs.

---

33. Dorothy Parker was a twentieth-century American poet, writer, and critic.

34. M. Raibert, *Good Writing* (1985), https://www.cs.cmu.edu/~pausch/Randy/Randy/raibert.htm.

35. W. Strunk & E. B. White, Elements of Style (2000, Fourth Edition).

§6.7.8 Three C's of Good Writing

Most writing texts address the three, four, or five-plus C's of writing: clear, coherent, concise, complete, cogent, and correct. Acknowledging the Power of Threes (see §6.8.2), we will stick with clear, coherent, and concise.

a. Clear

Imagine the following scenario in a home buying/selling negotiation:

> During the negotiations, they reduced the purchase price by $29,000. After further negotiations, they reduced the price an additional $5,000. With the purchase price being reduced a total of $34,000, then, they gave her clear instructions that they would not address any of their inspection concerns. She confirmed to them that she made this very clear to them. Therefore, they respectfully decline all of their inspection requests.

Notice the revised negotiation record below. The specific terms *sellers*, *buyers*, and *listing agent* are repeated; no pronouns are used. Why? Clarity! Repetition is not only acceptable where clarity is at issue, it is essential. Compare the paragraph above with the same paragraph below using specific nouns.

> During the negotiations, the sellers reduced the purchase price by $29,000. After further negotiations, the sellers reduced the price an additional $5,000. With the purchase price being reduced a total of $34,000, then, the sellers gave their listing agent clear instructions that the sellers would not address any of the buyers' inspection concerns. The listing agent confirmed to the sellers that she made this very clear to the buyers. Therefore, the sellers respectfully decline all of the buyers' inspection requests.

Clarity is important in all writing. Clarity is essential in legal documents.

b. Concise

If ever the term "less is more" had meaning, it is in the art of writing. Many books on writing include this command: "Omit needless words."[36] Some put it this way: "Omit surplus words."[37] You get the idea. Succinct, pithy, crisp writing is a joy to read.

---

36. W. Strunk & E. B. White, ELEMENTS OF STYLE (2000, Fourth Edition), 23.
37. R. C. Wydick, PLAIN ENGLISH FOR LAWYERS (2005, Fifth Edition), 7.

c. Coherent (a.k.a. Logical Flow)

Your writing is coherent if the reader can easily follow. It is critical to review your piece, in the end, to be sure it flows logically.

Again, the paragraph is king. Build coherence within each paragraph. One sentence should flow into the next. This can be accomplished by repeating key terms and using transition words. Also, build coherence between paragraphs. Use transitions to link one paragraph to the next.

Check coherence during the editing process. If you begin with a good outline, you may need less editing, but read it through to be sure it flows. Again, consider reading each topic sentence. Do the ideas follow? Your readers will appreciate the time spent checking for coherence.

§6.7.9 The Verb

A good verb can make a sentence come alive. OK, not bad, but let's see if we can do better. A good verb breathes life into a sentence. Can't you picture that? They do.

Search for your verbs. The payoff in your writing is dramatic.

Verbs also help with editing. As we were editing a previous page, we changed this sentence:

This is where your writing mechanics come in handy. Generally, "This is" and "there is" tend to be weak sentence starters. Those words don't really "tell." When editing your work, those can be the first things to go... though you may still find a few here.

The sentence now reads: *Good writing mechanics help communicate our thoughts effectively.* We found a better verb: *communicate.* The sentence provides more meaning.

The original version of the sentence, *This is where your writing mechanics come in handy,* is really not saying much. It simply says that writing mechanics are helpful in writing. But how? When we asked that question, the verb *communicate* came to mind because that is what we are trying to do; finding the right verb helps.

Rewriting and editing may have previously appeared as a chore. Finding verbs that tell, though, can be fun. And finding the right verbs will make a big difference in your writing. Verb choice is part of the carpenter's work, but it can come in again with the judge.

§6.7.10 Voice

Where style focuses on the structural aspect of writing, voice focuses on the author's tone. Voice reveals the author's personality. Is the word choice formal or casual? Are the sentences more direct, or is there extensive explanation? You may notice different voices throughout this book. The chapters are written by one of the book's authors. Do you notice a difference in voice?

§6.7.11 Word Choice

I know nothing in the world that has as much power as a word. Sometimes I write one, and I look at it until it begins to shine.

—Emily Dickinson

Just as an artist might use paint or charcoal to create a painting, a writer uses words to communicate ideas. When you really get down to making your writing great, you are following the advice of E. B. White in his seminal work, ELEMENTS OF STYLE: "Vigorous writing is concise. A sentence should contain no unnecessary words, a paragraph no unnecessary sentences, for the same reason that a drawing should have no unnecessary lines and a machine no unnecessary parts. This requires not that the writer make all his sentences short, or that he avoid all detail and treat his subject only in outline, but that every word tell."[38] With adequate time, with careful review, and with multiple rewrites, you can make "every word tell."

As mentioned in the sentence structure section, a strong focus on the subject-verb sentence construction will serve your writing well. So, along with the verb, choosing a good subject is important.

Some believe you must ascertain the perfect word for every sentence yourself; they disparage the use of the thesaurus. We disagree. A great feeling comes from finding the perfect word in the thesaurus. You certainly shouldn't be using it to find a more scholarly-sounding word; don't use a five-dollar word where a ten-cent word works perfectly. But the thesaurus can be a good tool. Don't hesitate to use it. Searching for that word is time well spent.

§6.8 Pulling It All Together in the Five-Paragraph Essay

Let's look at an example of a five-paragraph essay. We know you studied this in junior high. We have found, though, that many of our students have not studied writing in some time; they found the review helpful. If this is not your experience, please skip this example. You might want to take a quick look at the "rule of three," though (§6.8.2). It can be a powerful tool.

38. W. Strunk & E. B. White, ELEMENTS OF STYLE (2000, Fourth Edition), 23.

§6.8.1 The Five-Paragraph Essay Framework

Intro paragraph

Body paragraph 1

Body paragraph 2

Body paragraph 3

Conclusion paragraph

Imagine you are trying to persuade your company to pay for your master's degree. Let's use the Flowers paradigm. We start with the madman; we brainstorm and get something on paper.

Why should the company pay for your legal master's degree?

Jot down some ideas; don't worry about wordsmithing at this stage. You are simply brainstorming like a madman. Don't edit yourself here:

- What you learn will improve your work performance
- What you learn about the law can save the company money by avoiding legal errors
- Tuition reimbursement is an excellent benefit and will attract good employees
- It will also improve employee retention
- Employees will be happier and therefore more productive
- Employer may tie this benefit to the employee agreeing to stay with the company for a certain period
- Employee turnover is expensive for the company
- The employer may be able to deduct this benefit

Next, choose the three primary reasons that your company should pay for your legal master's degree. Why three?

§6.8.2 The Rule of Three (a.k.a. The Power of Three or The Magic of Three)

As with many writing "rules," you must remain flexible and use your own judgment. The rule of three isn't supported with scientific proof, but a review of journalism, marketing, and even fairy tales is enlightening (think Goldilocks and the Three Bears and the Three Little Pigs).

You may have two reasons and you may have five. Though it is only a generality, often three seems just right. Two might appear too thin, and with five you may lose impact. Three highlights a few important points without overdoing it.

In Carmine Gallo's book FIVE STARS: THE COMMUNICATION SECRET TO GET FROM GOOD TO GREAT, he tells us that "Apple is obsessed with the magical number 3.... Steve Jobs also realized that 'mere Humans' can only handle so much information. It's well-known among neuroscientists that people can easily remember up to three ideas or pieces of information. The longer the list, the less likely it is they'll remember it."[39]

A look at some of Apple's marketing on apple.com provides some examples:

- The first page with iPhone 13 Pro: "Oh. So. Pro."
- How to choose your MacBook:
    - "Choose your size."
    - "Choose your chip."
    - "Let it rip."

There are many examples in marketing. The magic three works.

§6.8.3 Drafting the Essay

Okay, back to our example. Let us decide on these three:

- What you learn will improve your work performance
- What you learn about the law can save company money by avoiding legal errors
- Tuition reimbursement is an excellent benefit and will attract top-notch employees

What is so useful about this approach is that these three reasons now become the topics of each of your three body paragraphs. These ideas inspire your three topic sentences. Then each body paragraph provides detail and support for the topic sentence. Those three ideas set up the organization for your essay and make the writing process much easier.

To begin our sample essay, we start with a thesis statement. This differs from a topic sentence in that it is more of an argument statement. It is helpful if it contains some specific details. It is a statement with which a reasonable person could disagree.

Your thesis statement explains what you are trying to communicate. So, the first thing you should do is draft a statement providing your central point to your reader. In our example, we are trying to persuade someone, so it is an argument statement. It is a statement with which a reasonable person could disagree.

39. C. Gallo, *Five Stars: The Communication Secrets to Get from Good to Great* (2018).

One possible thesis statement for our essay follows: By providing tuition reimbursement for its employees pursuing a legal master's degree, Smith Company would save money, observe improved employee performance, and recruit higher caliber employees.

You will start with an introductory paragraph that will include each of these three reasons. In doing so you have your organization set. Each of these reasons will provide the topic sentence for a support paragraph. Here is an example of one way to approach this topic:

In our post-pandemic economy, companies are in tight competition for top candidates. Many companies are offering top recruits increased salaries as well as increased benefits. One such benefit is tuition reimbursement. In fact, tuition reimbursement is a coveted benefit being offered by companies such as Starbucks, Walmart, Target, Amazon, UPS, Home Depot, and countless others.[40] *These companies have observed the rewards of offering tuition reimbursement. Smith Company would be wise to join the crowd. By providing tuition reimbursement for its employees pursuing a legal master's degree, Smith Company would save money, observe improved employee performance, and recruit higher caliber employees.*

Umbrella Paragraph

One such reward would be that your master's of legal studies degreed employee will save you money. This body paragraph will contain sentences that support the ways in which the master's prepared employee will save the company money (such as avoiding legal mistakes). Use specifics here.

In addition, work performance will improve as your employees learn more about business and the law. Provide a few sentences focused on the advantages of employees with this advanced legal knowledge.

Three Body Paragraphs

Finally, in this very competitive market in which companies are fighting over the top candidates, this tuition reimbursement benefit will attract the brightest and the best. This body paragraph should provide details and perhaps some supporting research about the benefits to companies who offer tuition reimbursement.

The investment that Smith Company makes in providing tuition reimbursement for the employee with a legal master's degree will be paid back tenfold. The company will save money, have more satisfied employees, and beat the competition by recruiting a very high caliber employee.

Conclusion

40. https://www.bestcolleges.com/news/analysis/2021/09/16/top-companies-offering-tuition-reimbursement/

EXERCISES

1. Draft some sentences that would support each of your body paragraphs.
2. Read the topic sentences aloud. Can you see that these provide a logical flow to the essay?
3. Discuss the difference between a thesis statement and a topic sentence.
4. Can you see how the conclusion paragraph circles back to summarize the essay?

§6.9 A Final Word: Excellent Writing... A Worthy Purpose

Consider for a moment Helen Keller, author and activist, who was both blind and deaf. She became deaf and blind after a severe illness before the age of two. With the help of a special teacher, Anne Sullivan, Helen was brought out of what she later referred to as "ignorance and darkness."[41]

The miraculous moment of communication is retold in books, plays, and movies. Anne Sullivan is signing the word *water* into Helen's hand while holding Helen's hand under an old fashion water pump. As Anne tells it, at the miraculous moment of communication, Helen's face bursts into a smile.[42] Communication. The thought of one person is grasped by another. It is a beautiful connection.

The written word is one very important and powerful means of communication. Hopefully this chapter provided motivation to work on your writing. As you sharpen your skills, your confidence will grow. You will hear from people at work who notice the improvement.

Pen poised, or computer keys waiting, write on!

---

41. H. Keller, The Story of My Life—The Classic Autobiography of Helen Keller (2019).

42. H. Keller, The Story of My Life—The Classic Autobiography of Helen Keller (2019).

CHAPTER SEVEN

Legal Analysis and Legal Writing

The ultimate authority must always rest with the individual's own reason and critical analysis.

—Dalai Lama

§7.1 Legal Analysis and Thinking Like a Lawyer

You may have heard the expression "thinking like a lawyer." What does this mean? Is thinking like a lawyer different than thinking like a businessperson or any other professional? Does it require special analytical skills unique to the legal profession? Is legal reasoning different than other forms of reasoning, or is it just reasoning "in a legal context"?[1] You will formulate answers to these questions as you proceed through this chapter.

Lawyers hone analytical skills to help them break down complex legal issues. Answering legal questions involves pinpointing an issue, finding the law that pertains to that issue, and then applying that law to a set of not-yet-decided facts. This helps determine what a judge might conclude regarding those facts. Is that thinking like a lawyer? Though the expression is often used, a precise definition of the phrase remains elusive.[2]

Thinking like a lawyer certainly involves legal analysis. Legal analysis is examining a complex legal problem, breaking it down, and viewing it from different angles to understand its underlying structure. Although often used interchangeably, legal analysis and legal reasoning are somewhat different. Legal reasoning uses logical thinking and analogy to reach a conclusion. Both are essential in answering legal questions and constructing strong legal arguments.

The concept of legal analysis is so important to understanding the law that some recommend that legal analysis be given comprehensive study throughout legal train-

1. S. R. Kedia, *Redirecting the Scope of First-Year Writing Courses: Toward a New Paradigm of Teaching Legal Writing*, 87 U. Det. Mercy L. Rev. (2010), 147, 159.

2. L. O. Natt Gant, *Deconstructing Thinking Like a Lawyer: Analyzing the Cognitive Components of the Analytical Mind*, 29 Campbell L. Rev. 413 (2007), 413.

ing.[3] Legal analysis "underlies every subject presented in law school and is the gateway to all lawyerly training."[4]

Judges also use legal analysis and reasoning to produce well-written legal opinions. Judges use "reflective thinking and the rules of deductive and inductive logic."[5] Reflective thinking, deductive reasoning, and inductive reasoning are also used to answer questions and construct arguments throughout the business world. Both inductive and deductive reasoning appear in our everyday thinking as well.

We now focus on these different types of legal reasoning. This sets the groundwork for understanding more complex legal issues and reading more complex legal cases. Strengthening your analysis skills will support your success in legal studies and the workplace.

§7.2 Types of Legal Reasoning

Two primary types of legal reasoning are important when new to legal studies: **rule-based reasoning** and **analogical reasoning**. We explore these at some length. We also mention policy-based and custom-based reasoning as you may notice that some judges employ them.

Generally, a judge should follow precedent. In the event, though, that societal values have changed, or a rule is patently unfair, a judge may employ **policy-based reasoning** to do what is best for society. To some, this is an important feature of fairness in our legal system. To others, this may appear to be legislating from the bench rather than a principled decision based on precedent.

Custom-based reasoning acknowledges that certain traditions are woven into the fabric of society, and though they may not be memorialized in the law, they are considered consequential.

Let us turn now to rule-based reasoning.

§7.2.1 Rule-Based Reasoning

Our legal system is based on the belief that the law is objective, and people will be treated similarly and fairly. The validity of this idea may certainly be questioned, but a judge's ruling should be based on legal rules. These rules must be applied equitably. Similar cases should be decided similarly.

---

3. J. A. Interdonato, *The Consummate Legal Education: Teaching Analysis as Doctrine*, 4 Concordia L. Rev. (2019), 68, 70.

4. J. A. Interdonato, *The Consummate Legal Education: Teaching Analysis as Doctrine*, 4 Concordia L. Rev. (2019), 68, 70.

5. R. J. Aldisert, M. Rasch, & M. P. Bartlett, *Opinion Writing and Opinion Readers*, 31 Cardozo L. Rev. 1 (2009), 20.

Rule-based reasoning is law based.[6] Answering a legal question with rule-based reasoning involves finding the relevant rule, applying that rule to the set of facts that comprise the legal question, and stating the likely answer.

Rule-based reasoning solves legal problems using **deductive reasoning**. Deductive reasoning is common in many disciplines. In law, "It operates through the application of the **syllogism**, with the rules serving as the major premises, the facts of the case providing the minor premises, and the legal result acting as the conclusion."[7]

You are likely familiar with deductive reasoning. We use it in our everyday thinking. Deductive reasoning, as noted, begins with a major premise, followed by a minor premise, and leads to a specific conclusion. It is sometimes called top-down reasoning; it proceeds from the general to the specific. An important point to remember about deductive reasoning is that the premises must be true for the conclusion to be true.[8]

An often-used example of deductive reasoning follows:

All men are mortal.

Socrates is a man.

Therefore, Socrates is mortal.

If the first two statements are true, you can be confident that the conclusion is true.

Can you see a potential problem with the conclusion in this example?

All students pay tuition.

John is a student.

Therefore, John pays tuition.

It is true that John is a student. Is it true that all students pay tuition? Perhaps some students are on athletic scholarships. It may be true that John pays tuition, but it is not guaranteed to be true. Whether we are entertaining a legal issue, or thinking about another topic, vetting information is vitally important to reach an accurate, true conclusion.

---

6. S. A. McMahon, *What We Teach When We Teach Legal Analysis*, 107 MINN. L. REV. 2511 (2023), 2521.

7. S. A. McMahon, *What We Teach When We Teach Legal Analysis*, 107 MINN. L. REV. 2511 (2023), 2518. Citing W. Huhn, *The Stages of Legal Reasoning: Formalism, Analogy, and Realism*, 48 VILL. L. REV. 305 (2003), 309.

8. Two true statements followed by a conclusion is called a syllogism.

Pause for Reflection Vetting information is important in making sound decisions. Vetting information is also important before taking action.

- Can you think of a time in the past week when you made a decision based on information you received from another person or news source? How did you determine that the information was true?
- Can you think of a time in the past month when you took action based on information you received from a salesperson, newspaper, friend, or family member? How did you vet the information? Were you pleased with the outcome?

Deductive reasoning is used frequently in the law. Consider this example regarding posted speed limits. You were driving on a stretch of highway with a posted speed limit of 55 miles/hour (major premise). You are stopped by the police for driving 65 miles/hour on that stretch of highway (minor premise). You are guilty of speeding (conclusion). How might you avoid being guilty of speeding in this situation? You would need to disprove one of the first two statements.

Here is another legal example of deductive reasoning:

Legal question—Can Clark park 12 feet from a fire hydrant?

Relevant rule—In this jurisdiction you must park at least 15 feet from a fire hydrant.

Answer—You cannot park 12 feet from a fire hydrant.

With a grip on rule-based reasoning, we now turn to case law and analogical reasoning.

§7.2.2 Analogical Reasoning

Where rule-based reasoning is law based, **analogical reasoning** is case based.[9] Answering a legal question with analogical reasoning involves finding the relevant precedent cases and comparing the facts and holding of the precedent case to your set of facts to reach a conclusion. Analogical reasoning uses **inductive reasoning**. Where deductive reasoning proceeds from the top down, inductive reasoning proceeds from the bottom up. Inductive reasoning begins with specifics and moves to the general. When synthesizing specific rules from several cases to form a general rule, you are using inductive reasoning.

We use analogical reasoning in everyday life. Imagine you approach your boss to request a raise. You are a vice president, and you find out that you are making $10,000 less than Gayle, another vice president. You explain to your boss that your jobs are

9. S. A. McMahon, *What We Teach When We Teach Legal Analysis*, 107 MINN. L. REV. (2023), 2511, 2521.

very similar. You set out your facts compared to Gayle's facts. You both manage the same number of people, you are responsible for the same revenue, and you work the same hours. You should be making the same salary. Your boss searches for distinguishing facts and points out that Gayle has been here five years longer than you. You respond that you have been in the business seven years longer than Gayle. You see how this goes. Finding similar facts that support your position and **distinguishing facts** to show why unfavorable facts do not apply can strengthen an argument.

Finding the facts to compare or distinguish is not always easy. It would be extremely rare to find a fact pattern in a precedent case that is identical to the facts of the situation you are examining. How do you know which facts to compare? Novices in the art of analogical reasoning are generally good at comparing the facts. A more seasoned practitioner realizes that a nuanced approach is necessary. That is, in addition to comparing the facts from a current case to a precedent case, one must understand the court's reasoning.[10] An example will help clarify.

Pause for Reflection Factory Shoe Example

Assume you are a factory worker walking into the factory. As you enter the vestibule you see a sign that says NO LIGHT SHOES ALLOWED. You are standing with three fellow workers. Each of you is wearing the following footwear:

- You—brown steel-toed boots
- Joe—black tennis shoes
- Mary—navy flip-flops
- Gary—white sandals

Who is allowed to enter? Does light mean in color or weight?

Compare these facts:

- Light shoes and brown steel-toed boots
- Light shoes and black tennis shoes
- Light shoes and navy flip-flops
- Light shoes and white sandals

How do you compare? You must know the rationale. If this is a paint factory, perhaps they recommend darker shoes because of paint splatter. In that case, the white boots would not be allowed.

Assume the sign says this: Protect your feet from falling hazards and other injury: NO LIGHT SHOES ALLOWED

Who is allowed to enter? The steel-toed boots are heavy, so they would be allowed.

---

10. Other legal scholars believe the rule comes first, not the facts. They contend that the judge looks for the rule first and the facts fit second. See F. Schauer & B. A. Spellman, *Analogy, Expertise, and Experience*, 84 U. Chi. L. Rev. 249 (2017), 257.

Again, the answer depends on the rationale behind the rule. You can see that comparing the workers' shoes to the "light shoes" on the sign, without understanding the rule, does not tell the workers who are allowed to enter. Once they know the rule is for foot protection, they can decide which shoe facts are relevant. This example is meant to demonstrate the importance of understanding the rule and the court's rationale in a precedent case. Here is a legal example of the same principle.

Assume that only case law addresses the fire hydrant issue in this case.

Legal question—Can Clark park twelve feet from a fire hydrant?

Precedent case—In *City v. Jones,* Jones parked thirteen feet from a fire hydrant and was found guilty.

Precedent case—In *City v. Smith,* Smith parked five feet from the fire hydrant and was found not guilty.

Likely answer—What do we need to know to determine whether Clark can park twelve feet from the fire hydrant based on these precedent cases?

We mentioned that the rationale for the rule is important in determining which facts to compare. In the above example, can you see that simply comparing the facts is not enough? Can you think of any reason why the court found Smith not guilty? Perhaps Smith had a disability, and the court made a rule exception for someone disabled. Perhaps Smith was driving a motorcycle, and the court made a rule exception for motorcycles. You can see that it is important to know the court's reasoning in precedent cases to know which facts in the Clark case are important.

Many believe that this analogical reasoning distinguishes legal analysis.[11] Understanding legal reasoning methods helps move the novice in legal studies toward legal literacy.

We next explore a framework used by many law students and lawyers to structure legal arguments. Both rule-based and analogical reasoning are used within this structure. This organizational structure is especially useful for someone new to the art of legal analysis.

---

11. F. Schauer & B. A. Spellman, *Analogy, Expertise, and Experience*, 84 U. Chi. L. Rev. 249 (2017).

§7.3 IRAC, an Organizational Tool for Legal Analysis

IRAC is an organizational tool used to analyze and answer legal questions. The acronym stands for Issue, Rule, Application, and Conclusion. Any lawyer will be familiar with IRAC. It is a very helpful initial framework for legal analysis and is taught to first-year law students across the country.

Legal scholars differ in their opinions regarding IRAC's continued utility. Some think it too rigid and simplistic.[12] Others find that it is a great starting point to organize a legal argument or understand a legal case. We fall into the latter camp. IRAC is a good place to start understanding that flexibility and artistry unfold with experience.

For those of you who are mathematically inclined, you might find the relationship of IRAC to math intriguing. Abraham Lincoln claimed that studying mathematical reasoning enhanced his study of law.[13] Theorems and proofs in upper-level mathematics have a similar organizational structure to some legal structures such as IRAC.[14] Math, like legal reasoning, also employs inductive and deductive reasoning.

Professor Maria Termini demonstrates the similarities in deductive reasoning between legal syllogisms and those in mathematical proofs. Both employ a major premise and minor premise that lead to a conclusion. She also shows the similarities in inductive reasoning, comparing a mathematical theorem to the inductive reasoning used in synthesizing precedent cases.[15]

Some disagree with the comparison between math and legal reasoning, perhaps thinking of the law more as art than science. Christopher Langdell, who instituted the case method of teaching law, claimed that law is a science.[16] Regardless of one's position on the issue, math, science, and the law all require analytical skills to ensure success.

Many variations of the IRAC theme exist: CRAC, CREAC, and CREXAC[17] to name a few.[18] Most variations appear to expand the rule element. As you learned in

---

12. Laura P. Graham, *Why-Rac? Revisiting the Traditional Paradigm for Writing about Legal Analysis*, 63 U. Kan. L. Rev. 681 (2015).

13. M. Termini, *Proving the Point: Connections between Legal and Mathematical Reasoning*, 52 Suffolk U. L. Rev. 5 (2019), 7–8.

14. M. Termini, *Proving the Point: Connections between Legal and Mathematical Reasoning*, 52 Suffolk U. L. Rev. 5 (2019), 7–8.

15. M. Termini, *Proving the Point: Connections between Legal and Mathematical Reasoning*, 52 Suffolk U. L. Rev. 5 (2019), 19.

16. M. Termini, *Proving the Point: Connections between Legal and Mathematical Reasoning*, 52 Suffolk U. L. Rev. 5 (2019), 27–28.

17. CRAC is conclusion, rule, application, conclusion. CREAC is conclusion, rule, explanation, application, conclusion. CREXAC is conclusion, rule, explanation, exceptions, application, conclusion.

18. M. Termini, *Proving the Point: Connections between Legal and Mathematical Reasoning*, 52 Suffolk U. L. Rev. 5 (2019), 13.

Chapter Two, the rule of law comes from cases as well as statutes and regulations in a common law[19] system. In the absence of a statute or regulation controlling an issue, the court will look to common law. Even if a statute applies, case law may be necessary to explain or define certain terms. How you weave together, analyze, and apply case law is a critical part of legal analysis.

Studying IRAC can also help you read legal opinions as many judges organize their cases around **IRAC**. Judges set forth the legal question (**issue**) in the case, provide the statutes, cases, and regulations (**rule**) that help answer the legal question, and provide the reasoning (**application**) they used in reaching the ruling (**conclusion**).

Let's look more closely at the components of IRAC.

Issue:

As previously stated, the issue is the legal question that an individual or a court is attempting to answer. There are several ways to state the issue. We recommend the whether/when format. Generally, the whether clause should contain a very brief statement of the law. The when clause contains a brief statement of the relevant facts. Example: Whether an employer violates the Americans with Disabilities Act (ADA) when the employer refuses to offer reasonable accommodations to an otherwise qualified employee.

Rule:

The rule of law in a given jurisdiction is found by researching statutes, regulations, and case law. The "R" of IRAC often requires broader thinking. Synthesizing precedent cases and finding the complete rule require practice.

Application:

This is the heart of legal analysis. You have a legal question (issue) based on specific facts. To predict what the legal answer might be, you find the applicable rule. If there is a statute or regulation, you begin there. In the ADA example above, you notice several terms that may need clarification. What constitutes an accommodation? What is a reasonable accommodation? Who is considered an employee? What is an otherwise qualified employee? Most statutes have a section that defines terms. Even with that, you would likely need to search the case law to see how these terms were defined in precedent cases.

---

19. Though common law and case law are often used interchangeably, they are actually slightly different. Common law refers to cases of first impression. That is, the case is before the judge and there are no previous statutes or regulations addressing the facts before the court. This term originated in England when a judge would ride from town to town and resolve disputes among the people. Once a decision was made, it was "common" to all the land. Case law, on the other hand, refers to a case that interprets an existing statute or regulation.

You are also looking for cases in your jurisdiction that have similar facts. Of course, what constitutes *similar* is another question.

You can see that the application section can become quite complex. Applying that rule to the new set of facts is an art that takes practice.

Conclusion:

The conclusion provides an answer to the legal question. The conclusion statement should provide an idea of how certain the writer is about the conclusion. It might begin with "it is likely," or "it is highly likely," or "it is unlikely." This provides the reader with an idea of certainty.

IRAC is a good starting point to organize a legal argument or answer a legal question. More complex legal issues will require a more flexible, advanced approach. The framework of IRAC, however, is an excellent foundation upon which to build.

In addition to IRAC assisting in legal analysis, you will see below that it is also a good starting point in legal writing. Specifically, IRAC can be quite helpful in drafting the discussion section of a legal memo (see § 7.5).

§ 7.4 Legal Writing

Like all good writing, legal writing must be clear, concise, organized, and logical, and, of course, use good grammar. What differentiates legal writing from other forms of writing? The way an argument is structured in legal writing is somewhat different than you might find in other writing. In addition, the legal writing style is different.

In expository writing, say in a college essay, one might pull out the thesaurus and search for words that say the same thing but in a different way. The aim is to avoid being repetitive. In legal writing, you do not avoid repetition. On the contrary, you are careful to use the same term to make the meaning clear to the reader. If you are writing about an employer, you do not write employer, boss, mentor, etc. Use the same term sentence after sentence to remove any doubt about your meaning. Clarity is key.

Lawyers write the following types of documents:

- Legal briefs, which are documents to the court presenting legal arguments supporting one of the parties in a lawsuit. This is distinguished from a case brief, discussed in Chapter Three, which is a personal tool to help one understand a legal case.
- Drafted legal documents
- Correspondence
- Office memoranda are objective documents used to answer legal questions. The parts of a memo are standardized.

In drafting these documents, legal writers use both objective writing and persuasive writing depending on the objective. You should become proficient at both persuasive and objective writing. Let's consider how these two styles differ.

Persuasive writing takes a position. It provides a strong argument for one party, or perhaps in support of an idea. Once a lawyer has a client, she looks at the facts and law in the best interest of her client.

You likely use persuasion every day. For example, you want to take a vacation in Arizona, and your partner wants to vacation in Colorado. How do you make your case? In general, it's best to lead with your strongest argument.

Here are a few other tips when drafting a persuasion piece. Make the first and last sentences in your paragraph strong. Tuck unwanted, but necessary, information in the middle. You don't want to be deceitful, but you don't need to highlight your weaknesses either.

Objective writing is unbiased. When you are predicting an outcome, you want to remain objective. If you went to a lawyer with a legal question, wondering if you had a good case, you would want her to be objective. You don't want to spend your time and money if your chance of bringing a successful lawsuit is poor.

You can likely think of many examples in which objective writing is important in the workplace. For example, you are tasked with finding which one of two locations would be best for a new branch of your company. You do the research and write a report presenting the relevant, unbiased facts. Discerning the relevant facts is not always easy. More difficult is keeping your biases at bay. Look at the counterargument to see where holes in your thinking may be. Be willing to see both sides and present an objective view.

In expository writing, you construct a thesis statement and then, paragraph by paragraph, you prove it. Your proof can come from many places. Generally, you want vetted sources so that the reader can check your conclusions.

Legal writing is also backed by authority. The reader is not interested in your opinion; the reader is interested in what the law says. You may see a legal document in which every sentence is cited. This is true in secondary sources about the law, especially law review articles. A legal opinion with case support will include legal citations for every case.

We next look at the legal memo. This document is used to answer legal questions. It should be written objectively. You are trying to determine how a court might decide a legal question. We provide a few examples below.

§7.5 The Legal Memorandum (The Office Memo)

The legal memo is a written document that analyzes a legal question and predicts how a court would likely rule on the issue. Lawyers in firms across the country write legal memos using a similar format. Legal memos may also be used in business legal departments and government offices. Studying the legal memo will help to further understand legal analysis.

The parts of a legal memo include the question presented, the brief answer, the statement of facts, and the discussion section. Again, these are fairly standard across the country. When first writing a legal memo it may seem that parts are quite repetitive. Understanding the various parts will help explain why this may be so.

Legal memos are often written by an associate in a law firm to be read by a partner. The question presented and brief answer, and even the statement of facts to some degree, will appear repetitive. The question presented and brief answer can be read quickly to ascertain the conclusion of the research. The discussion section can be read to get a more complete understanding of the answer.

The discussion section of the legal memo can also be broken down into smaller parts, though these parts are not labeled. The discussion section generally includes the following parts:

- Umbrella paragraph—The umbrella paragraph provides a general overview of the issue and includes the general rule.
- Rules synthesis—The applicable rule controlling the issue is pulled together from statutes, regulations, and case law.
- Application section—The application section applies the rules to the facts presented. It is where the legal analysis takes place. Notice that the application section of the office memo follows IRAC quite closely.
- Conclusion—The conclusion provides the reader with an answer to the legal question. As mentioned in discussing IRAC above, the conclusion statement should include the certainty of the answer: it is likely, it is highly likely, it is not likely, it is very unlikely.

You may wonder why we focus on the legal memo when it is unlikely that you would need to draft one. Studying the office memo helps to better understand legal analysis. Below we draft an office memo based on a simple, non-legal fact pattern. Starting with non-legal language will make it easier to see the memo construction and observe the analysis in the Cooper Family Curfew Hypothetical (§7.5.1). We then follow with a memo that includes legal language: Parents Responsible for Children's Torts Hypothetical (§7.5.2).

§7.5.1 Cooper Family Curfew Hypothetical

Consider the following scenario. The Cooper family has four children all around high school age. The kids are very busy with different activities and are running in many different directions. The Cooper parents were concerned that the family home was not properly secured at night; the kids had left the garage door open a few times after coming in late. They were also concerned for the kids' safety as there had been an increase in crimes in the neighborhood, including a break-in at the next-door neighbor's house last month. Finally, the Cooper parents work early in the morning, so they try to be in bed by 11pm. The Cooper parents,[20] therefore, enacted the following curfew rule (statute):

All Cooper family members must be home by 11pm; this rule will be strictly enforced. The only exception is in the case of an emergency.

We will now consider the Jack Cooper case. Jack is one of the four Cooper children. Please read the following facts. Assume that we are trying to decide whether the court (Cooper parents) will find Jack guilty of breaking the curfew rule.

Jack Cooper was out at the movies with his girlfriend, Donna. Jack was walking home at 10:30pm after dropping his girlfriend, Donna, off at her house. When Jack was about three blocks from home, Donna called him hysterical. Her dog, Sprinkles, got out of the house and Donna was afraid he would get hit by a car. Jack changed direction and went back to Donna's house to help find the dog. When they found the dog, Jack hurried to get back home. He walked in the door at 11:30pm.

To determine how the Cooper parents might rule, we examine three precedent cases. You can assume that these three cases are in the same neighborhood (jurisdiction) as the Jack Cooper case. Carey, Jimmy, and Margi are all Cooper children.

Case 1:

Three days ago, Carey got a ride home from basketball practice from her friend Sue. They pulled up in front of the house at 10:45pm and were in a conversation about Sue, the team's point guard. Sue was very upset because the coach had just told her that she would not be starting in the next game because a freshman point guard was going to replace her. Carey was trying to comfort her. Carey walked into the house at 11:10pm.

Parents' Holding: Carey is guilty of breaking the Cooper family curfew rule. Even though Carey was in front of the house at 10:45, by "house" the parents mean within the walls of their house. Carey argued that she was being kind and helping a friend. The parents said that though she was being kind, comforting a friend about basketball was not an emergency. There have been recent crimes in their neighborhood ,including next door. The parents do not think it safe for her to be walking in after they are in bed and have secured the house. Guilty.

Case 2:

Two weeks ago, Jimmy was walking home from the library intending to be home at 11pm. He had just turned onto the street of the Coopers' home. Five houses from his home lived a neighbor and family friend, Mrs. McKenna. She was elderly and walked with a walker. Jimmy saw Mrs. McKenna in her driveway lying next to her walker. She was conscious but could not get up.

20. Note that for this hypothetical the Cooper parents serve as both legislators and judges.

Jimmy called 911 and waited for an ambulance to arrive. In the commotion, he neglected to call home; he walked into the house at 11:30pm.

Parents' Holding: Even though Jimmy was thirty minutes late, his parents found him not guilty. His parents said that in an emergency situation where a Cooper child needs to provide vital help, a curfew delay is forgiven. Jimmy could not leave Mrs. McKenna on the driveway alone; he had to wait for the ambulance to arrive. Not Guilty.

Case 3:

Last month Margi was home at 10:45pm. Her father thought he heard one of the other kids out in front of the house. He told Margi to go out and tell them to come in. When Margi went outside, it was not one of her siblings, but one of the kids down the block who went to school with Margi. They started talking about a teacher they both had in class, and Margi lost track of time. Margi walked into the Cooper house at 11:10pm.

Parents' Holding: Margi broke the curfew rule. Even though Margi was helping her father by going outside to bring in one of the kids, she got distracted. This was not an emergency. Margi argued that she was only trying to help her father. The parents found that the delay was not vital, and further, Margi should not have been hanging around outside that late at night. Guilty.

Let's draft an office memo to determine the fate of Jack Cooper.

OFFICE MEMORANDUM

To: Persons reading this book

From: Persons writing this book

Date: September 24, 2023

Re: Jack Cooper case—late coming home because he helped a friend find her dog

Question Presented

Whether Jack Cooper will be found guilty of breaking the Cooper family curfew rule when he came home at 11:30pm because he was helping a friend find her dog.

Brief Answer

Yes. The family rule, which is strictly enforced, states that all Cooper family members must be home by 11pm. except in the case of emergency. The court would not likely find that Jack's dog-searching was an emergency.

Statement of Facts

Jack Cooper was walking home at 10:30pm after dropping his girlfriend, Donna, off at her house. When Jack was about three blocks from home, Donna called him hysterical. Her dog got out of the house, and she was afraid he would get hit by a car. Jack changed direction and went back to Donna's house to help find the dog. When they found the dog, Jack hurried to get back home. He walked in the door at 11:30pm.

Discussion

Umbrella Paragraph

The law established and strictly enforced in the Cooper household is that "[a]ll Cooper family members must be home by 11pm." (cite curfew rule) The Cooper parents instituted this rule because several crimes have been committed in their neighborhood and they are concerned for their children's safety. Their next-door neighbor had a break-in just last month. In addition, the Cooper parents work early in the morning, so they try to be in bed by 11pm. Finally, in the past few months, the kids left the garage door open after coming in late. The parents want to secure the house before they go to bed.

Rule Synthesis

Home means to be inside the house; it does not mean to be in front of the house in a car. (cite Case 1) An exception can be made in an emergency situation. (cite Case 2) A delay is not pardoned in which a child was being kind and helpful, but was in a non-emergency situation. (cite Case 3)

Application Section (Applying the Rule to the Jack Cooper facts)

It is likely that Jack Cooper's parents will find him guilty of breaking the family curfew rule. Like Carey in Case 1, Jack was helping a friend. Jack's act of helping find the dog of a friend who was frightened was similar to Carey who was comforting a friend who had received some disturbing news. It is likely that the Cooper parents would see these acts as kind, but both situations were avoidable and not emergencies. As Carey was found guilty, it is likely that Jack would be found guilty, too.

Jack would argue that helping a friend find her dog who had run away and could be hit by a car or taken by a stranger was similar to Jimmy's actions in Case 2. It is likely, though, that the Cooper parents would distinguish the Jimmy case finding that his act of calling 911 to help an elderly neighbor constituted "vital help" (cite Case 2), and though kind, Jack's helping a friend find her dog was not "vital."

In addition, the parents would likely highlight that the rule is strictly enforced. As an example, Margi was home on time. She only left the house at the request of her father. She also argued that she was only ten minutes late. Jack was also only ten minutes late. The rationale in the precedent case focused on safety. As neither Margi nor Jack's actions were vital, constituting an emergency, they were guilty.

Based on the curfew rule of law and the three precedent cases, Jack Cooper will likely be found guilty.

Here we mention an important point: Focus on the law, not your opinion. This is sometimes difficult. Perhaps you think the Cooper parents are too harsh. Should Jack have left Sprinkles running loose? Should Carey have cut off the conversation with her friend who was crushed? It doesn't matter what we think. What matters is what the law says. Keep your emotions at bay.

In the future, however, if you find a law patently unfair, you may work to change it. Examples of unfair laws that have been changed are noteworthy. See, for example, *Brown v. Board of Education* that held that racial segregation of public schools was unconstitutional.[21] *Shelley v. Kraemer*, in overturning two state supreme court decisions, held that racially restrictive covenants are unenforceable.[22] Unethical laws should be challenged; others should be followed.

We now turn to a second hypothetical that has more legal terminology. Notice the similarities in reasoning with the Cooper case above.

§7.5.2 Parents Responsible for Children's Torts Hypothetical

We present a second hypothetical that will tie together many of the important concepts covered in this chapter. The non-legal example of the Cooper family above demonstrated how you employ both rule-based reasoning (the curfew law) and analogical reasoning (the three precedent cases).

The following provides a more realistic legal scenario. This case involves an Ohio statute that provides that parents are liable for the torts of their minor children. (Remember from the *Palsgraf* case in Chapter Three that a tort is a civil, wrongful act that injures another person or property.) The question in this case is whether the parents of a ten-year-old boy will be liable for the damage caused when he threw a baseball through another family's car windshield.

Begin to read the legal memo drafted below; the statement of facts will orient you to the problem. Note the whether/when format of the question presented. Read through the start of the rules paragraph.

Question Presented

Whether defendant parents will be found liable under Ohio law for the property damage caused by their ten-year-old son when he stole a baseball from a display case in plaintiffs' living room and two days later threw the ball, breaking the windshield of the plaintiffs' van and damaging the collector's item baseball.

Brief Answer

Yes. Ohio Revised Statute 3109.09 provides that parents are liable for property damage caused by their child if the child "commits acts cognizable as a 'theft offense.'"

Statement of Facts

Thomas Rhode is a ten-year-old boy who lives in Fairlawn, Ohio, a suburb of Akron. He is the son of Mary and Calvin Rhode and lives in their home. On Saturday afternoon, June 18, 2005, Mary and Calvin went to visit their friends Madeline and Joe Granger. The Grangers have a nine-year-old son, David, who has become friends with Thomas. At around 4pm both Thomas and David were playing a video game up in David's room, and the four parents went out to the back deck to have a cocktail before dinner.

Unbeknownst to the parents, David and Thomas came downstairs and headed toward the kitchen for some chips and lemonade. While walking through the living room, Thomas saw a baseball in a display case. Thomas took the ball and put it in his pocket;

---

21. *Brown v. Bd. of Educ.*, 347 U.S. 483 (1954).
22. *Shelley v. Kraemer*, 334 U.S. 1 (1948).

David was in the kitchen ahead of Thomas and did not see him take the ball. After getting the snack from the kitchen, the boys went outside to play.

Two days later, Thomas was invited to the Grangers' to play with David. When they were in the front yard, Thomas took the baseball from his pocket, and intending to throw it to David, he threw it at the Granger family's van and cracked the windshield. When the baseball cracked the windshield, the baseball was also damaged. It was a collector's item as it was signed by Pete Rose and the "great eight" of the Cincinnati Reds 1976 World Series Championship team. The Grangers are suing Thomas's parents for $9,000 in damages.

Ohio Revised Code §3109.09 (in pertinent part)
Liability of parents for destructive acts or theft by their children.

(B) Any owner of property, including any board of education of a city, local, exempted village, or joint vocational school district, may maintain a civil action to recover compensatory damages not exceeding ten thousand dollars and court costs from the parent of a minor if the minor willfully damages property belonging to the owner or commits acts cognizable as a "theft offense," as defined in section 2913.01 of the Revised Code, involving the property of the owner.

Discussion

Umbrella Paragraph

The liability of Mary and Calvin Rhode for the damage caused by their minor son turns on the application of Ohio Revised Code 3109.09. Ohio Revised Code 3109.09 was enacted in 1965 to decrease "juvenile delinquency, vandalism and malicious mischief" by attaching parental liability to their child's willful destruction of property. *Allstate Ins. Co. v. Jaeger*, 2009 Ohio App. LEXIS 4843 citing *Conover v. McCutcheon*, 1990 Ohio App. Lexis 1329 (April 4, 1990). The statute was amended in 1978 to add a provision that increased parental liability in the case of a "theft offense" by their child. The legislature amended the statute in response to Ohio Supreme Court's decision in *Peterson v. Slone*, 56 Ohio St. 2d 255 (1978) that held that parental liability only attached when the child willfully caused damage to property, even when the child stole the property that was subsequently damaged. The legislature acted to provide recompense to a property owner whose property was damaged by a child stealing the property causing damage and financial loss.

First part of the Rules Paragraph

The controlling statute, Ohio Revised Code 3109.09, provides in pertinent part that "[a]ny owner of property,... may maintain a civil action to recover compensatory damages not exceeding ten thousand dollars and court costs from the parent of a minor if the minor willfully damages property belonging to the owner or commits acts cognizable as a "theft offense," as defined in section 2913.01 of the Revised Code, involving the property of the owner." So 3109.09 now imposes parental liability in two situations:

1. when a minor child willfully causes damage to another's property, or

2. when the minor child takes the property of another without permission that may be considered a theft offense under 2013.01 and causes damage to the property.

EXERCISE

We think you are ready to draft your first application section. Don't expect the language to be perfect. Just going through the process of trying to compare the facts of the precedent cases to the Granger case will really advance your legal thinking.

We have drafted three fictional legal cases below. We kept the fictional cases brief to simplify the exercise. Write one paragraph comparing the Rhodes facts to Case 1 below. Then write another paragraph comparing the Rhodes facts to Case 2, and then a third paragraph comparing the Rhodes facts to Case 3.

Review the material on the application section in §7.5. Then look back at the application section of the Cooper hypothetical in §7.5.1.

You will use rule-based reasoning to apply Ohio Revised Code §3109.09. You will use analogical reasoning to do fact-to-fact comparisons with the three fictional precedent cases provided.

Consider the following questions: Did Thomas willfully break the windshield of the Grangers' car when he threw the baseball? Would taking the baseball two days prior to the incident likely be considered a theft offense? Does the year of the case matter in Ohio?

Now, read through the fictional cases. Read all three cases. Then draft your three paragraphs. Begin with Case 1. After you have written all three paragraphs, decide the best order to present your analysis.

You begin the application section of a legal memo with your conclusion. We will start you off with a conclusion statement.

In the Granger case, it is very likely that a court would find Mary and Calvin Rhode liable for the damage caused by their minor son, Thomas.

Now, begin to read, analyze, and draft your three paragraphs.

Case 1:

Steven Jones, sixteen years old, drives to school every day with his neighbor, Susan Hayley, who is eighteen years old. On September 28, 2000, Susan picked up Steven and drove to school. She parked the Hayley family car in the student parking lot, and they both got out and walked into the school. When they got into the building, Steven said he left one of his books in the car. Susan gave him the keys and proceeded to meet some friends before class. Steven went out into the parking lot, started the car, and pulled out of the parking lot. His first class didn't start for thirty minutes, so he decided to go for a little joyride before school. He had just gotten his driver's license and was excited to drive, but he didn't want to be late for class, so he was headed back to the parking lot. As he pulled into the lot, he hit a parked car. Both the parked car and the Hayleys' car were damaged. The Hayleys sued Steven's parents for damages. The court found for the Hayleys in the amount of $5,500. The court found that this was a theft offense under Ohio Revised Statute 3109.09.

Case 2:

Carla Owens, six years old, was playing with a cat who belonged to the O'Briens, the next-door neighbors of the Owens family. It was 95 degrees out and the cat seemed very hot and Carla wanted to help cool the cat off. The cat ran over to the O'Briens' open basement window, and the cat jumped in. Carla saw a hose by the window. She turned on the hose and stuck it through the window to cool off the cat. The O'Briens sued Carla's parents for $2,000 in damages to their finished basement. The court found in favor of Carla's parents.

Case 3:

Danny Winters, thirteen years old, chased a ball he had accidentally hit into the neighbor's garage. When he entered the garage, he saw a blue two-wheel bike about the same size as his own bike. His bike was at home but had a flat tire, and Danny was anxious to go for a ride on this beautiful day. He jumped on the bike and headed out of the garage. He rode down the driveway and turned down the street. His house was at the top of a hill, and as he rode down the hill, he gained some speed. He then hit some gravel, swerved, and lost control. He hit a tree. Luckily, he fell off the bike just before impact, and he was not hurt. The bike, however, was damaged. This was a limited edition, custom-built mountain bike worth several thousand dollars. The neighbor-bike-owners sued Danny's parents for damages. The court found in favor of the neighbor.

In drafting these paragraphs, you were using legal reasoning. How did you do? Don't be surprised if you found it difficult. Having completed this exercise will help you read and understand legal cases in the future. These skills take time to develop. You are off to a good start.

We now return to where we started: thinking. Throughout this book we provide reflections and exercises to help sharpen your analytical thinking. Hopefully, a final look at thinking and the idea of "suspended conclusion" below will inspire a more flexible way to approach problem solving.

§7.6 Legal Analysis and "Thinking Like a Thinker"

After studying legal analysis and thinking like a lawyer, we turn to the thinking process generally. We look to the "underlying cognitive processes"[23] that support all thinking. In so doing, we highly recommend Donald J. Kochan's article *Thinking Like Thinkers: Is the Art and Discipline of an "Attitude of Suspended Conclusion" Lost on Lawyers?*[24] In this article, Professor Kochan examines John Dewey's book HOW WE THINK.[25]

---

23. L. O. Natt Gant, *Deconstructing Thinking Like a Lawyer: Analyzing the Cognitive Components of the Analytical Mind*, 29 CAMPBELL L. REV. 413 (2007), 415.

24. D. J. Kochan, *Thinking Like Thinkers: Is the Art and Discipline of an "Attitude of Suspended Conclusion" Lost on Lawyers?* 35 SEATTLE U. L. REV. 1 (2011).

25. D. J. Kochan, *Thinking Like Thinkers: Is the Art and Discipline of an "Attitude of Suspended Conclusion" Lost on Lawyers?* 35 SEATTLE U. L. REV. 1 (2011).

Dewey's work focuses on the "attitude of suspended conclusion."[26] By this, Dewey explains the importance of careful reflective thought before reaching a final conclusion. "Reflective thinking, in short means judgment suspended during further inquiry.... To maintain the state of doubt and to carry on systematic and protracted inquiry—these are the essentials of thinking."[27]

"To reflect means to turn the matter over in the mind, to view it from various angles, to consider carefully the various possibilities of solution."[28] As humans we tend to want a solid answer, and we are anxious to arrive at that answer. It takes a concerted effort to think deeply and carefully before we draw a conclusion.

This process applies not only to good legal analysis but to all good analytical thinking. Certainly, a physician must examine a patient's medical history, scans, tests, and lab results before reaching a conclusive diagnosis. In addition to the patient's information, the physician must also consider her own extensive medical knowledge. Similarly, a vice president charged with the task of finding a new location to open another office branch must research and analyze data carefully while suspending conclusion. In making risk assessments, a compliance officer must gather information and relevant knowledge to institute a suitable compliance plan. Reaching conclusions about specific identified risks prematurely could lead to liability or even injury.

As Dewey cautions, however, this is not easy. A critical, analytical thinker "embraces doubt, accepts confusion and anxiety, examines alternative suggestions, overcomes impatience and habitual tendencies to rush toward an answer, and otherwise avoids the impulsive tendencies toward a premature conclusion."[29] The key is to maintain an open mind as you evaluate ideas, consider all the relevant angles, test your positions and don't get too focused on one notion until the answer is clear.

Some contend that this kind of thinking should be taught in law schools. Like Kochan, we think this should be taught in every discipline. Each of us could benefit from practicing suspended conclusion in our professions, our relationships, and our everyday lives. Because we are focused here on the law, however, we next consider how suspended conclusion applies specifically in the legal arena.

---

26. D. J. Kochan, *Thinking Like Thinkers: Is the Art and Discipline of an "Attitude of Suspended Conclusion" Lost on Lawyers?* 35 Seattle U. L. Rev. 1 (2011).

27. D. J. Kochan, *Thinking Like Thinkers: Is the Art and Discipline of an "Attitude of Suspended Conclusion" Lost on Lawyers?* 35 Seattle U. L. Rev. 1 (2011), 3.

28. D. J. Kochan, *Thinking Like Thinkers: Is the Art and Discipline of an "Attitude of Suspended Conclusion" Lost on Lawyers?* 35 Seattle U. L. Rev. 1 (2011), 62. Citing Dewey.

29. D. J. Kochan, *Thinking Like Thinkers: Is the Art and Discipline of an "Attitude of Suspended Conclusion" Lost on Lawyers?* 35 Seattle U. L. Rev. 1 (2011), 62. Citing Dewey.

§7.7 Suspended Conclusion and the Law

Be curious, not judgmental.[30]

—Ted Lasso

To a certain degree suspended conclusion is inherent in our legal system. A judge and jury, for example, must suspend conclusion in an effort not to rush to judgment.[31] Even after all evidence is heard and all witnesses have been called, the case is not over. After both sides have presented their cases, deliberation begins. A jury retires to the jury room to discuss the case and attempt to reach a joint decision. At the trial court level, if it is a bench trial (no jury), one judge hears the case. When the case concludes, the judge retires to her chambers to deliberate. At the appellate or supreme court level, several judges or justices discuss the case and attempt to reach a conclusion. Both judge and jury must suspend conclusion until careful, reflective examination and thought has occurred.

More to the point for us, analyzing statutes and case law requires a willingness to be open and remain flexible in our thinking. We must avoid jumping to conclusions, or perhaps more tempting, to draw the conclusion that we think is fair or that we find favorable. Like a jury and a judge, to reach sound conclusions, we must remain flexible in our thinking and open to possibilities.

§7.8 Conclusion

Good legal writing requires many of the same writing skills as all good writing: clarity, conciseness, and logical flow. Good legal writing is also based on considered legal analysis.

Analytical thinking is important in studying the law, but it is not unique to it. Sharpening your analytical skills will help in thinking about and solving problems. These are valued skills in the workplace.

Vetting information upon which you are making important decisions is essential. You may have heard the expression "garbage in, garbage out." Quality decisions are based on true, quality input.

---

30. Said by Ted Lasso, the lead character in the Apple TV program of the same name. This quote was inaccurately attributed to Walt Whitman.

31. D. J. Kochan, *Thinking Like Thinkers: Is the Art and Discipline of an "Attitude of Suspended Conclusion" Lost on Lawyers?* 35 Seattle U. L. Rev. 1 (2011), 62, 67.

Finally, being flexible in your thinking, looking at information from various perspectives, and suspending conclusions will lead to better decisions. Individuals as well as society can benefit from such careful consideration.

EXERCISES

1. What is rule-based reasoning? Provide an example.
2. What is analogical reasoning? Provide an example.
3. What is the purpose of an office memorandum (also called a legal memo)?
4. Why do you need to understand the rationale of a precedent case when comparing those precedent cases to a not-yet-decided fact pattern?
5. Explain the concept of suspended conclusion.
6. Why is suspended conclusion important in the law?

CHAPTER EIGHT

Business Writing

BY LINDSAY DUNBAR[1]

I have made this letter longer than usual because I lack the time to make it shorter.

—Blaise Pascal (1656)[2]

§8.1 Basics of Good Business Writing

If you're like most other master of legal studies students, your current or desired position requires significant writing. You're probably writing in your day-to-day business almost every day. Unlike other types of writing we've discussed so far, business writing seems to suffer most from the writer's greatest foe: time.[3] Writing in business is often done in tremendous quantities under tremendous time pressure. The volume of email most employees receive and are expected to draft in one day is overwhelming.[4] And yes, remember, that even writing an email is writing.

Business writing is also often done in a different format than some of the writing we've already discussed. Your day-to-day work might include short emails between meetings, presentations pitching ideas, or policies for varied audiences. You will still need strong analytical skills in these different activities, but you will also need to understand best practices for tailoring your message to the medium.

1. Lindsay Dunbar is a graduate of Northwestern University and Northwestern Law. After law school she was an AmLaw litigation associate at a Chicago law firm. Lindsay served as Assistant Dean of Graduate and Online Education at Loyola University Chicago School of Law for several years. She also taught Introduction to Legal Studies and Legal Writing, an online course for Legal Masters students in the Health Law and Compliance & Enterprise Risk Management programs. This course is designed to introduce fundamental concepts of the US legal system, legal analysis, and legal writing to the Legal Masters student. Lindsay now manages a team of executive recruiters who place associates at mid-sized and large law firms across the Midwest.

2. Pascal, B. (1656). *The Provincial Letters.* Forgotten Books. Blaise Pascal was a French mathematician (1623–1662).

3. L. Brown, *Does Business Writing Matter Anymore? The Answer Seems To Be "Yes,"* FORBES (2019, April 26), https://www.forbes.com/sites/laurambrown/2019/04/26/does-business-writing-matter-anymore-the-answer-seems-to-be-yes/?sh=278b9b023284.

4. M. Plummer, *How to Spend Way Less Time on Email Every Day*, HARVARD BUSINESS REVIEW (2019, January 22), https://hbr.org/2019/01/how-to-spend-way-less-time-on-email-every-day.

The principles of good business writing are the same as those we've discussed already in previous chapters: proper planning, strong mechanics, audience identification, and appropriate tone. The trick in business writing is to do all these things quickly enough to meet deadlines. This requires familiarity with your audience and its needs, a strong grasp of professional tone, and some simple tricks that can help you plan and execute most types of writing under time pressure. This chapter will address how to improve your writing in common business scenarios.

§8.1.1 Your Audience

Just like in any other type of writing, successful business writing must first begin by identifying the purpose of the writing and who will be reading it. We've established that, in all good writing, it is critical to identify your audience. In legal writing, your audience is often the court, opposing counsel, or your client. In business writing, your audience varies. Business writing can include a brief email to a colleague, a presentation to convince a client, or a policy that must be understood by everyone in the company.

Start by considering the types of writing you do in a typical workday, work week, or even quarter (and yes, again, count emails!). Like the students we surveyed for this book, you may find that your writing mostly falls into the following categories:

1. Emails
2. Presentations
3. Reports
4. Policies

Or perhaps most of your writing takes the same form, but it must achieve different purposes. Consider, then, what you are most often trying to do in your writing. Are you trying to:

1. Update or Report
2. Persuade or Sell
3. Resolve
4. Propose

Identifying the purpose of your communication will help you determine how best to approach your audience, including the form your writing will take—be that an email, a formal letter, or a PowerPoint presentation.

Then, identify your audience. Is this an internal communication or an external communication? A well-known client or a brand-new client? Further, what's the reader's level of sophistication and expertise in the topic? Most importantly, what time pressure is the reader under? You may tailor your communication a bit based on your answers to these questions. You might greet a long-time client with "Hi

Siobhan!" instead of "Dear Ms. Roy." There are, however, certain principles that will rarely, if ever, steer you wrong, no matter the reader.

§8.1.2 Brief Is Best

First, as in all writing, brief is best. Concise writing is a "courtesy to your readers. Show them that you value their time."[5] If you feel under time pressure *writing* it, assume that the receiver is similarly time pressured *reading* it. Most people now read almost everything on their phone and only read a small fraction of what they receive.[6] To break through the clutter, a short, clear, communication wins the day.

We've already discussed in Chapter Six that your writing should be in the active voice and free from extraneous clauses. In a business communication, brevity must extend beyond syntax and grammar. You must also keep the message itself simple.[7] Instead of providing an exhaustive evaluation of every possible point or argument, you should provide only the most salient elements and leave nuances for a face-to-face or phone conversation.[8] We'll discuss how to tailor these key points to the message format later in this chapter.

§8.1.3 Professional

Above all else in business writing, your communication must be professional. This goes beyond appropriate tone for the intended audience and correct grammar. Remember that business communication, unlike much of the writing you do for your academic program, is often done under time pressure. You may be writing an email between meetings, responding to a text message, or chatting in an instant message platform to a colleague.

No matter the form your business writing takes, remember two important points each time you put fingers to keyboard:

1. The business owns your communication and can view it at any time.
2. Would you want what you are about to type on the front page of the NEW YORK TIMES?[9]

---

5. S. Leith, WRITE TO THE POINT: A MASTER CLASS ON THE FUNDAMENTALS OF WRITING FOR ANY PURPOSE (2018), 212.

6. M. Plummer, *How to Spend Way Less Time on Email Every Day*, HARVARD BUSINESS REVIEW (2019, January 22), https://hbr.org/2019/01/how-to-spend-way-less-time-on-email-every-day.

7. B. Birchard, *The Science of Strong Business Writing*, HARVARD BUSINESS REVIEW (2021, July 1), https://hbr.org/2021/07/the-science-of-strong-business-writing.

8. B. Birchard, *The Science of Strong Business Writing*, HARVARD BUSINESS REVIEW (2021, July 1), https://hbr.org/2021/07/the-science-of-strong-business-writing.

9. S. Leith, WRITE TO THE POINT: A MASTER CLASS ON THE FUNDAMENTALS OF WRITING FOR ANY PURPOSE (2018), 228.

These pieces of advice can be easy to remember when you are drafting an important memo to a client, but hard to keep in mind when you are firing off a quick response to an email that upsets you or chatting with a colleague on a break.

Keep in mind that all your written communications on your company devices or network, no matter how personal, are company property and can be searched by the company at any time.[10] Where possible, keep your personal business separate from your business. Use a separate, personal email account for your non-work correspondence and store personal information on your home computer.

Perhaps more important than where you say something is *what* you say. We spend a considerable amount of time at work, and it's no wonder that our colleagues can become close confidantes. As more of our communication is done by email, text, and chat, things we may have previously said verbally or, worse, never said at all, now have a permanent, digital record. There's no denying that you mocked the boss's favorite tuna fish lunch or, worse, that you said something inappropriate or illegal about a client or colleague, when you put it in writing.

Many lawyers will tell you that a best practice is never to put something in writing that you wouldn't want published on the front page of the newspaper. Another adage is never to put something in writing you wouldn't want a close relative, for example, your grandmother, to know you've said. The reason for this is simple: what you write is discoverable. During our time in legal practice, the authors of this book reviewed reams of emails during the discovery phase of litigation. The authors of those emails probably didn't think that anyone would be reading the quick note they fired off on their Blackberry ten years earlier, let alone that those hastily drafted words would be at issue in a lawsuit. What you say in an email, a text, or a chat can become evidence. Whenever you write, no matter how insignificant that writing may seem, assume it will be read, and possibly read much more widely than you intended.

Recent technological developments also mean that at least some of your business is likely to be done over instant message, text, or social media. More and more consumers and employees prefer communicating via these quick, seemingly informal methods.[11] When using these tools, keep in mind that these are still written, professional communications. While you don't need to be overly formal, use good basic etiquette (don't text late at night), don't say anything you don't want someone else to read, and keep your tone polite and professional.[12] If you choose to send a text or instant message, do not also call or email, and if the recipient is unlikely to know

10. S. Leith, Write to the Point: A Master Class on the Fundamentals of Writing for Any Purpose (2018), 228.

11. G. Macomber, *Council Post: Implement Business Text Messaging To Draw More Local Customers*, Forbes (2021, December 17), https://www.forbes.com/sites/forbesbusinesscouncil/2021/12/17/implement-business-text-messaging-to-draw-more-local-customers/?sh=df7da78731a6.

12. G. Macomber, *Council Post: Implement Business Text Messaging To Draw More Local Customers*, Forbes (2021, December 17), https://www.forbes.com/sites/forbesbusinesscouncil/2021/12/17/implement-business-text-messaging-to-draw-more-local-customers/?sh=df7da78731a6.

who is texting, let them know it's you at the outset.[13] Unless you are similarly situated in the office hierarchy, consider a thoughtful greeting and sign off as well, but don't let the messaging continue beyond its use.

For example, when I meet my similarly situated colleague Steve at conferences, our exchange often looks like this:

- Lindsay: Steve, I'm looking forward to seeing you at the exhibit hall tomorrow at 8 am. We are in booth 2152.
- Steve: Great, see you tomorrow. Do you need me to bring anything other than my computer?
- Lindsay: No, thank you for asking. Our booth is set. See you tomorrow morning!

When I'm texting an employee that reports to me, I typically only text if I genuinely need to do so. You might reserve these texts for emergent situations when an email will just not do. For example:

- Lindsay: Hi Kelly, it's Lindsay. The weather tomorrow looks dangerously icy. I'm writing to let you know the office will be closed. Please plan to work from home tomorrow. Please let me know you've received this message at your convenience.

This writer may be too conservative, but I prefer not to text my boss unless it is absolutely necessary and I know it is her preferred method of communication. In the rare instance I might need to do so, I would use a tone similar to that I use for my own employees. For example:

- Lindsay: Hello Maryellen. I am on my way to the meeting, but the red line is down across the city and I'm stuck on the tracks. I apologize. I'll be there as soon as I can, but Patrick will begin the presentation in my absence.

As with all communications, know your company and your audience's preferences. If your employees prefer to text and you are comfortable doing so, use your best judgment and your best manners!

§8.2 Types of Business Writing

With these basic principles in mind, let's address some of the most common types of business writing. As noted above, it's most important that you always first pay attention to your audience, which includes taking careful notice of the norms and

---

13. G. Macomber, *Council Post: Implement Business Text Messaging To Draw More Local Customers*, FORBES (2021, December 17), https://www.forbes.com/sites/forbesbusinesscouncil/2021/12/17/implement-business-text-messaging-to-draw-more-local-customers/?sh=df7da78731a6.

requirements of your office, boss, or client. These guidelines are just that—guidelines—to help you as you prepare common documents.

§8.2.1 Email

Master of legal studies students reported that they write emails more than any other kind of communication. Again, remember that even the shortest email is still a type of writing. It reflects on you and builds a relationship with your reader. Here, we offer a few general tips that apply to all business emails. At the conclusion of this section, we consider a few formats for common types of business emails.

a. Subject Line

The subject line of your email is meant to grab the reader's attention. This is your opportunity to draw the reader in and capture their very limited attention. Most people do not open all the emails they receive.[14] Consider using your subject line as your call to action. What do you need from your reader, when do you need it, and why do you need it from *them*?

Consider, for example, that you need your boss to provide comments on a draft presentation you've created for a client. The presentation is coming up next week and you know your boss will be out of town for several days just before the presentation. Which might be a more effective subject line?

1. Attached: Draft presentation for McCallister Security for Review
2. McCallister Security Update: Please Respond
3. Your McCallister Deck: Comments by COB Friday
4. McCallisterpres.pptx
5. Your McCallister Pitch Next Tues: Can You Review by Friday?

Your answer might depend some on your boss and how they prefer to be addressed, but certainly choices three and five are stronger than the others. These options call out what you need (review/comment), when you need it (by Friday), and why you need it from them (they are doing the pitch).

b. Once Again, Brief Is Best

Though we've continually discussed the importance of brevity, nowhere is it more important than in email. Many people will read only the preview pane or are reading an email on their phone and won't scroll down beyond the first screen.[15] You must get to the point immediately. If you've crafted a strong subject line, your reader

14. S. June, *Could Gen Z Free the World From Email?* New York Times (2021, July 10), https://www.nytimes.com/2021/07/10/business/gen-z-email.html.

15. S. Leith, Write to the Point: A Master Class on the Fundamentals of Writing for Any Purpose (2018), 230.

should know a bit about what to expect. In your first line, consider the most important piece of information you must convey. This might include a question you need answered or a solution you are presenting to a problem. Start here and then provide additional context, as needed, in the rest of the email.

It is the rare circumstance that would require, or even permit, an email of longer than a few paragraphs. Most email communications should be able to fit within your phone screen or, at most, require only one swipe of your thumb to read the full message. If, after careful editing, you really feel your message is too complicated to pare down to a few short paragraphs, consider a novel solution: picking up the phone.

c. A Word about Greetings

In recent years, younger generations of employees have taken to social media to bemoan the use of the phrase "I hope this email finds you well."[16] After the COVID-19 pandemic, they explain, many aren't well and nearly all are wishing your email had never found them.

How you greet your audience in an email sets the tone for your interaction. In some cases, where your relationship with the person is already well established, you may be able to jump right in with the key information. For a colleague you correspond with several times a day, it might be all right to say something like:

> Patrick:
>
> I need the latest data for Summer 2024 by Friday morning for the McCallister pitch. Will you please send it to me when you finish your updates on Thursday afternoon?

What to do about someone you don't correspond with very often or when you think it's appropriate to strike a more formal tone? Again, consider your tone. You can, of course, spend a few of your precious words on a warm, if formal opener. It *is* time to retire "I hope this email finds you well," but you could consider a greeting that appeals to a common connection or a recent success. Consider for example:

> Mr. McCallister:
>
> I enjoyed your presentation last month at the HCCA Compliance Institute.
>
> Or
>
> Kevin:
>
> My colleague Buzz sends his regards and thought I should connect with you about some new products here at Compliance Solutions LLC.

---

16. T. Herrera, *I Hope This Email Finds You Well*, New York Times (2020, August 20), https://www.nytimes.com/2020/08/19/smarter-living/coronavirus-how-to-write-better-emails.html

Or

Mr. McCallister:

Congratulations on McCallister Security's recent award with Compliance Week!

You can also consider forgoing the greeting if your overall tone is warm and inviting. Remember, you only have a small window—literally—to capture your reader's attention, so consider jumping right in:

Mr. McCallister:

Compliance Solutions LLC has a new product that I believe will save your company considerable money and time.

Note, though, that when doing business abroad, it's critical to understand and respect local custom. A brief email that cuts right to the chase may be expected by some U.S. readers, but many international readers may prefer or require a more formal or less direct opening line.[17]

d. Signing Off

Remember that closing your email is just as important as opening it. Your email signature is a case where technology can work for you or *really* work against you. Here are a few common courtesies and professional niceties to consider:

- Turn off the automated message from your phone provider that says your message was sent from a mobile device.[18] Even worse are those that ask the reader to "excuse any typos as this message was sent on the go." Nearly all messages are sent on the go these days and have been for more than a decade now. As we've mentioned, good grammar and typo-free drafting speak to your credibility. Don't let your phone call out your errors or, worse, tell your reader you don't care about making them.
- Include your contact information in your email signature line. Most email providers make it possible to include an automated signature with every email. As an additional courtesy to your reader, include your phone number and email address. This will also help them if they ever need to search their email for your contact information in the future.
- Tread carefully, however, when using your email signature to give your communications "personality." Business email signatures do not need to include your favorite quote or inspirational messages for the reader.

---

17. E. Barton, *Master the Art of Global Email Etiquette*, BBC (2013, November 7), https://www.bbc.com/worklife/article/20131106-lost-in-translation

18. S. Hershkowitz-Coore, How to Say It to Sell It: Key Words, Phrases, and Strategies to Build Relationships, Boost Revenue, and Beat the Competition (2014), 205.

- The same requirement goes for font. Keep your fonts a reasonable size, avoid creative or stylized fonts, and avoid colors that are difficult to read or multiple colors.
- One exception to the personal information in the signature line is to consider including your pronouns in your email signature. As a courtesy to the person returning your email, who may not know you well or at all, let them know if you prefer to be addressed as he/him, she/her, or they/them.

e. Features to Avoid

Some email clients include certain features that may tempt you, particularly in times of stress. Though your experience may vary, we recommend using the following three features rarely, if at all:

i. The "High Priority" Email

On a tight deadline or when emailing someone to follow up *yet again*, that little red exclamation point can seem like a great solution. Marking your email as "high priority" seems like a good way to convey that your message is just that—high priority. In our experience, it generally conveys a different message: that you, not your reader, should dictate their priorities and that you believe you can cut the line.[19] If your message truly is urgent, again, consider picking up the phone or, if possible, stopping by the reader's office. If neither is possible, make the best possible use of your subject line and greeting to spur the reader to action.

ii. The Read Receipt

The read receipt similarly sends the message that you, not your reader, is the most important party in this exchange. Requesting a read receipt is a passive aggressive method to convey the same sentiment as the high priority mark. You are telling your recipient that you don't trust them enough to respond to you in a timely fashion and thus are keeping tabs on when they read your latest message. Email is, of course, a good method to keep a record of your correspondence but consider whether your need to know about whether your email was opened and when could come at the expense of your rapport with your recipient.

iii. The Recall

We've all hit send on an email only to realize that we've made an error. Whether that means you've sent your message to everyone in the company when you meant to send it only to your best friend or you included the wrong attachment, you might think about "recalling" your message. In our experience, this feature often does the opposite of what it intends. The recall will join the inbox after your original message.

---

19. S. Leith, Write to the Point: A Master Class on the Fundamentals of Writing for Any Purpose (2018), 213.

Though the feature is meant to replace or retract the original message, it only does so if the recipient opens the recall email *before* they open the original email.[20] Odds are, most recipients will have already opened the original email before your recall message arrives and your recall message will only draw attention to your error. Or, worse, your recall message will drive them straight to their inbox to look for your original message, which they might have otherwise ignored. Though sometimes recalling might be necessary for sensitive or confidential information, think twice before drawing additional attention to the issue. Oftentimes a simple apology will suffice, and you can rest assured that the inadvertent communication will be buried in the river of email we all receive by the end of the day.

f. Features to Find

Please consider using these productivity features.

i. Send Later or Schedule Send

We've all written an angry response to an email that tests our patience. Hopefully these emails end up being deleted or composed only in your head. If you must commit your response to the written word, consider using the Send Later or Schedule Send feature. This allows you to set a later time for your email to send—perhaps twenty-four hours later, when cooler heads may have prevailed. Your email will stay in your drafts until the time you choose. Just remember to change or delete it if you do change your mind!

As a manager, you might also use this feature as a kindness to your employees. A manager might have ideas for her staff at odd hours or over the weekend. Instead of sending a brain dump on a Saturday morning and ruining their weekend, she uses the Send Later feature to make sure they don't receive her messages until the work week begins. This allows her to send her non-urgent requests and allows her team to enjoy their weekend.

ii. Delay Delivery

Many email clients also allow you to create rules to delay delivery of all your emails.[21] Even a short delay on delivery can help you avoid those minor email disasters like the wrong recipient or a missing attachment. Consider setting up a short delay on all your messages, particularly if you are regularly communicating high-

---

20. *Recall or replace an email message that you sent in Outlook for Windows - Microsoft Support*, Support.microsoft.com (n.d.), https://support.microsoft.com/en-us/office/recall-or-replace-an-email-message-that-you-sent-35027f88-d655-4554-b4f8-6c0729a723a0.

21. *Delay or schedule sending email messages in Outlook for Windows - Microsoft Support*, Support.microsoft.com (n.d.), https://support.microsoft.com/en-us/office/delay-or-schedule-sending-email-messages-in-outlook-for-windows-026af69f-c287-490a-a72f-6c65793744ba. Note that Gmail, in addition to scheduling send, also allows you to set up to thirty seconds to "unsend" your email, which is different from recalling an email in Outlook. See *Send or unsend Gmail messages - Computer - Gmail Help*, Support.google.com (n.d.), https://support.google.com/mail/answer/2819488?hl=en&co=GENIE.Platform%3DDesktop.

stakes or confidential information that could use one final proofread even after you hit send.

g. Drafting Your Message

With these basic courtesies and tips in mind, let's now consider how to go about crafting your message. Remember, as always, that your messages should first conform to the style rules and norms of your company. However, there are a few ways of organizing your emails that can help you organize your thoughts and convey your points quickly and clearly.

i. Summarizing Legal Information

As you are studying the law, you may soon need to summarize a court decision, statute, or regulation, particularly as it relates to an issue for your unit or company, if you haven't already. You may also regularly be in the position of raising issues to your in-house or outside counsel. We recommend some version of the IRAC format when summarizing legal information over email.

IRAC, as you recall from Chapter Seven, stands for Issue, Rule, Application, and Conclusion. This format lends itself well to the concise communication needed for the email medium. It allows you to communicate most of the critical details in one short paragraph.

Consider, for example, that you are asked to evaluate whether a newly decided case impacts your company's training requirements. You might summarize this information in an email as follows:

> Dear Mr. Maverick:
>
> I am writing to summarize my analysis of the 5th Circuit's recent decision in *Goose v. Air Force*. The issue is whether this decision requires us to update reporting procedures for our annual compliance trainings. In the *Goose* case, the court held that companies must now retain training records for five years. We are only maintaining records for a period of 750 days. To comply with this ruling, we should update our record retention to at least a five-year period.

This email quickly identifies why you are writing, the issue, the rule, how the rule will apply to your company, and your conclusion. Can you identify each of these elements in the email?

You can similarly use the CRAC formula: Conclusion, Rule, Application, Conclusion. This allows you to get your answer to the reader right away. This would look something like:

> Dear Mr. Maverick:
>
> We need to update our training record retention policy to a five-year period. The 5th Circuit's recent decision in *Goose v. Air Force* held that companies must retain training records for five years. Currently, we only retain records

> for 750 days. We'll need to move to something closer to 2,000 to comply with the ruling. I would be happy to discuss implications for the IT team with you at your convenience.

This email uses a different tone but conveys the same information.

What if you are asked to summarize several cases? You can, of course, write up a short IRAC summary for each. You might also consider a one-line, high-level summary for each case with the offer to discuss each in more detail in a follow-up memo or conversation. Consider, for example, that you've been asked to examine the record retention policies across several courts in your area. Your summary email might look something like this:

> Dear Mr. Maverick:
>
> I'm writing with a summary of my research into training record retention requirements. Here are the key cases to consider:
>
> > *Goose v. Air Force* (5th circuit, 2022): Requires retention of five years of training records
> >
> > *Kazansky v. Mitchell* (7th circuit, 2019): Requires retention of three years of training records
> >
> > *Charlie v. Merlin* (2nd Circuit, 2017): Requires retention of two years of training records
>
> The circuits are split on the retention issue. I would be happy to provide additional information in a more detailed memo or schedule a meeting to discuss the implications for our organization.

Here, you've given a top-line summary of the case holdings on the key issue you are evaluating. It gives your reader enough information to decide if they need to know more and doesn't overwhelm them with information. Though the law may sometimes be complicated to understand, it needn't be complicated to report.

ii. Reporting Information

You may also need to report information to a supervisor or colleague. Your office may have a standard or preferred format for email reports. For those that don't, the format that often works best here is like the format you might use as a journalist—the inverted pyramid.[22]

Recall that most readers are only scanning the information that fits on the first page of their phone, so the key details and most important details need to come at the beginning of the email. This should be answers to the common who, what, where,

---

22. S. Leith, Write to the Point: A Master Class on the Fundamentals of Writing for Any Purpose (2018), 205.

why, and how of your report as well as any call to action. Any additional detail can come toward the end of the email, if you determine it must be included at all.

Consider, for example, you have recently attended a conference and are asked to report back your learnings. Start your drafting process by considering your big questions: Where did you go? Why did you attend? What did you learn? Who did you meet? How will your trip help the company? Finally, what, if anything, do you need from the person you are writing to as a next step? Your report might look something like this:

> Dear Donna:
>
> I just returned from the annual Compliance Managers conference in San Antonio. I'm grateful to you for the opportunity to earn the continuing education units necessary to maintain my compliance certification.
>
> The best presentation I attended was Sam Seaborn's "Top 10 Mistakes Your Company Is Making in Cybersecurity." I was surprised to see at least two areas where we can improve. I spoke with Sam after his presentation and he agreed to share his presentation slides, attached here. I think we should consider hosting a training for the compliance team with Sam next quarter. Should I coordinate with your assistant to schedule this training?

Here, the email identifies the where (Compliance Managers conference), the what (a top presentation), the who (Sam Seaborn), and the call to action (improve our processes by bringing Sam in for a training). This short email gives your reader enough information to continue the discussion, which you may do via a meeting, phone call, or subsequent emails.

If you are asked for a more complete report with additional details, these details can come after your introductory summary. You can use the first paragraph of your email as a type of executive summary to address the key points and call to action and then subsequent paragraphs to provide richer context should the reader decide to read further.

Consider, for example, that you are asked to summarize Sam's presentation to the rest of your team. You might start your email this way:

> I attended Sam Seaborn's "Top 10 Mistakes Your Company Is Making in Cybersecurity" last week. Sam shared his slides with me, and they are attached here for your review. The top action items for our department are that we must:
>
> 1. Implement stronger password requirements
> 2. Require multi-factor authentication
> 3. Review which users on our network should have administrative privileges
>
> These items will enhance our network security and may reduce the risk of cyber-attacks.

Stronger Passwords: Length over Complexity

Our current password requirement is seven characters, which must include a number, a special character, and one capital letter. Passwords must be changed every nine months. Sam and other cybersecurity experts recommend that length trumps complexity in password management. We should implement longer passwords or passphrases of at least 15 characters.

Stronger Passwords: When to Change

Though past experts recommend requiring a password change every 90 days, we know that employees are frustrated by too-frequent password changes. The current recommendation is to change passwords in the event of the breach.

This excerpt begins with the top-line takeaways and then briefly summarizes additional relevant information.

Though it's most important to know your company's expectations and your readers preferences, this inverted pyramid structure should help you draft email reports that will garner attention and results.

iii. Selling or Convincing

There are several good books that detail the nuances of sales and marketing communication.[23] If your primary job is in one of these areas, you should familiarize yourself with the best practices in the field. The primary difference for a sales email is to pique the reader's interest in the direct benefits to them before stating your call to action.[24]

Some of the same concepts you use to write a persuasive essay also apply to the sales email format. Your goals are to:

1. Drive interest: start your email with a personal appeal or a "grabber"
2. Raise awareness of your product or service: describe for the reader what you are offering
3. Explain direct benefits: tell the reader how your proposal helps solve their specific problem
4. Call to action: explain the next steps and deadlines

Your email might look something like this:

---

23. See, e.g., F. Luntz, Words that Work: It's not What You Say, It's What People Hear (2015); W. Zinsser, On Writing Well (2013).

24. S. Leith, Write to the Point: A Master Class on the Fundamentals of Writing for Any Purpose (2018), 205.

Mr. McCallister:

Compliance Solutions LLC has a new product that I believe will save your company considerable money and time [Grabber]. Our new compliance dashboard provides quick and easy compliance reporting that can be transferred to presentations or converted to graphics with the click of a button [Awareness of product]. The dashboard saves you the trouble of managing multiple spreadsheets and tracking systems, and saves time when preparing reports to the board [Direct benefits].

I'd love to show you how easy the product is to use and give your team the opportunity to test its features. Do you have time for me to stop by the offices for a demo in the next two weeks? [Call to action and deadline].

Sales and marketing professionals use additional tools of the trade to close the deal, but this basic format should help you organize your thoughts the next time you need to persuade someone.

iv. Apologizing

Unfortunately, all of us need to apologize from time to time. Though the preferred method for a sincere apology is face to face if possible or over the phone in a pinch, sometimes an email may be the only form available or the correct method for the situation. This may be the case if time is of the essence or you are apologizing to a group. In these instances, consider the following organization:

State the situation

Seriously acknowledge the issue

Sincerely apologize

Solve the problem

Seek forgiveness

For example, let's imagine you missed a meeting with a client because of a calendar issue. You might apologize as follows:

Dear Mr. McCallister:

I'm sorry I missed our meeting today at your offices [Situation]. My unexplained absence was an unprofessional waste of your time [Acknowledgment]. I regret that I inadvertently booked two appointments simultaneously and wish I would have called you to confirm our appointment [Apologize]. I've incorporated a new method to manage my booking process to avoid this issue in the future [Solution 1]. I would be happy to reschedule our discussion at your convenience or transfer your account to another representative [Solution 2]. I hope you'll give me another chance to meet with you in the future [Forgiveness].

Though apology emails are difficult to write, it's important to maintain the same techniques you use for all good writing. Remember to strike the appropriate tone. An overwrought, hand-wringing apology doesn't read as sincere, especially over email. A clear, professional email accepting responsibility should suffice.

h. Word on Font, Bullets, and Numbering

Some experts suggest the use of strategic bolding, bullet points, or lists to break up long blocks of text and draw a reader's attention. You must know your reader and whether such techniques are likely to encourage a response or turn them off completely. Different readers have different preferences with respect to the font and layout of your email communications.

Typically, concise emails will help you avoid the need for special fonts to call out relevant information. Some emails, though, may suffer from TLDR syndrome (too long, didn't read). If you think this might be the case, consider bolding key information or takeaways or using bullet points to draw the reader's eye. Consider the difference between these two emails:

> Dear Patrick:
>
> I'm working on the McCallister pitch. I need a few pieces of data from your team to proceed. In particular, I'm looking for sales figures from 2020–2022, team biographies and headshots, and the screenshots you took of the dashboard for the Seaborn pitch. Do you think you can get these to me by Friday? I would be very grateful for your help.
>
> OR
>
> Dear Patrick:
>
> I need some help collecting items for the McCallister pitch. Can you send the following items by **5 pm on Friday?**
>
> - Sales figures from 2020–2022
> - Team bios
> - Team headshots
> - Dashboard screenshots from the Seaborn pitch
>
> Thanks for your help!

Which email do you prefer? Which is easier on the eyes? Which seems more likely to result in a complete response?

§8.2.2 Presentations

In nearly every type of career, at some point we must leave the land of email and communicate verbally. Perhaps the most feared form of business communication is the live presentation. Whether you are an accomplished public speaker or break out in a cold sweat just thinking about public speaking, an organized and visually appealing presentation goes a long way toward winning over your audience.

As with other forms of business communication, different organizations have different requirements for presentations. Your office may require a particular template or may not permit the use of certain presentation platforms. For example, at Amazon, there are no PowerPoint presentations in meetings. Instead, everyone reads a six-page memo at the beginning of the meeting before discussing.[25]

Assuming these specifics don't apply to your organization or presentation, there are a few key points that will help clarify your message and hold the reader's attention. There are many fine books, tutorials, and organizations that can help you hone your presentation skills. Here, we intend to provide just a few basic tips to get you started on the right foot.

a. Presenting as Storytelling: Organizing Your Information

One of the primary ways we connect as humans is through storytelling.[26] Our mind is trained to listen for narratives and, if you pay careful attention, you may find your own mind thinks in sentences, not bullet points. Many presenters, though, present information abstractly, with bullet points, or as sound bites. Thinking of your presentation as telling a story may help you as you craft your presentation.

The same tools that drive good writing drive good presentations. Presenters can still use the "madman, architect, carpenter, and judge" framework when drafting presentations (review § 6.3 and § 6.4). Consider preparing for your presentation by brainstorming about how you would explain the information if you were sharing it as a story. How might you explain the information at a dinner party? Don't be afraid to use complete sentences.[27]

Once you've brainstormed what you want to say, consider the progression of the story and logical flow. Imagine you are taking your reader on a journey through the information and are using your presentation's organization as navigational guideposts.[28] Avoid taking your listener on long detours or pointless roundabouts.

Instead, consider this formula.

---

25. Amazon, *Letter to Shareholders 2017* (2017), https://s2.q4cdn.com/299287126/files/doc_financials/annual/Amazon_Shareholder_Letter.pdf.

26. C. Gallo, *What the Best Presenters Do Differently*, Harvard Business Review (2022, April 27), https://hbr.org/2022/04/what-the-best-presenters-do-differently?utm_source=pocket-newtab.

27. C. Gallo, *What the Best Presenters Do Differently*, Harvard Business Review (2022, April 27), https://hbr.org/2022/04/what-the-best-presenters-do-differently?utm_source=pocket-newtab.

28. C. Anderson, *How to Give a Killer Presentation*, Harvard Business Review (2013), https://hbr.org/2013/06/how-to-give-a-killer-presentation.

i. Establish Your Bona Fides

Draw the listener in with information to establish your credibility as a presenter. Why should they listen to you on this topic?[29] Perhaps you have a story that establishes your expertise, particular credentials, or even time invested in the subject.

A particularly good example of establishing credibility is Brene Brown's Ted Talk, "The Power of Vulnerability."[30] She begins by telling a story of an event planner requesting information about how to describe Brown in information for an upcoming talk. The event planner tells Brown that, rather than calling her a researcher, she'd like to call her a "storyteller" to encourage more attendance at the talk. Brown concludes the anecdote by saying, "And I thought, you know, I am a storyteller. I'm a qualitative researcher. I collect stories; that's what I do. And maybe stories are just data with a soul."[31]

This quick introduction tells the reader more about the presenter without sharing a boring biography or a list of accomplishments. Instead, Brown uses a story to establish that she is a storyteller and highlights her work as a researcher. She's primed her audience to expect a good story supported with research.

ii. Grab the Listener's Attention

As with most writing, it's crucially important to draw the reader in early in your presentation. You've established why they should listen *to you* in general, but you must also establish why they should listen *at all.* Many of the best presenters will do this much as an attorney tackles an opening statement, by beginning with a compelling argument or powerful question for the audience to consider.[32]

If you know enough about your audience, you can consider opening your presentation with their pain point. What problem do they have that needs solving?[33] If you don't know the answer to that, consider starting with the goal of your presentation.[34] What are you here to accomplish?

---

29. M. Theriault, *9 Tips for More Powerful Business Presentations*, FORBES (2013, November 4), https://www.forbes.com/sites/allbusiness/2013/11/04/9-tips-for-more-powerful-business-presentations/?sh=5b44d6213089.

30. B. Brown, "The Power of Vulnerability," Ted Talk (2010, December 23), https://www.ted.com/talks/brene_brown_the_power_of_vulnerability/.

31. B. Brown, "The Power of Vulnerability," Ted Talk (2010, December 23), https://www.ted.com/talks/brene_brown_the_power_of_vulnerability/.

32. S. Hershkowitz-Coore, HOW TO SAY IT TO SELL IT: KEY WORDS, PHRASES, AND STRATEGIES TO BUILD RELATIONSHIPS, BOOST REVENUE, AND BEAT THE COMPETITION (2014), 116.

33. S. Hershkowitz-Coore, HOW TO SAY IT TO SELL IT: KEY WORDS, PHRASES, AND STRATEGIES TO BUILD RELATIONSHIPS, BOOST REVENUE, AND BEAT THE COMPETITION (2014), 116.

34. M. Theriault, *9 Tips for More Powerful Business Presentations*, FORBES (2013, November 4), https://www.forbes.com/sites/allbusiness/2013/11/04/9-tips-for-more-powerful-business-presentations/?sh=5b44d6213089.

You can also consider drawing your reader in with a rhetorical question or a powerful piece of data.[35] Put yourself in your listener's shoes for a moment and consider what they might want to know or ask, then answer that question to draw their attention.

iii. Provide Your Solution

Most presentations are a method to share how you can solve a problem. Even if you are presenting research or data, you want the listener to understand why your work is important and how it helps them. If you provide too much detail, abstract explanations, or generalized information, you risk losing your listener. Instead, use specific, concrete examples or additional stories to illustrate your point.

Instead, think of yourself as a mystery novelist. "Many of the best talks have a narrative structure that loosely follows a detective story. The speaker starts out by presenting a problem and then describes the search for a solution. There's an 'aha' moment, and the audience's perspective shifts in a meaningful way."[36] Take your listener on this mysterious journey and surprise them with your solution!

iv. Prepare for Questions

Some sophisticated presenters permit questions throughout or pausing at key points for questions if you believe you can do so without losing the thread of your presentation.[37] If the thought of answering questions on the fly gives you hives, the best strategy is to prepare for the Q&A period at the conclusion of your remarks. When doing so, two tips can help you feel more comfortable.

First, prepare a few questions ahead of time in case no one asks any questions at all![38] This is another opportunity for you to provide your solutions or draw out listener concerns. Anticipate what you think your listener will be wondering about at the end of your remarks and start there.

Second, prepare answers to difficult questions.[39] What do you anticipate will be a sticking point for the listener? What are the counter-arguments to your point? What question are you most worried about answering? If you prepare for these questions

---

35. M. Theriault, *9 Tips for More Powerful Business Presentations*, FORBES (2013, November 4), https://www.forbes.com/sites/allbusiness/2013/11/04/9-tips-for-more-powerful-business-presentations/?sh=5b44d6213089.

36. C. Anderson, *How to Give a Killer Presentation*, HARVARD BUSINESS REVIEW (2013), https://hbr.org/2013/06/how-to-give-a-killer-presentation.

37. S. Hershkowitz-Coore, HOW TO SAY IT TO SELL IT: KEY WORDS, PHRASES, AND STRATEGIES TO BUILD RELATIONSHIPS, BOOST REVENUE, AND BEAT THE COMPETITION (2014), 138.

38. M. Theriault, *9 Tips for More Powerful Business Presentations*, FORBES (2013, November 4), https://www.forbes.com/sites/allbusiness/2013/11/04/9-tips-for-more-powerful-business-presentations/?sh=5b44d6213089.

39. M. Theriault, *9 Tips for More Powerful Business Presentations*, FORBES (2013, November 4), https://www.forbes.com/sites/allbusiness/2013/11/04/9-tips-for-more-powerful-business-presentations/?sh=5b44d6213089.

in advance, you can be prepared with examples and data for your toughest audience members.

v. Always Be Closing

At the conclusion of the Q&A period, most experts recommend a second closing or another call to action for your listener. Leave time to restate your key objective, the information you most want your listener to remember, or next steps.[40] Don't lose your opportunity to remind the listener of how you can help them or the importance of your information.

b. PowerPoint Tips

There are many excellent guides and tips for how to make the best use of PowerPoint. In this section we seek to highlight a few common recommendations that can make the most impact on your presentation materials.

i. The 10-20-30 Rule

Guy Kawasaki, of Apple fame, famously subscribes to the 10-20-30 rule.[41] He recommends that your presentation "have ten slides, last no more than twenty minutes, and contain no font smaller than 30 points."[42] Though his recommendations arise from watching venture capitalists pitching their investors, the general framework should work well for many types of presentations.

In particular, Kawasaki notes, "If you must use more than ten slides to explain your business, you probably don't have a business."[43] The same might be said of other areas. If you need more than ten slides to explain your ideas or your research, you likely don't have a strong enough handle on the material to present it. Kawasaki's ten recommended slides may not fit perfectly with your particular presentation, but there are a few that should work no matter your topic. These include starting with the problem, then providing your solution, explaining projections and milestones, and concluding with a summary and call to action.[44] Using these slide topics as the skeleton of your presentation may help you distill your thoughts and organize your presentation.

---

40. S. Hershkowitz-Coore, How to Say It to Sell It: Key Words, Phrases, and Strategies to Build Relationships, Boost Revenue, and Beat the Competition (2014), 130.

41. G. Kawasaki, *The 10/20/30 Rule*, Guy Kawasaki (2016, October 24), https://guykawasaki.com/the_102030_rule/.

42. G. Kawasaki, *The 10/20/30 Rule*, Guy Kawasaki (2016, October 24), https://guykawasaki.com/the_102030_rule/.

43. G. Kawasaki, *The 10/20/30 Rule*, Guy Kawasaki (2016, October 24), https://guykawasaki.com/the_102030_rule/.

44. G. Kawasaki, *The 10/20/30 Rule*, Guy Kawasaki (2016, October 24), https://guykawasaki.com/the_102030_rule/.

A shorter slide deck should also help you avoid the dreaded phenomenon of "death by PowerPoint."[45] This phrase is commonly used when a presenter drones on and on about their topic or flips through slides full of text or boring images. A shorter slide deck allows additional time for questions or more thorough discussion of your material.[46]

ii. A Picture Is Worth a Thousand Words

Kawasaki also recommends a 30-point minimum font for slides. While 30-point may be shockingly large to some academics, it does support the common recommendation to avoid using too many words on any given slide.[47] This helps you avoid the most common presentation mistake—reading your slides to the audience. Remember that your PowerPoint is designed to jog *your* memory as you present and not to provide every piece of information to your viewer. If you wanted to provide that level of detail or wanted your listener to read the material, you could have chosen some other format to present your information, like a memo or email.

If possible, you should avoid long blocks of text or long bulleted lists in small fonts.[48] Instead, you may want to use a compelling image to tell the story on your slide.[49] When choosing images, though, be careful in your selections. You will want to find images that truly illustrate your point, avoiding common graphics like a cog, a wheel, or a question mark, and searching images that truly represent your idea.[50]

Also, choose your images carefully to provide thoughtful representation. Make sure to consider what message your images might send to your audience. For example, are you representing powerful positions with images of exclusively white men? Remember that every image tells a powerful story, and that story includes "a narrative about race, class and gender"[51] that you must examine. There are several recent

---

45. J. Wakefield, *How to Avoid "Death by PowerPoint,"* BBC NEWS (2015, December 18), https://www.bbc.com/news/technology-35038429.

46. G. Kawasaki, *The 10/20/30 Rule*, Guy Kawasaki (2016, October 24), https://guykawasaki.com/the_102030_rule/.

47. J. Wakefield, *How to Avoid "Death by PowerPoint,"* BBC NEWS (2015, December 18), https://www.bbc.com/news/technology-35038429; Microsoft, *Tips for Creating and Delivering an Effective Presentation*, Support.microsoft.com (n.d.), https://support.microsoft.com/en-us/office/tips-for-creating-and-delivering-an-effective-presentation-f43156b0-20d2-4c51-8345-0c337cefb88b.

48. B. Ravilious, *28 Great PowerPoint Presentation Tips & Techniques*, PARTICIPOLL (2019, October 8), https://www.participoll.com/powerpoint-presentation-tips/.

49. B. Ravilious, *28 Great PowerPoint Presentation Tips & Techniques*, PARTICIPOLL (2019, October 8), https://www.participoll.com/powerpoint-presentation-tips/.

50. J. Wakefield, *How to Avoid "Death by PowerPoint,"* BBC NEWS (2015, December 18), https://www.bbc.com/news/technology-35038429; Microsoft, *Tips for Creating and Delivering an Effective Presentation*, Support.microsoft.com (n.d.), https://support.microsoft.com/en-us/office/tips-for-creating-and-delivering-an-effective-presentation-f43156b0-20d2-4c51-8345-0c337cefb88b.

51. S. Gordon, *How Stock Images Can Reinforce Racism*, AXIOS (2021, November 13), https://www.axios.com/2021/11/13/how-stock-images-can-reinforce-racism.

solutions for finding more inclusive stock images, including stock image sites that highlight "diversity across race, ethnicity, gender, ability and age."[52]

iii. Choose Your Template Carefully

Since PowerPoint is such a visual medium, you should choose a template that improves the overall visual appeal of your presentation. If your company requires a particular branded template, you should use it, but make note of whether the font style is easy to read and the colors are appealing. Ideally, your template should include subtle, consistent backgrounds and a good contrast between the background color and your font color.[53] Avoid overly bright colors or a background in one color and a font in the same color of a different tone. PowerPoint now comes with some built-in templates that can enhance your presentation's style and even includes a design suggestions feature that can give you some ideas to customize the look of each slide.

You should also avoid overuse of the animations feature.[54] Though many prefer to avoid all animations, some may like to use a minimal animation between slides. Avoid wild animations, like dissolve effects, and avoid animations for every bullet point. These tend to distract the viewer rather than hold their interest.

iv. Do You Need Slides at All?

In recent years, new presentation methods have tried to unseat the PowerPoint juggernaut. These include Canva and Prezi, both excellent tools if you know how to use them well. The templates in these platforms tend to be more design focused (Canva) and more interactive (Prezi). You should explore these options if you'd like to further enhance your presentations, but be sure to familiarize yourself with the features before presenting and make sure they will work well with the technology in the room on presentation day.

Finally, consider whether you need slides at all. Though an effective slide deck can enhance your presentation, a bad one can really detract. Consider again the Ted Talk. Many of Ted's most popular or best presenters don't use slides to support their presentation.[55]

---

52. S. Gordon, *How Stock Images Can Reinforce Racism*, Axios (2021, November 13), https://www.axios.com/2021/11/13/how-stock-images-can-reinforce-racism.

53. Microsoft, *Tips for Creating and Delivering an Effective Presentation*, Support.microsoft.com (n.d.), https://support.microsoft.com/en-us/office/tips-for-creating-and-delivering-an-effective-presentation-f43156b0-20d2-4c51-8345-0c337cefb88b.

54. B. Ravilious, *28 Great PowerPoint Presentation Tips & Techniques*, ParticiPoll (2019, October 8), https://www.participoll.com/powerpoint-presentation-tips/.

55. J. Wakefield, *How to Avoid "Death by PowerPoint,"* BBC News (2015, December 18), https://www.bbc.com/news/technology-35038429; Microsoft, *Tips for Creating and Delivering an Effective Presentation*, Support.microsoft.com (n.d.), https://support.microsoft.com/en-us/office/tips-for-creating-and-delivering-an-effective-presentation-f43156b0-20d2-4c51-8345-0c337cefb88b.

§8.2.3 Other Common Communications—Know Your Company

Though email and presentations are the two most commonly used communications, our master of legal studies students also report that they engage with other types of business writing. Like these students, you may find that your job includes writing the next most common documents: policies and memos. Though the most important rule for these types of communications is to follow the practices or templates available at your company, this section provides a few additional tips for these documents. We also provide a short note on the business letter, an infrequent but still sometimes required type of business writing, and conclude with some tips for executive summaries.

a. Policies

Policies, perhaps more than any other type of business writing, require deep knowledge of your company and audience.[56] Policy drafting requires unique consideration of who the policy will cover, how it will be implemented, and how success will be assessed. These topics are beyond the scope of this book. If your primary responsibilities include drafting policy, you might consider a full course on policy drafting or reading more widely on the subject.[57] For our purposes, consider these few tips about approaching a policy drafting assignment. Notice how closely these steps mirror the general guidelines for good writing.

i. Start with Assessment in Mind

Though *having* policies is a good place to start for any compliance program, regulators also pay careful attention to how your policies are implemented and assessed.[58] It is not enough to draft the policy, distribute it, and require employee acknowledgment.[59] Instead, as you begin the process of drafting a new policy, consider how your company will measure successful implementation. What metrics will show that employees are following the policy and that the policy you've drafted is successfully achieving its aims?

Exploring these questions requires you to use similar tools to those you would use in any good writing project. You must consider your audience. Often, your audience

---

56. Many programs include coursework in policy, including Loyola's MJ program, which currently offers the very popular Drafting Policies & Procedures course.

57. Many programs include a course in policy drafting. For additional reading in the area, consider consulting the International Standards Organization as a jumping off point: https://www.iso.org/standards.html.

58. H. Chen & E. Soltes, *Why Your Compliance Programs Are a Million-Dollar Waste of Time*, Harvard Business Review (2018, March), https://hbr.org/2018/03/why-compliance-programs-fail.

59. H. Chen & E. Soltes, *Why Your Compliance Programs Are a Million-Dollar Waste of Time*, Harvard Business Review (2018, March), https://hbr.org/2018/03/why-compliance-programs-fail.

will be your entire global workforce; readers may have widely varied roles or levels of sophistication. As you prepare to draft, recall that you are an expert in the area writing to an inexpert audience. Don't assume that the audience has your level of familiarity or interest in the subject.[60] Further, don't assume that because you know something, others "should" know as well.[61]

You should also consider the end goal of each policy. By creating it, what outcome are you hoping to achieve or avoid?[62] Keeping these outcomes in mind can help you draft a policy tailored to achieve these goals and avoid creating policies just for the sake of having them. Make sure to involve stakeholders in this assessment. Consider not only who will need to read and follow the policy, but also who will need to enforce it and under what conditions.[63]

Finally, keep in mind that policies and procedures are distinct but related concepts.[64] Policies should explain what the rule is; procedures are related to implementation of that policy.[65] Your policy might be that all employees are entitled to ten days of paid time off. The related procedure would explain how an employee should request that time off, perhaps by filling out a specific form or contacting their supervisor, and would also list consequences for failing to request time off using the appropriate methods. Policies may be broad concepts or specific rules, but procedures should be reasonably specific and lacking in ambiguity where possible.[66] Think of policies as more like a statute. Policies provide information about what the rule is, the reason it was created, where, when, and to whom it applies, who enforces the rule, and the consequences for breaking the rule.[67] A procedure is more like a regulation explaining more specifics about how the rule will be enforced and the steps an individual needs to take to comply with the broader policy.

---

60. *Ten Style Tips for Writing an Effective Code of Conduct*, Ethics & Compliance Initiative (2018), https://www.ethics.org/resources/free-toolkit/style-tips/.

61. N. Campbell, Writing Effective Policies and Procedures: A Step-by-Step Resource for Clear Communication (1998), 11.

62. N. Campbell, Writing Effective Policies and Procedures: A Step-by-Step Resource for Clear Communication (1998), 31.

63. N. Campbell, Writing Effective Policies and Procedures: A Step-by-Step Resource for Clear Communication (1998), 11.

64. *Guide to Writing Policy and Procedure Documents*, Administrative Policy, UC Santa Cruz (n.d.), https://policy.ucsc.edu/resources/images/GuidetoWritingPolicy.pdf.

65. N. Campbell, Writing Effective Policies and Procedures: A Step-by-Step Resource for Clear Communication (1998), 2–3.

66. N. Campbell, Writing Effective Policies and Procedures: A Step-by-Step Resource for Clear Communication (1998), 18.

67. N. Campbell, Writing Effective Policies and Procedures: A Step-by-Step Resource for Clear Communication (1998), 18.

ii. Plain English Drafting

It is absolutely essential that policies and procedures be written in "Plain English" and avoid legalese.[68] Your audience for these documents is highly varied and may include both those with an in-depth knowledge of the area as well as novices. To best ensure compliance, you must be able to reach all readers with direct, concise, simple language.[69]

Plain English drafting requires that your audience be able to "find what they need, understand what they find, and use what they find to meet their needs."[70] Much like every other piece of writing we've discussed, policies and procedures should be thoughtfully organized, concise, and easy to read.[71] Just as you would in other writings, you should lead with the most important information and guide your reader with headings, topic sentences, and transition words.[72] Keep sentences and paragraphs short, eliminate extraneous words, and use active voice.[73] Where possible, use strategic charts, visuals, or examples.[74] In short, continue to use the same good writing principles and strategies you would use for any other piece.

iii. Require Review

Effective policies require buy-in across your organization. Accordingly, you should attempt to write policies using a multidisciplinary team or require review by a variety of stakeholders.[75] Your code of conduct drafting process, for example, might include representatives from human resources, information technology, compliance, risk management, and various other units of the business, including managers or supervisors.[76] If writing with a team is not practical for the scope or time-

---

68. H. Chen & E. Soltes, *Why Your Compliance Programs Are a Million-Dollar Waste of Time*, Harvard Business Review (2018, March), https://hbr.org/2018/03/why-compliance-programs-fail.

69. H. Chen & E. Soltes, *Why Your Compliance Programs Are a Million-Dollar Waste of Time*, Harvard Business Review (2018, March), https://hbr.org/2018/03/why-compliance-programs-fail.

70. *Federal Plain Language Guidelines*, Plainlanguage.gov (2011), https://www.plainlanguage.gov/guidelines/.

71. *Federal Plain Language Guidelines*, Plainlanguage.gov (2011), https://www.plainlanguage.gov/guidelines/.

72. *Federal Plain Language Guidelines*, Plainlanguage.gov (2011), https://www.plainlanguage.gov/guidelines/.

73. *Federal Plain Language Guidelines*, Plainlanguage.gov (2011), https://www.plainlanguage.gov/guidelines/.

74. *Federal Plain Language Guidelines*, Plainlanguage.gov (2011), https://www.plainlanguage.gov/guidelines/.

75. *Suggested Guidelines for Writing a Code of Ethics/Conduct* (n.d.), https://www2.deloitte.com/content/dam/Deloitte/in/Documents/risk/Board%20of%20Directors/in-gc-suggested-guidelines-for-writing-a-code-of-conduct-noexp.pdf.

76. *Suggested Guidelines for Writing a Code of Ethics/Conduct* (n.d.), https://www2.deloitte.com/content/dam/Deloitte/in/Documents/risk/Board%20of%20Directors/in-gc-suggested-guidelines-for-writing-a-code-of-conduct-noexp.pdf.

line of your project, you should at least require review by a variety of stakeholders before finalizing the policies or procedures.

You may also need or want to involve various stakeholders in your research process. There are some areas of your business or field where you may not be an expert or where your policies might benefit from additional insight from experts.[77] You may solicit information via email or survey or wish to conduct interviews with key stakeholders.[78] These insights may help you avoid making assumptions about the knowledge or needs of various parts of your audience.

iv. Revise, Revise, Revise

A core principle of effective policies is assessing employee understanding and monitoring compliance.[79] Accordingly, you should be prepared to revise and revisit your policies regularly. Your company may choose to assess understanding and implementation using a variety of best practices, but be sure that whatever process you use includes regular review.[80] This is particularly relevant for those of you working in areas where regulations are frequently updated and will need to be monitored. Outdated policies can pose significant risk for your organization.[81] When working with your organization to draft and manage policies, be sure to include a regular review cycle and consider other triggering events that require review outside of this regular cycle.[82] Even the best written policies can be dangerous if they aren't regularly revisited.

b. Memos

Though many communications in business have long been replaced by email, there are still occasions that may require a formal memo. Though there are many types of memos, from those designed to solve a problem to those intended to summarize or report information, we'll provide some general principles for business memos. As with all other types of business writing, keep in mind that your company

77. N. Campbell, Writing Effective Policies and Procedures: A Step-by-Step Resource for Clear Communication (1998), 34.

78. N. Campbell, Writing Effective Policies and Procedures: A Step-by-Step Resource for Clear Communication (1998), 34.

79. Mitratech Holdings, *What Is Policy Management? And Why Does It Demand New Solutions?* JD Supra (2021, January 6), https://www.jdsupra.com/legalnews/what-is-policy-management-and-why-does-2046376/.

80. *Suggested Guidelines for Writing a Code of Ethics/Conduct* (n.d.), https://www2.deloitte.com/content/dam/Deloitte/in/Documents/risk/Board%20of%20Directors/in-gc-suggested-guidelines-for-writing-a-code-of-conduct-noexp.pdf.

81. R. Bradley, *Council Post: The Importance of Updating Your Policies and Compliance Terms*, Forbes (2019, April 18), https://www.forbes.com/sites/theyec/2018/04/13/the-importance-of-updating-your-policies-and-compliance-terms/?sh=67911bbb106b.

82. R. Bradley, *Council Post: The Importance of Updating Your Policies and Compliance Terms*, Forbes (2019, April 18), https://www.forbes.com/sites/theyec/2018/04/13/the-importance-of-updating-your-policies-and-compliance-terms/?sh=67911bbb106b.

may have a particular preferred format or specific requirements. You should always follow your company's preferred method if possible. However, we find the following tips to be generally applicable to most memos.

PARTS OF THE MEMO

Business memos differ in some ways from the legal memos we discussed in Chapter Seven. Business memos may serve different purposes than the traditional legal memo. Most legal memos provide objective, predictive analysis, while business memos may be used to persuade, recommend, report, or inform. Business memos, unlike legal memos, may vary in length and detail but are typically quite short.[83] Business memos much longer than two pages might need to be evaluated for whether the memo is the best format for the information provided. [84]

Business memos, like legal memos, do generally require similar sections regardless of the memo's purpose. Though the content may vary depending on your purpose, any business memo usually includes:

HEADING

Like a legal memo, the heading of a memo informs your reader of key details about your analysis, including who the memo is directed to, how recently it was prepared, and the key subject.

Start your heading with a "To" line. This line should identify your primary audience by name and title.[85] As you would with an email, if more than one recipient is needed, you may list all on the same line either alphabetically or by seniority, depending on your company's custom.[86] Identify yourself in the "From" line by name and title as well.

Your heading should also include the date, written out fully instead of numerically.[87] This can help avoid confusion when working with international audiences, as the U.S. custom for numerical dates differs from other countries. For example, you would date your memo with "January 1, 2023" instead of 1/1/23.[88]

Your subject line is where you should employ many of your good writing tips. The subject line should be specific enough to allow the reader to understand exactly what

---

83. P. Connor, *Business Memos*, Writing@CSU, Colorado State University (2009), https://writing.colostate.edu/guides/guide.cfm?guideid=73.

84. P. Connor, *Business Memos*, Writing@CSU, Colorado State University (2009), https://writing.colostate.edu/guides/guide.cfm?guideid=73.

85. P. Connor, *Business Memos*, Writing@CSU, Colorado State University (2009), https://writing.colostate.edu/guides/guide.cfm?guideid=73.

86. P. Connor, *Business Memos*, Writing@CSU, Colorado State University (2009), https://writing.colostate.edu/guides/guide.cfm?guideid=73.

87. P. Connor, *Business Memos*, Writing@CSU, Colorado State University (2009), https://writing.colostate.edu/guides/guide.cfm?guideid=73.

88. P. Connor, *Business Memos*, Writing@CSU, Colorado State University (2009), https://writing.colostate.edu/guides/guide.cfm?guideid=73.

the memo is about with a quick glance.[89] It should be concise but clearly identify the key points you wish to convey. Consider which better prepares your reader for your analysis: "Please Welcome New Staff" or "Amy Roberts Joins Compliance Training Team as Senior Manager."

Finally, you may be able to make use of existing templates either in your organization or Microsoft Word to prepare and format this section of your memo. Your company may have a preferred order of information or font, and Microsoft Word provides several templates for memos that can remind you of these necessary sections.

INTRODUCTION

The first paragraph of your memo should generally begin with a statement of the memo's key objective.[90] This sentence should indicate why you are writing to this group at this time. In some cases, this direct approach may need to be softened. This method might be used if your audience is not receptive to the content, if the news you are reporting is bad, or if you are attempting to persuade or sell to your reader.[91] In this case, you may want to use a lighter hand in introducing your purpose, providing some softer background information that then guides the reader into the body of the memo. Use your judgment to determine which style will best match your audience and purpose.

The introductory paragraph should also include a short summary of the key background information relevant to understanding the subject.[92] Where relevant, you should also acknowledge the request you are responding to or the specific task you are addressing.[93] The entire introductory segment should be brief—usually no longer than three or four sentences.

BODY

You can use a variety of formats to organize the body of your memo. You may wish to revisit some of the strategies discussed earlier in this chapter about organizing an email. Many of these formats will also work well in a memo, which is a similarly short and relatively informal communication. You'll need to identify which organizational structure will work best for your message and audience.

89. P. Connor, *Business Memos*, Writing@CSU, Colorado State University (2009), https://writing.colostate.edu/guides/guide.cfm?guideid=73.

90. P. Connor, *Business Memos*, Writing@CSU, Colorado State University (2009), https://writing.colostate.edu/guides/guide.cfm?guideid=73.

91. V. Williams, *Emails, Memos and Letters*, Pressbooks.bccampus.ca (2020), https://pressbooks.bccampus.ca/businesswritingessentials/chapter/chapter-7-2/.

92. V. Williams, *Emails, Memos and Letters*, Pressbooks.bccampus.ca (2020), https://pressbooks.bccampus.ca/businesswritingessentials/chapter/chapter-7-2/.

93. *Parts of a Memo*, Purdue Writing Lab, https://owl.purdue.edu/owl/subject_specific_writing/professional_technical_writing/memos/parts_of_a_memo.html.

The body section of your memo should provide support for your main solution or argument as well as key informational details relevant to understanding your conclusion.[94] If your memo does not fit neatly into one of the existing formats, like STAR (situation, task, action, result) or IRAC (issue, rule, application, conclusion), you may consider organizing your information from most general to most specific or from your strongest argument to your weakest. Whatever format you choose, you'll want your reader to have the most important information first, since, as we know, many readers only read a small portion of the entire document.

Most memos should address only one topic or recommendation. Accordingly, the body will usually be limited to only a few paragraphs. Longer memos may need to be divided into separate documents or, at the very least, should make use of clear organizational headings.[95] As a business memo is less formal than a legal memo or other business communications, you should also feel free to make use of bullet points where appropriate.[96] Continue to use other best practices for business writing: a professional but not overly formal tone and concise, Plain English drafting principles.

CONCLUSION

The conclusion of the memo should briefly reiterate any key points or arguments and close with a call to action for the reader. Much like presentations or emails, your concluding words should politely but clearly tell the reader what you need them to do and why you need them to do it based on the findings you've shared in the body paragraphs.[97] The conclusion, like the introduction, should typically only require one short paragraph.[98] This is your opportunity to make the ask of your audience and guide them toward action, so be clear, concise, and direct.

ATTACHMENTS AND OTHER CLOSING INFORMATION

As noted above, many memos have been replaced by email. Think of the memo as the hard copy version of email. Just like an email, you may need to provide attachments to the memo. This might be additional reports, research, or data. If you do need to provide this information, you should list the attachment at the end of the

---

94. P. Connor, *Business Memos*, Writing@CSU, Colorado State University (2009), https://writing.colostate.edu/guides/guide.cfm?guideid=73.

95. P. Connor, *Business Memos*, Writing@CSU, Colorado State University (2009), https://writing.colostate.edu/guides/guide.cfm?guideid=73.

96. V. Williams, *Emails, Memos and Letters*, Pressbooks.bccampus.ca (2020), https://pressbooks.bccampus.ca/businesswritingessentials/chapter/chapter-7-2/.

97. D. Teten, *How to Write A Memo that People Will Actually Read*, FORBES (2013, August 1), https://www.forbes.com/sites/davidteten/2013/08/01/how-to-write-a-memo-that-people-will-actually-read/?sh=6bc4f1bd2cc9.

98. P. Connor, *Business Memos*, Writing@CSU, Colorado State University (2009), https://writing.colostate.edu/guides/guide.cfm?guideid=73.

memo as an enclosure.[99] You should only include these attachments if you have referenced them elsewhere in the memo.[100]

On a separate line, you may list an attached or referenced document in one of several ways, including:

- Enclosure: Name of Document
- Enclosures: Number of Documents Enclosed
- Enc. or Encs. (here, you do not list the enclosures, but just notify the reader that a document or documents are also enclosed)

Further, just as you may CC another recipient on an email, you may also CC them in a memo. These recipients may not be the primary intended audience, but still need a copy of the document. If that's the case, you can list them on a separate line that reads as follows:

- cc: Name or Names of Additional Recipients[101]

Though a memo assignment can be daunting, if you apply similar principles to your memo drafting that you do to drafting appropriate business emails, you should succeed in creating effective business memos.

c. Business Letters

Though email is quicker and more frequent, sometimes a formal business letter may be appropriate. These documents are typically the most formal business communications and require a great deal of care.[102] Taking the time to draft a letter typically means that the nature of your communication is particularly important, formal, or sensitive. Business letter-worthy situations can include formal thank you letters, official sales letters, important announcements, recommendation letters, or information that needs to be formally preserved for legal purposes.[103]

The formal nature of letters requires careful attention to two key points. First, your letter is directed to a specific person who will be spending the time to read your words in print. You should show the recipient that you value them and their time by

---

99. P. Connor, *Business Memos*, Writing@CSU, Colorado State University (2009), https://writing.colostate.edu/guides/guide.cfm?guideid=73.

100. *Parts of a Memo*, Purdue Writing Lab (n.d.), https://owl.purdue.edu/owl/subject_specific_writing/professional_technical_writing/memos/parts_of_a_memo.html.

101. P. Connor, *Business Memos*, Writing@CSU, Colorado State University (2009), https://writing.colostate.edu/guides/guide.cfm?guideid=73.

102. . Williams, *Emails, Memos and Letters*, Pressbooks.bccampus.ca (2020), https://pressbooks.bccampus.ca/businesswritingessentials/chapter/chapter-7-2/.

103. . Williams, *Emails, Memos and Letters*, Pressbooks.bccampus.ca (2020), https://pressbooks.bccampus.ca/businesswritingessentials/chapter/chapter-7-2/.

using appropriate forms of address and making your letter easy to understand.[104] Second, your letter is a paper permanent record that you have signed. Your signature explains for all the world that you affirm the contents of the communication.[105] As with all communications, make your letters clear, well-organized, and, most of all, truthful.

i. Formatting

There are many fine guides available to guide you in formatting your letter, and most word processing programs also include templates to guide you. Your letter may be "block formatted" meaning that all paragraphs are left-justified or modified block, with the sender and recipient address as well as the body being left-justified and the date and closing being tabbed to the center.[106]

Most letters should include the sender's address, or a letterhead, the date, and the recipient's address as the first content. You should then open the letter with the formal salutation "Dear" followed by the recipient's formal name. This name can be in the form of Mr./Ms./Dr. Last Name or, if you are uncertain of gender, First and Last Name or their formal Title and Last Name. If you know the recipient well, you may also choose to use their first name.[107]

For example, you could address a letter to Pat Dunlap, Dean of Students, in several ways:

- Dear Ms. Dunlap:
- Dear Dean Dunlap:
- Dear Pat Dunlap:
- Dear Pat:

If you are particularly concerned about the preferred address, it is acceptable to call the company or do some research on the company website to determine the appropriate address.

The remainder of your letter should include your body paragraphs and should close with a formal sign off, such as "Sincerely," followed by your handwritten signa-

---

104. S. Leith, Write to the Point: A Master Class on the Fundamentals of Writing for Any Purpose (2018), 212.

105. P. Connor, *Business Letters*, Writing@CSU, Colorado State University (2009), https://writing.colostate.edu/guides/guide.cfm?guideid=71.

106. *The Basic Business Letter*, Purdue Writing Lab (2018), https://owl.purdue.edu/owl/subject_specific_writing/professional_technical_writing/basic_business_letters/index.html.

107. *The Basic Business Letter*, Purdue Writing Lab (2018), https://owl.purdue.edu/owl/subject_specific_writing/professional_technical_writing/basic_business_letters/index.html.

ture and then your typed name. As with memos, include a notation of any attachments or other recipients also receiving a copy of the letter.[108]

ii. Organization

Unlike other business writing, business letters typically follow only one organizational format. You should open with a short, polite statement of the key point. This opening statement should be one line only if possible.[109]

The remainder of your body should include only one point per paragraph. Start with the information that most supports your opening statement and continue from there. Each paragraph should be concise and make good use of topic sentences. As with other writing, review your topic sentences to be sure they flow logically from one point to the next and clearly articulate your argument for your reader.[110]

Your letter should close with a brief restatement of your main point or reason for writing and, if appropriate, a call to action. The entire letter should be, at most, two typed pages. Keep in mind that certain types of letters, such as cover letters or letters of acceptance, may require specific formats outside the scope of this discussion.

d. Executive Summary

Some types of business communication are best accompanied by a short executive summary, particularly if your communication is directed to a high-ranking or busy recipient. They are most often used for long communications, such as long reports or presentations.[111] These summaries are designed to share the most important points of the longer document for readers who are unlikely to have the time to read and digest the full details. Much like a legal memo, these are documents written by you—the expert in the subject—to share with someone with less information or expertise in the supporting research and material.

As with all business documents, be aware if your company has a preferred method for executive summaries. Regardless of format, an executive summary should be brief—typically less than one page.[112]

---

108. *The Basic Business Letter*, Purdue Writing Lab (2018), https://owl.purdue.edu/owl/subject_specific_writing/professional_technical_writing/basic_business_letters/index.html.

109. S. Leith, Write to the Point: A Master Class on the Fundamentals of Writing for Any Purpose (2018), 212.

110. *The Basic Business Letter*, Purdue Writing Lab (2018), https://owl.purdue.edu/owl/subject_specific_writing/professional_technical_writing/basic_business_letters/index.html.

111. D. LeCourt, *Executive Summaries*, Writing@CSU, Colorado State University (1999), https://writing.colostate.edu/guides/guide.cfm?guideid=76.

112. *Abstracts and Executive Summaries.* (n.d.). Purdue Writing Lab. Retrieved January 21, 2024, from https://owl.purdue.edu/owl/subject_specific_writing/writing_in_engineering/handbook_on_report_formats/abstracts_and_executive_summaries.html

Begin with a clear statement of your findings. The statement should be one concise sentence that tells your reader what they most need to know about your report. For example, if you are summarizing the information in a longer quarterly business review, your opening statement might read:

> The sales team exceeded our quarterly sales target by 5% despite a 10% decrease to our advertising budget last quarter.

Then, you should provide a brief statement of the report or document's specific recommendation. You should be as accurate as possible here to summarize the decision you believe the reader should make based on your findings. For example, if you've exceeded your sales goals and want to maintain your market position, your findings may support a recommendation to increase your advertising budget:

> We recommend an incremental budget increase of 2% from current levels to support the media team's efforts to continue to exceed targets in the highly competitive fourth quarter.

Once you've summarized the key recommendation or finding, you should briefly summarize other key results or information that justifies your findings.[113] This may be a short paragraph or, in some cases, a few short paragraphs providing relevant information about the ultimate recommendation. With our sales team example, you might provide a short sentence or two summarizing the market or any relevant data you're reporting in the quarterly business review. Your justification could include:

> The competitive landscape analysis indicates that our chief competitor, ABC Company, is likely to repeat last year's fourth quarter efforts and saturate the market with a 10% increase in its advertising budget. To continue to win on our key search terms in our target market, we recommend a modest increase in current spending levels.

Your executive summary should allow the reader to quickly, but accurately, understand your recommendation and the reasons supporting it.

§8.3 Conclusion: Business Writing Is Just Writing

Though this chapter provides several specific tips for various types of business writing, remember that all business writing is *writing*. If you keep the core principles for good writing in mind, you can transform from a novice or apprehensive business writer into a strong, confident business writer.

---

113. *Abstracts and Executive Summaries.* (n.d.). Purdue Writing Lab. Retrieved January 21, 2024, from https://owl.purdue.edu/owl/subject_specific_writing/writing_in_engineering/handbook_on_report_formats/abstracts_and_executive_summaries.html

EXERCISES

1. What are the four key principles of good business writing?
2. True or False: All your written communications on your company devices or network are company property and can be searched by the company.
3. The subject line of an email is like what other writing technique?
4. What is one email feature you can use to help resolve any mistakes in your emails?
5. What structure is recommended for reporting information in an email?
6. Strong presentations make use of what common method of human connection?
7. What is the difference between a policy and a procedure?
8. What are the key sections of a business memo?

PART III

ETHICS

CHAPTER NINE

Ethics

Ethics is a formal, rational, systematic examination of the rightness and wrongness of human actions.[1]

—Edmund Pellegrino (1920–2013)

§9.1 What Is Ethics?

Perhaps, in your professional role, you may work with legal issues that have ethical implications. For example, you may be involved in compliance monitoring, contract review, employment litigation, or international business disputes. Any of these situations as well as others may raise ethical issues that you must address. We hope to build a basic understanding of the key ethical concepts and how they may impact your business.

A comprehensive treatise on ethics is beyond the scope of this text, but we wish to address the topic to help prepare you for ethical issues that may arise in your professional life. This topic is especially important in an evolving area like master of legal studies professionals without a well-defined set of rules for conduct and practice. Ethics and compliance infractions abound, and they can carry a hefty price tag.[2]

In this chapter, we consider some foundational ethical theories to give you a grounding in commonly used ethical language, ask you to reflect on the values that underlie your decision-making processes, and offer some problem-solving frameworks. First, a few simple working definitions. For our purposes, morality is the concept of right and wrong. Morality can be individual, group (for example, a professional code of ethics discussed later in this chapter), and societal. Ethics is the systematic reflection of the moral principles that govern behaviors. However, values are the principles or standards of behavior that are most important to an individual.

1. E. D. Pellegrino, *Toward a Reconstruction of Medical Morality*, 6 American Journal of Bioethics 65 (2006), 71.

2. J. Jaeger, *Top Ethics and Compliance Failures of 2019*, ComplianceWeek.com (2019, December 27), https://www.complianceweek.com/opinion/top-ethics-and-compliance-failures-of-2019/28237.article.

Pause for Reflection Identify Your Values

1. What influences formed your value set? Often, these are family, cultural, and religious influences, teachers, mentors, friends, and wider influences such as what we read and the media we watch or listen to.
2. Think about how you might evaluate professional values in a colleague.
3. Reflect on how you typically respond to others whose values may differ.
4. Take some time to identify your values.

Identifying your values is a first step in dealing with ethical issues; however, standing alone, our values inform, but do not fully assist us in solving ethical dilemmas.

Moral development suggests that moral reasoning requires moral sensitivity, moral character, moral judgment, and moral motivation. These were explored by Rest and Narvaez and have been applied in the area of business ethics.[3] Moral sensitivity requires an individual to recognize that there is an ethics issue present by analyzing the salient features of a situation. Moral judgment requires a person to weigh their options, assessing the good and bad in each option.[4] In moral motivation, the individual knows the right thing to do and must be willing to take the moral course of action despite personal cost and take personal responsibility for outcomes.[5] Moral character involves inner strength, perseverance, and courage to do the right thing.

Ethical situations may be found in different realms—individual, organizational, and societal.[6] Ethical situations can also be categorized:[7]

Ethical conflict: when duties, values, or goals conflict.

Ethical dilemma: principles or values suggest two or more courses of action.

Ethical silence: everyone knows there is an ethical issue, but no one is talking about it.

---

3. J. R Rest & D. Narváez, (Eds.), MORAL DEVELOPMENT IN THE PROFESSIONS: PSYCHOLOGY AND APPLIED ETHICS (1994).

4. Rafael Morales Sanchez & Carmen Cabello, *The Role of Four Universal Moral Competencies in Ethical Decision-Making*, 116 JOURNAL OF BUSINESS ETHICS 4 (September 2013), 717–34, at 718.

5. Rafael Morales Sanchez & Carmen Cabello, *The Role of Four Universal Moral Competencies in Ethical Decision-Making*, 116 JOURNAL OF BUSINESS ETHICS 4 (September 2013), 717–34, at 718.

6. L. L. Swisher, L. E. Arslanian, & C. M. Davis, *The Realm-Individual Process-Situation (RIPS) Model of Ethical Decision Making*, 5 HPA RESOURCE 3 (October 2005).

7. L. L. Swisher, L. E. Arslanian, & C. M. Davis, *The Realm-Individual Process-Situation (RIPS) Model of Ethical Decision Making*, 5 HPA RESOURCE 3 (October 2005).

§9.2 Main Ethical Theories

Ethical theories can be descriptive (describing the way things are) or normative/prescriptive (suggesting the way things should be). There are three main ethical theories:[8]

Deontological ethics: actions to comply with moral rules or duties.

Utilitarianism ethics: actions to maximize well-being for the greatest number of people.

Virtue ethics: focus on virtue to develop character.

When dealing with ethical issues, following specific ethical theories may lead to adhering to theoretical rules that may not be sensitive to our morals and that may be inconsistent with the goal of ethical decision making. A pragmatic approach is to be aware of the ethical theories but focus on using hands-on knowledge and daily problem-solving skills that can lead to practical and cost-effective solutions.[9] This practical approach applies to simple or repetitive ethical issues that an organization may encounter, which will likely be most cases; however, novel or complex ethical situations may require a more structured problem-solving framework as described below.

§9.3 Problem-Solving Frameworks

So far, we've looked at various ethical theories and reflected on values. But how does a person or a team resolve a particular ethical dilemma? Problem-solving frameworks have been developed to guide individuals through a systematic consideration of cases involving an ethical component. A pragmatic offering is found in the work of Robert J. Nash, an ethicist at the University of Vermont. He posits asking a series of nine questions listed below in considering cases involving ethics situations.[10] His is an applied ethics, considering the interplay of such factors as narrative, community, and virtue in ethical problem solving.

---

8. U. Gal, S. Hansen, & A. S. Lee, *Research Perspectives: Toward Theoretical Rigor in Ethical Analysis: The Case of Algorithmic Decision-Making Systems*, 23 Journal of the Association for Information Systems 6 (2022), 1634–61, https://doi.org/10.17705/1jais.00784.

9. M. Drascek, A. Rejc Buhovac, & D. Mesner Andolsek, *Moral Pragmatism as a Bridge Between Duty, Utility, and Virtue in Managers' Ethical Decision-Making*, 172 Journal of Business Ethics (2021), 803–19, https://doi.org/10.1007/s10551-020-04489-2.

10. R. J. Nash, Real World Ethics: A Holistic, Problem-Solving Framework (2007). Material taken from: Robert J. Nash, Spirituality, Ethics, Religion, and Teaching: A Professor's Journey (2002), and Robert J. Nash, "Real World" Ethics: Frameworks for Educators and Human Service Professionals (2002), https://kimberlymoynahan.com/wp-content/uploads/2012/03/popular-real-world-ethics.pdf.

1. What are the central moral issues in your case-dilemma?
2. What are the ethical conflicts in your case that make it an actual dilemma needing rigorous ethical analysis and resolution?
3. Who are the major stakeholders in your case?
4. What are some foreseeable consequences of the possible choices in your case/dilemma? What are some foreseeable principles?
5. What are some important background beliefs that you should consider in your case-dilemma?
6. What are some of your initial intuitions and feelings about your case-dilemma?
7. What choices would you make if you were to act in character in your case/dilemma?
8. What does your profession's code of ethics say regarding the relevant moral issues in your case-dilemma?
9. What is your decision in the case-dilemma, and do you have any nagging afterthoughts?[11]

Note that the final determination is informed but not answered by the profession's code of ethics and permits, and in fact requires consideration of underlying intuitions, consequences, and the perspectives of various stakeholders.

Here is another framework adapted from Swisher and Krueger-Brophy.[12] This approach, developed for use in medical ethics contexts, involves six steps:

1. Clearly articulate the problem: is this primarily an ethical problem?
2. Generate major options for action.
3. Identify major duties, rights, consequences, and virtues for all legitimate stakeholders. Consider legal, societal, and environmental influences.
4. Recognize conflicts between ethical principles and prioritize options.
5. Engage in moral creativity and imagination. Is there a compromise that preserves the most important values?
6. Select and complete the action and evaluate the process and outcome, including strengths, weaknesses, additional information that would have been useful, and any underlying biases of the decision-maker.

---

11. R. J. Nash, REAL WORLD ETHICS: A HOLISTIC, PROBLEM-SOLVING FRAMEWORK (2007). Material taken from: Robert J. Nash, SPIRITUALITY, ETHICS, RELIGION, AND TEACHING: A PROFESSOR'S JOURNEY (2002), and Robert J. Nash, "REAL WORLD" ETHICS: FRAMEWORKS FOR EDUCATORS AND HUMAN SERVICE PROFESSIONALS (2002), https://kimberlymoynahan.com/wp-content/uploads/2012/03/popular-real-world-ethics.pdf.

12. L. Swisher, & C. Krueger-Brophy, LEGAL AND ETHICAL ISSUES IN PHYSICAL THERAPY (1997).

Pause for Reflection Applying a Problem-Solving Framework

Consider this scenario: Imani has interviewed for a position as director of nursing (DON) at a local hospital near her home. She is excited to receive a phone call from the operational VP offering her the job. She is less excited when she hears the VP's request that she spend one day per week at the corporate office advising them on legal matters. "With that master of legal studies degree, you will be such an asset to the team. You won't have to worry about the DON duties on Wednesdays—the assistant DON is terrific—she will manage things while you're away."

Please apply one of the problem-solving frameworks to address Imani's ethical dilemma.

§9.4 Codes of Ethics

Professional codes of ethics may be looked at in certain professions for guidance in ethical decision making. However, codes of ethics generally provide a frame of reference or guidelines and may not envision the particulars of a specific case. In other cases, there may be no relevant code of ethics, which is the case for master of legal studies professionals as of the publishing date for this book. Still other situations involve teams of professionals that may have multiple professional codes of ethics, each with its own set of values and expectations. Consider, for example, a project that you may work on with a biomedical equipment company. You could be collaborating with members of the American Medical Association,[13] the American College of Surgeons,[14] the National Society of Professional Engineers,[15] the American College of Healthcare Executives,[16] the American Bar Association,[17] and the Biomedical Engineering Society,[18] each with its own discrete code of ethics and professional conduct. If a code of ethics for master of legal studies professionals is developed in the future, ethicist Nash would advise to refer to the relevant sections

13. Code of Medical Ethics overview | American Medical Association (amaassn.org), https://code-medical-ethics.ama-assn.org/.

14. Statement on Principles | ACS (facs.org), https://www.facs.org/about-acs/statements/statements-on-principles/#code.

15. Code of Ethics | National Society of Professional Engineers (nspe.org), https://www.nspe.org/resources/ethics/code-ethics.

16. code_of_ethics_web.pdf (ache.org), https://www.ache.org/-/media/ache/ethics/code_of_ethics_web.pdf?la=en&hash=F8D67234C06C333793BB58402D73741A4ACE3D9D.

17. Model Rules of Professional Conduct (americanbar.org), https://www.americanbar.org/groups/professional_responsibility/publications/model_rules_of_professional_conduct/.

18. Code of Conduct - Biomedical Engineering Society (bmes.org), https://www.bmes.org/bmes2023-policies.

when you are dealing with a moral issue and after you make a decision, to consider any afterthoughts that need to be addressed.[19]

§9.5 Compliance

A full analysis of compliance is beyond the scope of this book; however, a brief mention is in order. Depending on their size, companies may have separate compliance and ethics officers and departments, or they may fold them into a single department or individual.

Institutions should never practice in the unethical, illegal, and noncompliant realm and should consistently perform ethically and legally, in full compliance with all applicable laws and regulations. The more interesting cases for analysis involve areas that are less clear. Can an action be ethical and not compliant? For example, consider a situation in which an individual breaks a law to save a person's life. Alternatively, what about an action that is compliant but not ethical? Consider the concept of a profiteer or individual that utilizes market position to charge exorbitant prices. Martin Shkreli raised the price of the Daraprim drug over 5,000 percent and was called "the most hated man in America" in the press.[20] Examples of arguably excessive profits in the defense industry have been well publicized.[21] Oftentimes, executives defend their profit-seeking actions as falling within the law.

What do compliance and risk management professionals need to be mindful of to stay compliant? Here, it may be instructive to review behaviors that may lead to compliance violations. For instance, consider the concept of ethical fading.[22] Ethical fading suggests that individuals may make decisions with ethical implications with self-deception. We believe we are acting under our principles while the ethical aspects fade into the background, and the moral elements become obscured. Enablers of self-deception include language euphemisms, slippery slopes, errors in perceptual causation, and misconstrued judgments about moral responsibility. Language euphemisms involve terms that soften the adverse impact of business decisions, like

---

19. Robert J. Nash, "Real World" Ethics: Frameworks for Educators and Human Service Professionals (2002), https://kimberlymoynahan.com/wp-content/uploads/2012/03/popular-real-world-ethics.pdf.

20. A. R. Harris, *A Case Study in Compliance v. Ethics*, National Defense Magazine (2019, July 26), https://www.nationaldefensemagazine.org/articles/2019/7/26/a-case-study-in-compliance-vs-ethics.

21. A. R. Harris, *A Case Study in Compliance v. Ethics*, National Defense Magazine (2019, July 26), https://www.nationaldefensemagazine.org/articles/2019/7/26/a-case-study-in-compliance-vs-ethics.

22. A. E. Tenbrunsel & D. M. Messick, *Ethical Fading: The Role of Self-Deception in Unethical Behavior*, 117 Social Justice Research 2 (2004), 223–36.

"optics," "collateral damage," "right-sizing," and "transaction costs." Eventually, "we no longer see the questionable behavior they were designed to disguise."[23]

Under the slippery slope argument, we may fall prey to psychic numbing from sheer repetition of morally questionable behavior.[24] Similarly, we may make a series of small steps leading us further and further along an unethical path. Perceptual causation issues involve assumptions about the integrity of systems and the likelihood of human error. Self-interested motives may influence assignment of blame, encouraging us to consider certain systems as infallible and immutable.[25] Consider the assumption that nurses are always to blame for medication errors, when larger systemic issues may be at play, such as staffing inadequacy and delivery system design flaws. We may rely on legal maxims such as "buyer beware" that shift the moral agency to the victim. (He should have done his homework.) Another problem is framing. We may pose a decision as purely a legal decision or purely a business decision, without full (or any) consideration of its impact. Finally, there is the notion that no individual can be completely objective about their own actions.[26] Here are some real-life examples of these ethical behaviors.

§9.5.1 Slippery Slope Example

Adhering to Motorola's anti-bribery policy, CEO Robert Galvin refused to pay a requested bribe to a corrupt foreign official. Galvin stated that not only would there be no payment, "negotiations with the country were ended, and there would be no further negotiations with the country if the current political regime was in power. As Galvin explained, even if Motorola denied paying a bribe, no one would believe them—if one is going to bribe, one is probably willing to lie about it—and so there was no way Motorola could maintain its reputation and deal with the country."[27] Note that this occurred prior to the enactment of the Foreign Corrupt Practices Act[28] when Galvin was a rising executive.

---

23. A. E. Tenbrunsel & D. M. Messick, *Ethical Fading: The Role of Self-Deception in Unethical Behavior*, 117 Social Justice Research 2 (2004), 223–36.

24. A. E. Tenbrunsel & D. M. Messick, *Ethical Fading: The Role of Self-Deception in Unethical Behavior*, 117 Social Justice Research 2 (2004), 223–36.

25. A. E. Tenbrunsel & D. M. Messick, *Ethical Fading: The Role of Self-Deception in Unethical Behavior*, 117 Social Justice Research 2 (2004), 223–36.

26. A. E. Tenbrunsel & D. M. Messick, *Ethical Fading: The Role of Self-Deception in Unethical Behavior*, 117 Social Justice Research 2 (2004), 223–36.

27. A. Christina & T. L. Fort, *Finding the Fit: Why Compliance and Ethics Programs Should Seek to Match Individual and Corporate Values*, 63 Business Horizons 4 (2020), 451–62, at 452 https://www.sciencedirect.com/science/article/pii/S0007681320300318

28. 15 U.S.C. §§78dd-1

§9.5.2 Language Euphemism, Framing, and Ethical Fading Example

In the area of environmental justice, consider location decisions for factories and toxic waste dumps and mechanisms for building removal. Recently, destruction of a coal plant in the Chicago area released billowing clouds of toxic debris into the air in an impoverished neighborhood.[29] According to news reports, local residents were given little notice. The corporate executives responsible may have framed the decision in terms of a business decision (a language euphemism and framing decision). Additionally, the removal company may have relied on "standard operating procedures" (another language euphemism and framing decision) and a "just following orders" argument, thereby removing moral agency and shifting blame to the corporate client. No one likely considered the potential health consequences to the surrounding residents, or if they did, anticipated that there would be no public outcry. Any resultant lawsuits or damage to the corporate reputation would be chalked up to the cost of doing business. Ethical fading may have led executives to believe that local residents had a choice to move out of the neighborhood, failing to recognize the systemic and personal barriers faced by many individuals in poverty.

So, what is a leader to do to manage risks and ensure the organization acts legally, in compliance with all applicable laws, rules, and regulations, and ethically, especially if key players are unaware that they are making potentially unethical decisions? Again, you may have taken an entire course in risk management, but a helpful checklist from Thornton and Martin includes[30]:

1. What are the risks?
2. How can these risks be resolved?
3. What ethical concerns may arise?
4. Identify actions to address ethical concerns.

§9.6 Plagiarism and Artificial Intelligence

We conclude the ethics chapter with a brief discussion on plagiarism, failing to give credit to the original author. As you learned in Chapter Seven, legal writers are expected to cite their work heavily. Each direct quote must, of course, have quotation marks and include a citation, even if it involves referencing your own prior work. You commit plagiarism if you use someone else's idea without attribution. In addition, excessive paraphrasing is considered plagiarism. Inadequate attribution of ta-

---

29. A. Vinicky, *City Clampdown on Coal Plant Demolition "Too Little, Too Late,"* WTTW (2020), https://news.wttw.com/2020/04/12/city-clampdown-coal-plant-demolition-too-little-too-late.

30. M. Thornton & W. Martin, *Pandemics at Work: Convergence of Epidemiology and Ethics*, 32 Business Ethics Quarterly 1 (January 2022), 41–74, https//doi.org/10.1017/beq.2021.32.

bles and figures is also plagiarizing. A good rule of thumb is when in doubt, provide a citation. Fortunately for both students and faculty, software is available to help screen for possible plagiarism. We strongly advise you to run papers through one of these tools to avoid unintended consequences. Recent advances in generative artificial intelligence (AI) software pose new challenges. Some professors would consider work generated by generative AI to be plagiarism.

Pause for Reflection

Jessica Meyers has been an adjunct professor in a master of legal studies program for five years. Jessica has taught several courses within the curriculum. One of the assignments for the Introduction to the Law course is writing a five-page paper on the unauthorized practice of law in her state. Jessica receives a submission from one of her students that troubles her. She notices that the voice is distinctly different from other work by this student. Several areas of the paper are repetitive, and the tone is rather flat, with very consistent sentence length and a level of complexity that strikes Jessica as inauthentic for this writer. Jessica ponders what to do. If it turns out that this is AI-generated work, is it plagiarism?

Jessica speaks with her department chair, and he says other faculty members have shared similar concerns. The following week, the department meets to consider the issues posed by generative AI. They agree that there seems to be an issue with some students' work that suggests outside sourcing. The faculty want to reinforce plagiarism in all its forms at the start of each semester in each course. They plan to stress that students using online products cheat themselves as they do not develop the critical analysis and writing competencies the program emphasizes, using the metaphor that the tool is like turning to a fellow student for help with an assignment. By using others' work they are falsifying these competencies. Clarifying the requirements through discussion is permissible; turning in another student's work is not. Going forward, they agree to explicitly mention in course syllabi that AI-generated work will be considered plagiarism, how suspected AI-generated work will be detected and evaluated, and the consequences for violating the AI use policy.

A subcommittee begins work drafting guidelines and an AI use policy, turning to the evolving literature and drawing on the work of other universities. What would you include to ensure academic integrity, development of analysis and writing skills, and avoiding plagiarism?

Another subcommittee agrees to explore developing tools to detect this type of plagiarism such as watermarking that may offer promise at least for images.[31] The faculty also consider ways to use AI-generated work while helping students develop their skills.

---

31. A. Hern, *AI-Assisted Plagiarism? ChatGPT Bot Says It Has an Answer for That*, GUARDIAN (2022, December 31), https://www.theguardian.com/technology/2022/dec/31/ai-assisted-plagiarism-chatgpt-bot-says-it-has-an-answer-for-that. H. Zhong, J. Chang, Z. Yang, T. Wu, P. C. M. Arachchige, C. Pathmabandu, & M. Xue, *Copyright Protection and Accountability of Generative AI: Attack, Watermarking and Attribution*, WWW '23 Companion: Companion Proceedings of the ACM Web Conference 2023 (2023, March 15), 94–98, https://doi.org/10.1145/3543873.3587321.

One faculty member suggests using an AI-generated product as a first draft with an appropriate citation. Another professor notes that he gives an AI-generated memo to his class to dissect and critically analyze. The professor asks questions such as: "Is the legal analysis sound? Why or why not? What additional points would you add to the document? How would you fine tune the writing for clarity? What sources were used to create the paper? Are they trustworthy?"

Several faculty encourage their colleagues to embrace the new opportunities that generative AI may provide.[32] Some suggest that it is just a tool that students should be allowed to use, and that faculty need to become AI literate.[33] Opinions differ. What is yours? Some faculty suggest discussion early in the course to elicit students' views on the tools and come to a shared agreement on expectations, both in class and eventually in their professional lives. They emphasize that ultimately students need to understand and value the intellectual ownership of their work and their professional responsibilities to make sure it is correct.

It is imperative that you check with your instructor regarding their expectations as this is a newly developing tool and its authorized use is yet unclear. In addition, you may want to know whether your work is being graded in whole or in part by AI-generated tools and how your personal information is being protected when faculty use software tools to detect AI-generated work.

§9.7 Conclusion

In summary, this chapter has provided you with some fundamentals of what ethics is, the main ethical theories, some problem-solving frameworks, an explanation of professional code of ethics, and some potential unethical behaviors relating to compliance and risk management. Hopefully, this information will assist you in navigating the ethical challenges that you may encounter in your professional life.

---

32. W. M. Lim, A. Gunasekara, J. L. Pallant, J. I. Pallant, & E. Pechenkina, *Generative AI and the Future of Education: Ragnarök or Reformation? A Paradoxical Perspective from Management Educators*, 21 The International Journal of Management Education 3 (July 2023), 100790, https://doi.org/10.1016/j.ijme.2023.100790; Yogesh K. Dwivedi, Nir Kshetri, Laurie Hughes, Emma Louise Slade, Anand Jeyaraj, Arpan Kumar Kar, Abdullah M. Baabdullah, Alex Koohang, Vishnupriya Raghavan, Manju Ahuja, H. Albanna, M. A. Albashrawi, A. S. Al-Busaidi, J. Balakrishnan, Y. Barlette, S. Basu, I. Bose, L. Brooks, D. Buhalis, L. Carter, S. Chowdhury, T. Crick, S. W. Cunningham, G. H. Davies, R. M. Davison, R. Dé, D. Dennehy, Y. Duan, R. Dubey, R. Dwivedi, J. S. Edwards, C. Flavián, R. Gauld, V. Grover, M. Hu, M. Janssen, P. Jones, I. Junglas, S. Khorana, S. Kraus, S … & R. Wright, *Opinion Paper: So What If ChatGPT Wrote It? Multidisciplinary Perspectives on Opportunities, Challenges and Implications of Generative Conversational AI for Research, Practice and Policy*, 71 International Journal of Information Management (August 2023), 102642, https://doi.org/10.1016/j.ijinfomgt.2023.102642.

33. B. A. Anders, *Is Using ChatGPT Cheating, Plagiarism, Both, Neither, or Forward Thinking?* 4 Patterns 3 (2023), 100694, https://doi.org/10.1016/j.patter.2023.100694.

EXERCISES

1. What is the term for the principles or standards of behaviors that are most important to an individual?
2. What tool can you use to resolve a particular ethical dilemma?
3. What is the ethical situation called when everyone knows that there is an ethical issue, but no one is talking about it?
4. Which ethical theory focuses on maximizing well-being for the greatest number of people?
5. What is the language euphemism term that describes making a series of small steps leading further and further along an unethical path?

CHAPTER TEN

The Unauthorized Practice of Law

Knowledge is power.

—Sir Francis Bacon (1561–1626)

§10.1 Background

Master of legal studies programs have been around for many years. This has given the employment world plenty of time to appreciate the value of this advanced legal education. Some may wonder, however, if this education is preparing students to practice law without obtaining a license; it is not. Students of this degree do not intend to practice law, yet their careers or future careers require a foundational knowledge, or perhaps even a more specialized knowledge, of the law. Obtaining this knowledge is certainly not illegal or unethical.

Let's consider an analogy using a subject matter familiar to most of us: driving a car. Consider all the laws you need to know to operate a car. Violating these laws can lead to a citation or even to jail. To pass the driver's test, you need to know the rules and laws of the road. You are breaking the law if you drive without a valid license, drive above the posted speed limit, fail to wear a seat belt, drive while intoxicated, and the list goes on. But as you know, acquiring knowledge of the driving laws does not make you a traffic officer any more than knowing the law studied here makes you a lawyer. Yet you must study and know the driving laws, just as you should study and know the laws and regulations that govern your profession. A few examples follow.

A human resource specialist should know what questions are inappropriate and illegal to ask an interviewee. A few places to find helpful information would be Title VII of the Civil Rights Act of 1964,[1] the Americans with Disabilities Act,[2] and the Equal Employment Opportunity Commission regulations.

A benefits administrator might work with a lawyer in understating the Employee Retirement Income Security Act (ERISA).[3]

1. Civil Rights Act of 1964 §7, 42 U.S.C. §2000e et seq. (1964).
2. Americans With Disabilities Act of 1990, 42 U.S.C. §12101 et seq. (1990).
3. Employee Retirement Income Security Act of 1974, 29 U.S.C. §§1001–1461 (1974).

A health care worker in a hospital or nursing home should know the federal Medicare regulations as well as their state's restrictions regarding using chemical and physical restraints on patients.

Certainly, a nurse, physician, and pharmacist should be familiar with the Health Insurance Portability and Accountability Act (HIPAA)[4] to properly protect his or her patients' privacy.

In addition, many of us, as employees, have viewed required videos in the workplace regarding sexual harassment and discrimination.

While obtaining legal knowledge, therefore, is advantageous, the following sections highlight a few of the ways you need to proceed with caution in using that knowledge. Obtaining knowledge is never prohibited. How you use that knowledge, however, is an important consideration. What follows, then, is information regarding the **unauthorized practice of law.**

§10.2 The Unauthorized Practice of Law

Identifying the unauthorized practice of law is often difficult as highlighted by the Indiana Supreme Court in *State ex rel. Ind. State Bar Ass'n v. Diaz.*[5] The court acknowledged that non-attorneys could work on limited legal immigration issues in administrative proceedings as provided in the Code of Federal Regulations.[6] However, the court found the non-attorney guilty of engaging in the unauthorized practice of law.[7] The Indiana Supreme Court stated that it "has not attempted to provide a comprehensive definition of what constitutes the practice of law because the infinite variety of fact situations each must be judged according to its own specific circumstances."[8] While obtaining clear and comprehensive parameters regarding the unauthorized practice of law may be challenging, what follows provides some guidance.

§10.3 Practice of Law Regulated by States

What, then, is the master of legal studies student to understand about the unauthorized practice of law? It is important to know that each state regulates its practice of law. State definitions of the practice of law vary and are sometimes found in court

4. Health Insurance Portability and Accountability Act of 1996, Pub. L. No. 104-191, 110 Stat. 1936 (1996).
5. *State ex rel. Indiana State Bar Association v. Diaz*, 838 N.E.2d 433 (Ind. 2005).
6. *State ex rel. Indiana State Bar Association v. Diaz*, 838 N.E.2d 433, 437 (Ind. 2005).
7. *State ex rel. Indiana State Bar Association v. Diaz*, 838 N.E.2d 433, 448 (Ind. 2005).
8. *State ex rel. Indiana State Bar Association v. Diaz*, 838 N.E.2d 433, 443 (Ind. 2005).

cases, state laws, codes, and rules from the state bar.[9] This complicates the matter somewhat further in that some states have defined the practice of law by listing specific functions, other states have a vague or no single definition, while some states have chosen no definition leaving it to the court's review of specific facts. On August 11, 2003, the American Bar Association Task Force on the Model Definition of the Practice of Law provided guidance for states by recommending that:

> every state and territory adopt a definition of the practice of law... [including] that the practice of law is the application of legal principles and judgment to the circumstances or objectives of another person or entity,... [and] specify who may provide services that are included within the definition of the practice of law and under what circumstances, based upon the potential harm and benefit to the public. The determination should include consideration of minimum qualifications, competence, and accountability.[10]

Pause for Reflection Applying Your State Law

Consider this scenario: Max hops onto the elevator with his friend Greg. "Maybe we better schedule our annual golf outing a bit earlier next year. You are going to be busy!" Greg looks at him quizzically. Max says "I guess you haven't heard. For the draft of the next department budget, the boss asked me to reduce our outside legal counsel fees by 10%. She figured with your new master of legal studies degree that you could handle some of the legal work." Max shakes his head; he has explained to his boss that he is not getting a J.D., but rather a master of legal studies degree.

Questions: Find the rules that govern the practice of law in your state in the footnote below.[11]

1. Is there a section that seems relevant to Max?
2. If yes, please identify specific language.

Hopefully, you were able to identify your state's rules for Max to avoid the unauthorized practice of law.

---

9. American Bar Association, *Task Force on the Model Definition of the Practice of Law, State Definitions of the Practice of Law* (n.d.), https://www.americanbar.org/groups/professional_responsibility/task_force_model_definition_practice_law/.

10. American Bar Association, *Task Force on the Model Definition of the Practice of Law, Recommendation as Adopted August 11, 2003* (n.d.), https://www.americanbar.org/groups/professional_responsibility/task_force_model_definition_practice_law/.

11. American Bar Association, *Task Force on the Model Definition of the Practice of Law, State Definitions of the Practice of Law* (n.d.), https://www.americanbar.org/groups/professional_responsibility/task_force_model_definition_practice_law/.

§10.4 Concerns with States' Definitions of the Practice of Law

The Department of Justice and Federal Trade Commission (FTC) have expressed concern regarding some states' definitions of the practice of law. For example, in 2004, the FTC recommended not adopting the Massachusetts proposed definition of the practice of law, stating it "is not in the best interest of consumers, as it would prevent non-lawyers from providing services in competition with lawyers in situations where there is no clear demonstration that non-lawyer services would actually harm consumers. . . .This would likely raise costs for consumers and limit their choices."[12] In 2007, the FTC shared their belief regarding the Connecticut definition that "non-attorneys should be permitted to compete with attorneys in areas where no specialized legal knowledge and training is demonstrably necessary to protect the interests of consumers."[13] Additionally, in 2016, the FTC stated that North Carolina's "overbroad scope-of-practice and unauthorized-practice-of-law policies can restrict competition between licensed attorneys and non-attorney providers of legal services, increasing the prices consumers must pay for legal services, and reducing consumers' choices."[14] The definitions of the practice of law and what non-attorneys are permitted to do in each state is evolving as more non-attorneys are employed in multiple industries. So, let's look at some case examples regarding the practice of law.

§10.5 Examples of Courts' Interpretations of the Practice of Law

The following case examples illustrate the importance of understanding how your state defines the practice of law. "There is no mechanistic formula to define what is and what is not the practice of law. Rather, courts examine the character of the acts themselves to determine if the conduct is the practice of law."[15] In 1949, the court in *People ex rel. Illinois State Bar Ass'n*[16] explained that:

---

12. American Bar Association, *Task Force on the Model Definition of the Practice of Law, Proposed Definitions of the Practice of Law. Massachusetts, U.S. FTC/DOJ Comments on Draft Proposal Definition of the Practice of Law* (December 16, 2004), 1, https://www.americanbar.org/groups/professional_responsibility/task_force_model_definition_practice_law/.

13. American Bar Association, *Task Force on the Model Definition of the Practice of Law, Proposed Definitions of the Practice of Law. Connecticut, U.S. FTC Comments on Proposed Section 2-44A of the Rules of the Superior Court* (May 17, 2007), 1, https://www.americanbar.org/groups/professional_responsibility/task_force_model_definition_practice_law/.

14. American Bar Association, *Task Force on the Model Definition of the Practice of Law, Proposed Definitions of the Practice of Law. North Carolina, FTC/DOJ Letter to North Carolina Regarding the Definition of the Practice of Law in HB 436* (June 10, 2016), 2, https://www.americanbar.org/groups/professional_responsibility/task_force_model_definition_practice_law/.

15. *Downtown Disposal Servs., Inc. v. City of Chi.*, Docket No. 112040, 4 (Ill. 2012).

16. *People ex Rel. Bar Ass'n v. Schafer*, 404 Ill. 45, 87 N.E.2d 773 (Ill. 1949).

> the practice of law involves not only appearance in court in connection with litigation but also services rendered out of court, and it includes the giving of advice or rendering of any services requiring the use of legal skill or knowledge, such as preparing a will, contract or other instrument, the legal effect of which, under the facts and conditions involved, must be carefully determined.[17]

In a 2021 appellate court of Oregon case, *Mouktabis v. Amarou*,[18] the issue was whether a non-lawyer guardian *ad litem* is authorized to represent a party in court and if their conduct engaged in the practice of law.[19] Mouktabis asserted that as the plaintiff's guardian *ad litem*, he is "authorized to prosecute the case."[20] The court stated that the guardian *ad litem* represents the interests of the minor party but held that a guardian *ad litem* who is not an attorney is not authorized to practice of law.[21]

In a 2022 New York case, *Upsolve, Inc. v. Letitia James*,[22] the non-profit Upsolve trained non-lawyer volunteers to give legal advice to individuals pursued by debt collectors, raising the issue of the unauthorized practice of law.[23] The court ruled that Upsolve's program is protected by the First Amendment to provide their legal advice as speech and enjoined the New York attorney general from applying the unauthorized practice of law rules against Upsolve.[24] This decision broadens access to justice allowing non-lawyer volunteers in New York to provide certain legal advice.

§10.6 Unlicensed vs. Unauthorized Practice of Law

Non-lawyers are sometimes permitted to work within a limited scope on issues that might be considered the practice of law when they have specialized expertise, including but not limited to "divorce, immigration, estate planning, mortgage lending, real estate, insurance, accounting, . . . and others."[25] These activities are sometimes referred to as the "**unlicensed**" (as opposed to "unauthorized") **practice of law**.[26] So, you may be asking how does a non-lawyer avoid the unauthorized practice of law? Of course, holding oneself out as an attorney without a license consti-

17. *People ex Rel. Bar Ass'n v. Schafer*, 404 Ill. 45, 50 (Ill. 1949).
18. *Mouktabis v. Amarou*, 314 Or. App. 130, 499 P3d 881 (2021).
19. *Mouktabis v. Amarou*, 314 Or. App. 135 (2021).
20. *Mouktabis v. Amarou*, 314 Or. App. 132 (2021).
21. *Mouktabis v. Amarou*, 314 Or. App. 132, 137 (2021).
22. *Upsolve, Inc. v. James*, 604 F. Supp. 3d 97 (S.D.N.Y. 2022).
23. *Upsolve, Inc. v. James*, 604 F. Supp. 3d 97, 103 (S.D.N.Y. 2022).
24. *Upsolve, Inc. v. James*, 604 F. Supp. 3d 97, 103 (S.D.N.Y. 2022).
25. S. L. Buhai, *Act Like a Lawyer, Be Judged Like a Lawyer: The Standard of Care for the Unlicensed Practice of Law*, UTAH L. REV. (2006), 88.
26. S. L. Buhai, *Act Like a Lawyer, Be Judged Like a Lawyer: The Standard of Care for the Unlicensed Practice of Law*, UTAH L. REV. (2006), 88.

tutes the unauthorized practice of law.[27] In addition, non-lawyers must not perform tasks that only lawyers can do, including but not limited to giving legal advice that affects a person's rights or representing clients in court.[28] Here are some practical parameters to avoid the unauthorized practice of law.

§10.6.1 Giving Legal Advice and Counsel Requiring Legal Knowledge and Skill

"The core element of practicing law is the giving of legal advice to a client, and merely entering into such relationship constitutes the practice of law."[29] The key is whether performance of the activity requires a "trained legal mind" to understand "more than a layman's knowledge of the law" and possess "a high degree of legal skill."[30] Thus, providing legal advice and representing individuals in legal matters is considered the practice of law.[31] As such, non-lawyers should avoid using legal concepts to counsel someone on a specific situation.[32]

§10.6.2 Representing Others in Court

"The practice of law includes making it one's business to act for, and by the warrant of, others in legal formalities, negotiations, or proceedings."[33] Additionally, it was held by the Supreme Court of Indiana that the production of court motions and pleadings and communication to clients, done by legal office support staff without supervision from a licensed attorney, is the unauthorized practice of law.[34]

§10.6.3 Preparing Legal Documents that Secure Legal Rights

Courts have found that legal practice extends to preparing legal documents that preserve legal rights. For example, in *Franklin v. Chavis*,[35] a South Carolina court held that the practice of law includes the creation of legal documents when it requires providing "advice, consultation, explanation, or recommendations on matters of law."[36] In *Oregon State Bar v. Gilchrist*,[37] the court held that "personal contact

---

27. *Matter of Contempt of the Supreme Court*, 673 N.E.2d 755, 757 (Ind. 1996).
28. *Matter of Thonert*, 693 N.E.2d 563 (Ind. 1998).
29. *Noethtich v. State*, 676 N.E.2d 1078, 1083 (Ind. Ct. App. 1997).
30. *The People v. Goodman*, 366 Ill. 346, 356 (Ill. 1937).
31. *Matter of Thonert*, 693 N.E.2d 559 (Ind. 1998).
32. T. D. Morgan, *Professional Malpractice in a World of Amateurs*, 40 St. Mary's L. J. (2009), 894.
33. *Matter of Contempt of Mittower*, 693 N.E.2d 555, 558 (Ind. 1998).
34. *Matter of Thonert*, 693 N.E.2d 559, 563 (Ind. 1998).
35. *Franklin v. Chavis*, 371 S.C. 527, 640 S.E.2d 873 (S.C. 2007).
36. *Franklin v. Chavis*, 371 S.C. 527, 532 (S.C. 2007).
37. *Oregon State Bar v. Gilchrist*, 272 Or. 552, 538 P.2d 913 (Or. 1975).

between defendants and their customers in the nature of consultation, explanation, recommendation or advice or other assistance in selecting particular forms, in filling out any part of the forms, or suggesting or advising how the forms should be used in solving the particular customer's marital problems does constitute the practice of law and must be and is strictly enjoined."[38] However, an Indiana court held that filling in the blanks in legal documents was not the practice of law unless the answers required "considerations of significant legal refinement,... or legal consequences."[39] States have different interpretations of the practice of law so it is important to understand your state law.

§10.7 Know Your State Law

It bears repeating that what constitutes the practice of law is a state law matter. Some states expressly define the practice of law; others do not, relying on the courts for guidance. Definitions are challenging given the multi-faceted practice of law. Students are strongly urged to become familiar with the laws and bar association rules in their state regarding the unauthorized practice of law. The American Bar Association website provides the states' definitions of the practice of law.[40]

State bar associations' rules of conduct may contribute to the understanding of the unauthorized practice of law as do guidelines for paralegal practice. However, as master of legal studies professionals are not directly supervised by attorneys in many cases, lines blur for paralegal comparisons, but may provide broad guidance. For example, the court *In Matter of Easler*,[41] explained that paralegal work is not the practice of law "as long as they are limited to work of a preparatory nature, such as legal research, investigation, or the composition of legal documents, which enable the licensed attorney-employer to carry a given matter to a conclusion through his own examination, approval or additional effort."[42] However, the Supreme Court of New Jersey has found that a "paralegal who recognizes that the attorney is not directly supervising his or her work or that such supervision is illusory because the attorney knows nothing about the field in which the paralegal is working must understand that he or she is engaged in the unauthorized practice of law."[43]

---

38. *Oregon State Bar v. Gilchrist*, 272 Or. 552, 563-64 (Or. 1975).

39. *State ex rel. Indiana State Bar Association v. Diaz*, 838 N.E.2d 433, 444 (Ind. 2005).

40. American Bar Association, *Task Force on the Model Definition of the Practice of Law, State Definitions of the Practice of Law* (n.d.), https://www.americanbar.org/groups/professional_responsibility/task_force_model_definition_practice_law/.

41. *In the Matter of Easler*, 275 S.C. 400, 272 S.E.2d 32 (S.C. 1980).

42. *In the Matter of Easler*, 275 S.C. 400, 401 (S.C. 1980).

43. *In Re: Opinion No. 24 of the Committee on the Unauthorized Practice of Law*, 128 N.J. 114, 127 (1992).

Pause for Reflection Unauthorized Practice of Law

Consider this scenario: Len knocks on the door of the corporate attorney at the end of a long day of contract review. As the contract officer at a medium-sized business, he is thoroughly familiar with the ins and outs of the contracts they deal with on a daily basis. "Steve, do you have a minute? There is language in the new proposal from ABC that I have not seen before. I thought I had seen it all, but this one has me stumped." With a pained expression, Steve says, "Sorry man I cannot—I am slammed. Just getting this last memo out and then I must head to the airport—we are getting out of town for the long weekend and my wife will kill me if I miss the flight. I trust your judgment. And now that you have your master of legal studies degree, I was planning to talk with you about shifting some of my load to you—it has been crazy lately."

Questions:

1. What issues are involved here for master of legal studies graduates?
2. Would you categorize these as ethical or legal issues?
3. How should Len respond to this request?

Attempting to apply legal knowledge regarding the new contractual language as well as taking on Steve's legal work are some potential legal issues that could have made Len engaged in the unauthorized practice of law. Len should educate Steve on the work that he is qualified to do with his master of legal studies degree to avoid the unauthorized practice of law.

In summary, please make sure that you understand what constitutes the practice of law as defined by your state and to not engage in those activities to avoid the unauthorized practice of law.

EXERCISES

1. What is the term that allows non-lawyers to engage in what might otherwise constitute the practice of law within limited spheres where they have specialized expertise?
2. Is the practice of law regulated by the state or federal government?
3. Name three activities that constitute the unauthorized practice of law.
4. Which 2022 New York case broadened access to justice allowing non-lawyer volunteers to provide certain legal advice?

APPENDIX A

CFR Titles[1]

		Last Amended
Title 1	:: General Provisions	Dec 29, 2022
Title 2	:: Grants and Agreements	Oct 23, 2023
Title 3	:: The President	Mar 17, 2015
Title 4	:: Accounts	May 01, 2018
Title 5	:: Administrative Personnel	Jan 30, 2024
Title 6	:: Domestic Security	Jul 12, 2023
Title 7	:: Agriculture	Feb 01, 2024
Title 8	:: Aliens and Nationality	Jan 31, 2024
Title 9	:: Animals and Animal Products	Dec 14, 2023
Title 10	:: Energy	Jan 17, 2024
Title 11	:: Federal Elections	Jan 29, 2024
Title 12	:: Banks and Banking	Feb 01, 2024
Title 13	:: Business Credit and Assistance	Jan 29, 2024
Title 14	:: Aeronautics and Space	Dec 28, 2023
Title 15	:: Commerce and Foreign Trade	Jan 25, 2024
Title 16	:: Commercial Practices	Jan 31, 2024
Title 17	:: Commodity and Securities Exchanges	Jan 24, 2024
Title 18	:: Conservation of Power and Water Resources	Jan 29, 2024
Title 19	:: Customs Duties	Jan 31, 2024
Title 20	:: Employees' Benefits	Jan 23, 2024
Title 21	:: Food and Drugs	Jan 30, 2024
Title 22	:: Foreign Relations	Jan 08, 2024

1. https://www.ecfr.gov/titles.

Title 23	:: Highways	Jan 18, 2024
Title 24	:: Housing and Urban Development	Jan 01, 2024
Title 25	:: Indians	Jan 17, 2024
Title 26	:: Internal Revenue	Jan 22, 2024
Title 27	:: Alcohol, Tobacco Products and Firearms	Sep 28, 2023
Title 28	:: Judicial Administration	Jan 10, 2024
Title 29	:: Labor	Jan 24, 2024
Title 30	:: Mineral Resources	Jan 25, 2024
Title 31	:: Money and Finance: Treasury	Jan 25, 2024
Title 32	:: National Defense	Jan 26, 2024
Title 33	:: Navigation and Navigable Waters	Jan 30, 2024
Title 34	:: Education	Jan 26, 2024
Title 35	:: Reserved	
Title 36	:: Parks, Forests, and Public Property	Jan 29, 2024
Title 37	:: Patents, Trademarks, and Copyrights	Jan 17, 2024
Title 38	:: Pensions, Bonuses, and Veterans' Relief	Jan 23, 2024
Title 39	:: Postal Service	Jan 10, 2024
Title 40	:: Protection of Environment	Feb 01, 2024
Title 41	:: Public Contracts and Property Management	Jan 15, 2024
Title 42	:: Public Health	Feb 01, 2024
Title 43	:: Public Lands: Interior	Jan 25, 2024
Title 44	:: Emergency Management and Assistance	Jan 22, 2024
Title 45	:: Public Welfare	Feb 01, 2024
Title 46	:: Shipping	Feb 01, 2024
Title 47	:: Telecommunication	Feb 01, 2024
Title 48	:: Federal Acquisition Regulations System	Jan 24, 2024
Title 49	:: Transportation	Feb 01, 2024
Title 50	:: Wildlife and Fisheries	Feb 01, 2024

APPENDIX B

Docket for *Loper Bright Enterprises*[1]

No. 22-451	
Title:	**Loper Bright Enterprises, et al., Petitioners** **v.** **Gina Raimondo, Secretary of Commerce, et al.**
Docketed:	**November 15, 2022**
Lower Ct:	**United States Court of Appeals for the District of Columbia Circuit**
Case Numbers:	**(21-5166)**
Decision Date:	**August 12, 2022**
Questions Presented	

Date	**Proceedings and Orders**
Nov 10 2022	Petition for a writ of certiorari filed. (Response due December 15, 2022)
	Petition Appendix Certificate of Word Count Proof of Service
Nov 17 2022	Blanket Consent filed by Petitioner, Loper Bright Enterprises, et al.
	Blanket Consent
Dec 06 2022	Brief amicus curiae of New England Legal Foundation filed.
	Main Document Proof of Service Certificate of Word Count
Dec 09 2022	Brief amici curiae of Cato Institute, et al. filed.
	Main Document Proof of Service Certificate of Word Count
Dec 12 2022	Brief amici curiae of Competitive Enterprise Institute, et al. filed.
	Main Document Proof of Service Certificate of Word Count
Dec 13 2022	Motion for leave to file amicus brief filed by Pacific Legal Foundation.
	Main Document Proof of Service Certificate of Word Count

1. https://www.supremecourt.gov/docket/docketfiles/html/public/22-451.html

Dec 13 2022	Motion to extend the time to file a response from December 15, 2022 to January 17, 2023, submitted to The Clerk.
	Main Document
Dec 14 2022	Motion for leave to file amicus brief filed by Center for Constitutional Jurisprudence.
	Main Document Proof of Service Certificate of Word Count
Dec 15 2022	Motion to extend the time to file a response is granted and the time is extended to and including January 17, 2023.
Dec 15 2022	Brief amicus curiae of Independent Women's Law Center filed.
	Main Document Certificate of Word Count Proof of Service
Dec 15 2022	Brief amici curiae of West Virginia, et al. filed.
	Main Document Certificate of Word Count Proof of Service
Dec 15 2022	Brief amicus curiae of Southeastern Legal Foundation filed.
	Main Document Certificate of Word Count Proof of Service
Dec 15 2022	Motion for leave to file amicus brief filed by Christian Employers Alliance.
	Main Document Certificate of Word Count Proof of Service
Dec 15 2022	Brief amicus curiae of National Right to Work Legal Defense Foundation, Inc. filed.
	Main Document Certificate of Word Count Proof of Service
Dec 15 2022	Motion for leave to file amici brief filed by Relentless, Inc., et al.
	Main Document Proof of Service Certificate of Word Count
Dec 15 2022	Motion for leave to file amici brief filed by David Goethel, et al.
	Main Document Certificate of Word Count Proof of Service
Dec 15 2022	Motion of Advancing American Freedom for leave to file amicus brief not accepted for filing.(Duplicate submission) (December 20, 2022)
Dec 15 2022	Motion for leave to file amici brief filed by Advancing American Freedom, et al.(12/19/2022)
	Main Document Certificate of Word Count Proof of Service
Dec 15 2022	Brief amici curiae of Buckeye Institute, et al. filed.
	Main Document Certificate of Word Count Proof of Service
Jan 12 2023	Motion to extend the time to file a response from January 17, 2023 to February 16, 2023, submitted to The Clerk.
	Main Document

Jan 13 2023	Motion to extend the time to file a response is granted and the time is further extended to and including February 16, 2023.
Feb 16 2023	Brief of respondents Gina Raimondo, Secretary of Commerce, et al. in opposition filed.
	Main Document Certificate of Word Count
Mar 08 2023	DISTRIBUTED for Conference of 3/24/2023.
Mar 08 2023	Reply of petitioners Loper Bright Enterprises, et al. filed. (Distributed)
	Main Document Certificate of Word Count Proof of Service
Mar 27 2023	DISTRIBUTED for Conference of 3/31/2023.
Apr 10 2023	DISTRIBUTED for Conference of 4/14/2023.
Apr 17 2023	DISTRIBUTED for Conference of 4/21/2023.
Apr 24 2023	DISTRIBUTED for Conference of 4/28/2023.
May 01 2023	Motion for leave to file amicus brief filed by Pacific Legal Foundation GRANTED. Justice Jackson took no part in the consideration or decision of this motion.
May 01 2023	Motion for leave to file amicus brief filed by Center for Constitutional Jurisprudence GRANTED. Justice Jackson took no part in the consideration or decision of this motion.
May 01 2023	Motion for leave to file amicus brief filed by Christian Employers Alliance GRANTED. Justice Jackson took no part in the consideration or decision of this motion.
May 01 2023	Motion for leave to file amici brief filed by Relentless, Inc., et al. GRANTED. Justice Jackson took no part in the consideration or decision of this motion.
May 01 2023	Motion for leave to file amici brief filed by David Goethel, et al. GRANTED. Justice Jackson took no part in the consideration or decision of this motion.

May 01 2023	Motion for leave to file amicus brief filed by Advancing American Freedom GRANTED. Justice Jackson took no part in the consideration or decision of this motion.
May 01 2023	Petition GRANTED limited to Question 2 presented by the petition. Justice Jackson took no part in the consideration or decision of this petition.
Jun 02 2023	Motion for an extension of time to file the briefs on the merits filed. Main Document
Jun 05 2023	Motion to extend the time to file the briefs on the merits granted. The time to file the joint appendix and petitioners' brief on the merits is extended to and including July 10, 2023. The time to file respondents' brief on the merits is extended to and including August 30, 2023.
Jun 09 2023	Motion to dispense with printing the joint appendix filed by petitioners Loper Bright Enterprises, et al. Main Document Proof of Service
Jun 20 2023	Motion to dispense with printing the joint appendix filed by petitioners GRANTED. Justice Jackson took no part in the consideration or decision of this motion.
Jul 07 2023	Motion for a further extension of time to file the briefs on the merits filed. Main Document
Jul 07 2023	Motion to further extend the time to file the briefs on the merits granted. The time to file petitioners' brief on the merits is further extended to and including July 17, 2022. The time to file respondents' brief on the merits is further extended to and including September 15, 2023.
Jul 13 2023	Amicus brief of Atlantic Legal Foundation submitted. Main Document Certificate of Word Count Proof of Service
Jul 13 2023	Amicus brief of DRI Center for Law and Public Policy submitted. Main Document Certificate of Word Count Proof of Service

Glossary

Many of the definitions and explanations below are taken with permission from the free dictionary at the Legal Information Institute of Cornell Law School. These definitions are in quotes and LII is noted at the end of the material.

We recommend visiting the LII site. LII supports "open access to legal information." The general LII site is law.cornell.edu. The dictionary is at https://www.law.cornell.edu/wex.

The definitions with the asterisk before the term are from the United States Courts Glossary of Legal Terms: https://www.uscourts.gov/glossary.

Administrative Law: Administrative law and regulatory law are often used interchangeably; both deal with government agencies. They are distinguishable, however, in that regulatory law refers to the regulations promulgated by government agencies. Administrative law generally refers to the guidelines and rules that agencies must follow in promulgating and administering regulations.

Appellant: "Appellant is the party who appeals a lower court's judgment or order to a higher court. The appellant is dissatisfied with the outcome of the proceeding and seeks review by a higher court to overturn or modify the decision. In some courts, it is also referred to as a petitioner." LII

Appellee: "Appellee is the party against whom the appeal is filed and responds to and defends the appeal. The appellee is also referred to as the respondent. In contrast, the appellant is the party who appeals a lower court's judgment or order to a higher court." "For example: Plaintiff (P) sues Defendant and (D) and wins. D files an appeal. D is the appellant, and P is the appellee. If D wins the lawsuit and P files an appeal, the roles are reversed. P becomes the appellant and D is the appellee." LII

Authority: The United States Constitution grants authority to each of the three branches of government: to legislate, to execute, and to judge. The Constitution both limits the branches' authority and provides checks and balances.

When discussing the law, it is important to distinguish four types of authority:

- Primary authority is the law itself.
- Secondary authority explains and analyzes the law; law review articles and treatises are examples of secondary authority.
- Mandatory authority must be followed as it is binding or precedential.
- Persuasive authority can be persuasive, but it is not mandatory.

Primary Authority (the law) can be either mandatory or persuasive.

Secondary Authority is never mandatory but may be persuasive.

It is important to understand how these four terms relate.

Primary Authority: The law, including constitutions, statutes, case law, regulations. A court is bound by primary authority if it is from a case with a similar issue, in the same jurisdiction, and by a higher court.

Secondary Authority: "Secondary authority refers to statements about the law from unofficial commentators without the authority to establish legal rules in the relevant jurisdiction. Secondary authorities can provide valuable insights and guidance on legal issues, helping to clarify the application and implications of primary law. Common examples include law review articles and treatises. Although secondary authority may be persuasive, it is never mandatory." LII

Mandatory Authority: Mandatory authority must be followed as it is precedential. "Mandatory authority, unlike persuasive authority, describes legal authority that is binding and must be followed. All mandatory authority are primary sources of law. However, not all primary sources of law are mandatory authority because the jurisdiction affects whether a legal authority is mandatory or persuasive. A secondary source of law can never be mandatory authority. [W] hile the Constitution of the United States is mandatory authority in every state and every court in the United States, an individual state's constitution is mandatory authority only within the state's jurisdiction. In this situation, even though a state constitution is a primary source of law, it is not automatically mandatory authority." LII

Persuasive Authority: Persuasive authority may state an important rule, but it does not have the status of precedent. It can persuade the court, but it is not mandatory. "Persuasive authority, unlike mandatory authority, describes a source of law—primary or secondary—that carries some authoritative weight but that does not bind a court.

"Whether a court decision is persuasive authority or mandatory authority depends on the rank and jurisdiction of the courts involved. A decision by a lower court is persuasive authority for a higher court. Therefore, a decision by any other court is persuasive authority for the Supreme Court because it is the highest court in the United States. In general, a decision by a court of the same rank is persuasive authority. For example, trial court decisions are not binding in the same trial court. A decision by a court of one jurisdiction is persuasive authority for courts of another jurisdiction. For example, decisions by federal courts do not bind state courts and vice versa, and decisions by courts of other states do not bind the forum state court." LII

Canons or Canons of Construction Canons are "guiding principles for interpreting statutes."[1] "Canons of Construction is defined as a system of rules or maxims that is used to interpret the legal instruments such as statutes. There are several canons of construction such as *contra proferentem* and *ejusdem generis* that are used by attorneys or judges to interpret specific law. It is to be noted that canons of construction are not rules but rather they act as a principle that guides the interpretation of the text." LII

*__Case Law:__ "Case law is the law as established in previous court decisions. A synonym for legal precedent. Akin to common law, which springs from tradition and judicial decisions." uscourts.gov/glossary

Cause of Action: "A cause of action is a set of predefined factual elements that allow for a legal remedy. The factual elements needed for a specific cause of action can come from a constitution, statute, judicial precedent, or administrative regulation." LII

Certiorari (Writ of Certiorari): "Certiorari simply defined is a 'writ' by which a higher court (such as an appellate court) reviews some lower court's decision (such as a district court).

"When a party loses in a court of law, often said party is allowed to appeal the decision to a higher court. In some instances, parties are entitled to an appeal, as a matter of right. However, sometimes a party is not able to appeal as a matter of right. In these instances, the party may only appeal by filing a writ of certiorari. If a court grants the writ of certiorari, then that court will hear that case.

"Certiorari is generally associated with the writ that the Supreme Court of the United States issues to review a lower court's judgment. A case cannot, as a matter of right, be appealed to the U.S. Supreme Court. As such, a party seeking to appeal to the Supreme Court from a lower court decision must file a writ of certiorari.

"In the Supreme Court, if four Justices agree to review the case, then the Court will hear the case. This is referred to as 'granting certiorari,' often abbreviated as 'cert.' If four Justices do not agree to review the case, the Court will not hear the case. This is defined as denying certiorari.

"Most of the Justices participate in a 'cert pool,' meaning their law clerks collectively assign out among themselves the various petitions for certiorari (known commonly as 'cert petitions') and prepare memoranda for the Justices summarizing the issues and recommending whether or not the Court should grant certiorari. Critics of this process note the shrinking number of cases the Court has agreed to hear in recent years, theorizing that the 'cert pool' tends to increase the number of recommended denials." LII

---

1. Brannon, V. C. (2023, March 10). *Statutory Interpretation: Theories, Tools, and Trends.* Congressional Research Service. https://crsreports.congress.gov/product/pdf/R/R45153. p. 27.

***Chevron* deference: Note—the Supreme Court overturned the Chevron doctrine in *Loper Bright Enterprises v. Raimondo* (June 28, 2024) while this book was in process. We added the following information here to explain this update:** "*Chevron* deference is referring to the doctrine of judicial deference given to administrative action. It was coined after a landmark case, *Chevron U.S.A., Inc. v. Natural Resources Defense Council, Inc.*, 468 U.S. 837 (1984). In *Chevron*, the Supreme Court set forth a legal test as to when the court should defer to the agency's answer or interpretation, holding that such judicial deference is appropriate where the agency's answer was not unreasonable, so long as Congress had not spoken directly to the precise issue at question.

"*Chevron* was one of the most important principles in administrative law for 40 years. In June of 2024, the U.S. Supreme Court overturned the *Chevron* doctrine in *Loper Bright Enterprises v. Raimondo* stating: 'The Administrative Procedure Act requires courts to exercise their independent judgment in deciding whether an agency has acted within its statutory authority, and courts may not defer to an agency interpretation of the law simply because a statute is ambiguous; *Chevron* is overruled.'

"The scope of the *Chevron* deference doctrine was when a legislative delegation to an administrative agency on a particular issue or question was not explicit but rather implicit, a court may not substitute its own interpretation of the statute for a reasonable interpretation made by the administrative agency. Rather, as Justice Stevens wrote in *Chevron*, when the statute was silent or ambiguous with respect to the specific issue, the question for the court was whether the agency's action was based on a permissible construction of the statute.

"First, the *Chevron* deference required that the administrative interpretation in question was issued by the agency charged with administering that statute. Accordingly, interpretations by agencies not in charge of the statute in question were not owed any judicial deference. Also, the implicit delegation of authority to an administrative agency to interpret a statute did not extend to the agency's interpretation of its own jurisdiction under that statute.

"Generally, to be accorded *Chevron* deference, the agency's interpretation of an ambiguous statute had to be permissible, which the Court has defined to mean 'rational' or 'reasonable.' In determining the reasonableness for the particular construction of a statute by the agency, the age of that administrative interpretation as well as the congressional action or inaction in response to that interpretation at issue would be a useful guide; if Congress were aware of the interpretation when it acted or refrained from action, and when the agency's interpretation was not inconsistent with the clear statutory language.

"In subsequent cases, the Supreme Court narrowed the scope of *Chevron* deference, holding that only the agency interpretations reached through formal proceedings with the force of law, such as adjudications, or notice-and-comment rulemaking, qualify for *Chevron* deference, while those contained in opinion letters, policy statements, agency manuals, or other formats that do not carry the force of law are not warranted a *Chevron* deference. In such cases, the Court may have given a slightly less deferential treatment to the agency's interpretation, giving a persuasive value under the Court's '*Skidmore* deference' analysis.

"The Supreme Court overturned the *Chevron* doctrine in *Loper Bright Enterprises v. Raimondo* (2024) holding that it was inconsistent with the Administrative Procedure Act (APA) and gave unelected government officials too much authority.

"By overturning *Chevron*, the Court realigns the doctrine with the requirements of Section 706 of the Administrative Procedure Act, which stipulates that '[t]o the extent necessary to decision and when presented, the reviewing court shall decide all relevant questions of law, interpret constitutional and statutory provisions, and determine the meaning or applicability of the terms of an agency action.' *See Loper Bright.*

"According to the *Loper* Court, step 2 (implicit delegation of authority) of the *Chevron* test erred in that it 'requires a court to ignore, not follow, the reading the court would have reached' had it exercised its independent judgment as required by the APA. *See Loper Bright.* The command of step 2 of the *Chevron* test was inconsistent with not only the APA but also judicial practice prior to *Chevron* and Article III of the Constitution. *See also* Davies *Warehouse v. Bowles* and *Whitman v. American Trucking Associations*. *Loper Bright* rejects the premise that Congress' creation of an ambiguous statute means that Congress intended for an administrative agency to fill in the gaps. See *Loper Bright* and C. Sunstein, *Interpreting Statutes in the Regulatory State*, 103 Harv. L. Rev. 405, 445 (1989). Rather, the Court notes that many statutory ambiguities are unintentional and may not reflect the true intent of Congress. The mere fact that statutory ambiguity involves an administrative agency does not mean that the Courts are excused from their responsibility to fulfill their traditional role of statutory interpretation. *See Loper Bright* and *Chevron.*

"When faced with an ambiguous statute, the Courts should not blindly defer to an administrative agency's interpretation. Instead, when a statute appears to delegate authority to an administrative agency, 'the role of the reviewing court under the APA is, as always, to independently interpret the statute and effectuate the will of Congress subject to constitutional limits.' *See Loper Bright.* A Court engages in this task by recognizing 'recognizing constitutional delegations, fixing the boundaries of the delegated authority, and ensuring the agency has engaged in "reasoned decision-making" within those boundaries.' *See Michigan v. EPA* (quoting *Allentown Mack Sales v. NLRB*). Even though Courts will no longer blindly defer to an agency's interpretation of a statute, such an interpretation can still be especially informative to the Court 'to the extent it rests on factual premises within [the agency's] expertise.' *See Bureau of Alcohol, Tobacco and Firearms v. FLRA* and *Loper Bright*." LII

Circuit split: "Circuit split arises when two or more circuits in the U.S. Court of Appeals reach different decisions on the same legal issue. This disagreement means federal law is applied differently in different parts of the country, so that similarly situated litigants receive different treatment across jurisdictions. The existence of circuit split is one of the reasons for the U.S. Supreme Court to grant certiorari." LII

Civil court: "In reference to law, 'civil' is used primarily as a descriptive term to denote conflicts between private individuals. Where in a civil case two or more individuals or private entities (such as corporations) dispute their rights relative to each other (such as in a contract or a tort), a criminal case involves the government attempting on behalf of its citizens to punish a person for violating its criminal law." LII

Civic mindedness: An individual that is civic minded is focused on the common good. A civic minded person cares about the community's welfare. Importantly, the civic minded take action to promote what is best for the community.

*__Common Law:__ "The legal system that originated in England and is now in use in the United States, which relies on the articulation of legal principles in a historical succession of judicial decisions. Common law principles can be changed by legislation." uscourts.gov/glossary

Concurring opinion: "A concurring opinion is an opinion that agrees with the majority opinion but does not agree with the rationale behind it. Instead of joining the majority, the concurring judge will write a separate opinion describing the basis behind their decision.

"Concurring opinions are not binding since they did not receive the majority of the court's support, but they can be used by lawyers as persuasive material. There are some rare circumstances in which the concurring opinion eventually becomes law, such as in *Escola v. Coca-Cola Bottling Co.*" LII

Counterclaim: "A counterclaim is defined as a claim for relief filed against an opposing party after the original claim is filed. Most commonly, a claim by the defendant against the plaintiff." LII

*__Declaratory judgment:__ "A judge's statement about someone's rights. For example, a plaintiff may seek a declaratory judgment that a particular statute, as written, violates some constitutional right." uscourts.gov/glossary

*__Defendant:__ "In a civil case, the person or organization against whom the plaintiff brings suit; in a criminal case, the person accused of the crime.

"Defendant, in criminal cases, is the person accused of the crime. In civil cases, the defendant is the person or entity that is being sued by the plaintiff. In certain types of actions, the defendant is called the respondent. However, the term respondent is usually used to designate the person responding to an appeal." uscourts.gov/glossary

Dicta: "Dicta is short for the Latin phrase *obiter dictum,* meaning 'something said in passing.'

"Dicta in law refers to a comment, suggestion, or observation made by a judge in an opinion that is not necessary to resolve the case, and as such, it is not legally binding on other courts but may still be cited as persuasive authority in future litigation. Also referred to as dictum and judicial dicta. A dissenting opinion is also generally considered *obiter dictum.*" LII

Dissenting opinion: "A dissenting opinion refers to an opinion written by an appellate judge or Supreme Court Justice who disagrees with the majority opinion in a given case. A party who writes a dissenting opinion is said to dissent.

"Unlike majority opinions and similar to concurring opinions, dissenting opinions are not binding law and, therefore, future cases are not obliged to follow them. Nonetheless, dissenting opinions preserve minority viewpoints on contested legal issues and contribute to the public debate of these issues." LII

Federalism: "Federalism is a system of government in which the same territory is controlled by two levels of government. Generally, an overarching national government is responsible for broader governance of larger territorial areas, while the smaller subdivisions, states, and cities govern the issues of local concern.

"Both the national government and the smaller political subdivisions have the power to make laws and both have a certain level of autonomy from each other." LII

Holding of the case: "A court's decision on a matter of law in civil procedure is called a 'holding.' It frequently refers to a ruling on a crucial issue that decides the outcome of the entire case." LII

*__Injunction:__ "A court order preventing one or more named parties from taking some action. A preliminary injunction often is issued to allow fact-finding, so a judge can determine whether a permanent injunction is justified." uscourts.gov/glossary

Intervenor: "Intervening is entry into a lawsuit by a third party into an existing civil case who was not named as an original party but has a personal stake in the outcome. The nonparty who intervenes in a case is called an intervenor. The intervenor joins the suit by filing a motion to intervene, which must be timely and include a statement of the grounds for intervention and a pleading of the relevant claims or defenses. An intervenor can join the side of the plaintiff, defendant, or as adverse to both the plaintiff and defendant. In federal cases, Rule 24 of the Federal Rules of Civil Procedure governs intervention." LII

IRAC: IRAC is an acronym that stands for Issue, Rule, Application, and Conclusion. IRAC is a framework for analyzing legal problems. It is a helpful starting point for answering a legal question that is taught in many law schools across the country.

Though it provides a very good initial structure for analyzing legal questions, a more nuanced approach may be needed in more complex legal questions.

Issue of the case: "An issue is a point of controversy or disagreement between parties and is submitted to a court or other legal tribunal for resolution. An issue can be a question of fact or law, or both, and can arise in various stages of a legal proceeding, such as during pretrial discovery, at trial, or on appeal." LII

***Jurisdiction:** "The legal authority of a court to hear and decide a certain type of case. It also is used as a synonym for venue, meaning the geographic area over which the court has territorial jurisdiction to decide cases." uscourts.gov/glossary

Major Questions Doctrine: The Major Questions Doctrine provides that agencies cannot interpret statutes that contain consequential economic or political issues. The Doctrine was introduced by the United States Supreme Court in *Alabama Association of Realtors v. Department of Health & Human Services* (2021).

Motion: "A motion is a formal request made by any party for a desired ruling, order, or judgment. The party that makes the motion is known as the movant. A motion can be written or spoken, as the relevant rules require. Various motions can be made throughout a proceeding, but only after the initial complaint has been filed." LII

A motion is initiated by one of the parties of a legal case asking the court to decide a single issue about the case. There are several different types of motions including motions to dismiss and motions for summary judgment explained next.

Motion to Dismiss: A motion to dismiss is requested by either party at any time during the proceedings. The party is asking to dismiss the case; this can be done for one of many reasons. The party may claim, for example, that the plaintiff failed to state a cause of action. "A motion to dismiss is a formal request for a court to dismiss a case. The reasons for a dismissal vary greatly." LII

Motion for Summary Judgment: A motion for summary judgement is brought by one of the parties of a legal case. In this motion the party contends that there is no genuine issue of material fact and they should win the case as a matter of law.

"A summary judgment is a judgment entered by a court for one party and against another party without a full trial. In civil cases, either party may make a pre-trial motion for summary judgment. Rule 56 of the Federal Rules of Civil Procedure governs summary judgment for federal courts. Under Rule 56, in order to succeed in a motion for summary judgment, a movant must show 1) that there is no genuine dispute as to any material fact, and 2) that the movant is entitled to judgment as a matter of law. 'Material fact' refers to any facts that could allow a fact-finder to decide against the movant." LII

Natural Law: "In legal philosophy, natural law is a set of universal truths, principles, and rules that properly govern moral human conduct. In contrast to positive law, natural law is pre-existing and discovered through human reason and rational analysis. From a natural law perspective, the purpose of laws and the judicial system is to become as close to natural law as possible." LII

Negligence: "Negligence is the failure to behave with the level of care that a reasonable person would have exercised under the same circumstances. Either a person's actions or omissions of actions can be found negligent. The omission of actions is considered negligent only when the person had a duty to act (e.g., a duty to help someone because of one's own previous conduct).

"Negligence is a foundational concept of tort law. Some primary factors to consider in ascertaining whether a person's conduct lacks reasonable care are the foreseeable likelihood that the conduct would result in harm, the foreseeable severity of the harm, and the burden of precautions necessary to eliminate or reduce the risk of harm. The following five elements may typically be required to prove negligence:

- The existence of a legal duty that the defendant owed the plaintiff
- Defendant's breach of that duty
- Harm to the plaintiff
- Defendant's actions are the proximate cause of harm to the plaintiff
- Defendant's actions are the cause-in-fact of harm to the plaintiff

"Generally, members of society have entered a social contract that includes a duty to not cause harm to others. When considering legal duty as an element of negligence, there is a duty to act reasonably. When a jury is asked to determine if a defendant's actions were reasonable, the standard is what a reasonable person would have done in the defendant's situation." LII

Non-delegation doctrine: The non-delegation doctrine provides that Congress cannot delegate its law-making powers to another branch of government.

Plaintiff: "A plaintiff is the party who initiates a lawsuit in a civil matter. The plaintiff may be an individual or an entity. A plaintiff files a complaint with a court against the defendant, initiating the action. In bringing an action, a civil suit must be prosecuted in the name of real party in interest, so the plaintiff must be the person or a representative of the person who possesses a claim against the defendant.

"A plaintiff may also be referred to as a petitioner, especially in equity, although the term petitioner can also be applied to either the plaintiff or defendant on appeal, depending on who is presenting the case to the higher court for further proceedings." LII

Pluralistic Society: A pluralistic society is one in which the members of the society are of diverse backgrounds. This diversity may include, for example, race, religion, and cultural distinctions. The ideal is that these diverse groups not only coexist, but that they work together all as valuable members of the group.

Precedent: If a given case must be followed, we say that it sets precedent. Specific rules determine whether a case is precedential: a case in higher court in the same jurisdiction with closely related facts and issues is precedential. The precedential case has binding or mandatory authority.

Procedural Laws: "Law that establishes the rules of the court and the methods used to ensure the rights of individuals in the court system. In particular, laws that provide how the business of the court is to be conducted. Examples may be pleading requirements, discovery rules, or standards of review.

"In the U.S. federal court system, the Rules Enabling Act of 1934 provides the 'Supreme Court of the United States shall have the power to prescribe, by general rules, for the district courts of the United States and for the courts of the District of Columbia, the forms of process, writs, pleadings, and motions, and the practice and procedure in civil actions at law.' The result has been the Federal Rules of Civil Procedure, which provide a comprehensive guide as to how federal courts should conduct the administration of justice. Note, however, that the Federal Rules of Civil Procedure apply only in civil actions, and not to state rules of procedure. Each states follows its own system of civil procedure laws, many of which are modeled on or influenced by the federal rules.

"The federal court system also has a system of rules of criminal procedure. Rules of criminal procedure differ from those of civil procedure in that they include rules governing preliminary proceedings specific to criminal proceedings, such as arrest; they include rules governing grand juries and indictment; arraignment and notices of defenses; and particular issues pertaining to criminal trials. While distinct from substantive rights, procedural law can nevertheless greatly influence a case." LII. *See also* Substantive Laws.

Purposivism: Purposivism is a "statutory interpretation theory that focuses on addressing the issue that the legislature was trying to fix when it wrote the statute."[2]

Regulatory law: Administrative law and regulatory law both deal with government agencies and are often used interchangeably. They are distinguishable, however, in that regulatory law refers to the regulations promulgated by government agencies. Administrative law generally refers to the guidelines and rules that agencies must follow in promulgating and administering regulations.

Respondent: "The respondent is the party against whom a petition is filed, especially one on appeal. The respondent can be either the plaintiff or the defendant from the court below, as either party can appeal the decision thereby making themselves the petitioner and their adversary the respondent. Formerly, in the equity courts of common law, the defendant was always called the respondent. see also petitioner." LII

---

2. Brannon, V. C. (2023, March 10). *Statutory Interpretation: Theories, Tools, and Trends.* Congressional Research Service. https://crsreports.congress.gov/product/pdf/R/R45153. p. 12.

Settlement: "Approximately 95% of civil cases reach settlements at some stage (can be before, after, or during the trial)." LII

Shepard's citations: Shepard's is a system used in the law to track authorities like cases, statutes and regulations. Shepards is used to determine whether an authority is still good law.

Standing: "Standing, or *locus standi*, is capacity of a party to bring suit in court. A state's statutes will determine what constitutes standing in that particular state's courts. These typically revolve around the requirement that plaintiffs have sustained or will sustain direct injury or harm and that this harm is redressable. At the federal level, legal actions cannot be brought simply on the ground that an individual or group is displeased with a government action or law. Federal courts only have constitutional authority to resolve actual disputes." LII

***Stare Decisis*:** "*Stare decisis* is the doctrine that courts will adhere to precedent in making their decisions. *Stare decisis* means 'to stand by things decided' in Latin. When a court faces a legal argument, if a previous court [with binding authority] has ruled on the same or a closely related issue, then the court will make their decision in alignment with the previous court's decision. The previous deciding-court must have binding authority over the court; otherwise, the previous decision is merely persuasive authority. In *Kimble v. Marvel Enterprises*, the U.S. Supreme Court described the rationale behind stare decisis as 'promot[ing] the evenhanded, predictable, and consistent development of legal principles, foster[ing] reliance on judicial decisions, and contribut[ing] to the actual and perceived integrity of the judicial process.'" LII

Substantive Laws: Substantive laws are the laws "which governs the original rights and obligations of individuals. Substantive law may derive from the common law, statutes, or a constitution. For example, a claim to recover for breach of contract or negligence or fraud would be a common law substantive right. A state or federal statute giving an employee the right to sue for employment discrimination would also create a substantive right. Additionally, *Sibbach v. Wilson* (1941) illustrates how courts might approach the question of whether a law is substantive. There, the U.S. Supreme Court, in ruling that an order for a party to undergo a medical examination was a procedural and not a substantive matter, placed weight on the fact that no such substantive right existed in the common law and that no such statute touches on the matter." LII

Supremacy Clause: "Article VI, Paragraph 2 of the U.S. Constitution is commonly referred to as the Supremacy Clause. It establishes that the federal constitution, and federal law generally, take precedence over state laws, and even state constitutions. It prohibits states from interfering with the federal government's exercise of its constitutional powers, and from assuming any functions that are exclusively entrusted to the federal government. It does not, however, allow the federal government to review or veto state laws before they take effect." LII

Textualism: Statutory interpretation theory that maintains "(1) that a statute is a command from the legislature, (2) the meaning and legitimacy of which are discernible from the legislative enactment itself, and (3) are alterable only by legislative amendment."[3]

Further, "[t]extualism is a method of statutory interpretation that asserts that a statute should be interpreted according to its plain meaning and not according to the intent of the legislature, the statutory purpose, or the legislative history. Justice Antonin Scalia was considered one of the pioneers of originalism and textualism. Even if the textualist approach is commonly regarded as a conservative approach to the law, the rigor of its application can lead to progressive outcomes.

"In *Bostock v. Clayton Cnty.*, 140 U.S. 1731, 1734 (2020), Justice Neil Gorsuch (also widely viewed as Justice Scalia's heir) delivered an opinion prohibiting employment discrimination based on sexual orientation or gender identity with his reasoning based on textualism." LII

Tort: "A tort is an act or omission that gives rise to injury or harm to another and amounts to a civil wrong for which courts impose liability. In the context of torts, 'injury' describes the invasion of any legal right, whereas 'harm' describes a loss or detriment in fact that an individual suffers.

"The primary aims of tort law are to provide relief to injured parties for harms caused by others, to impose liability on parties responsible for the harm, and to deter others from committing harmful acts. Torts can shift the burden of loss from the injured party to the party who is at fault or better suited to bear the burden of the loss. Typically, a party seeking redress through tort law will ask for damages in the form of monetary compensation. Less common remedies include injunction and restitution.

"The boundaries of tort law are defined by common law and state statutory law. Judges, in interpreting the language of statutes, have wide latitude in determining which actions qualify as legally cognizable wrongs, which defenses may override any given claim, and the appropriate measure of damages. Although tort law varies by state, many courts utilize the Restatement of Torts (2nd) as an influential guide.

"Torts fall into three general categories:

- intentional torts (*e.g.*, intentionally hitting a person);
- negligent torts (*e.g.*, causing an accident by failing to obey traffic rules); and
- strict liability torts (*e.g.*, liability for making and selling defective products [*see* Products Liability).

---

3. Moncrieff, A. R. (2019). *Statutory Realism: The Jurisprudential Ambivalence of Interpretive Theory*. 72 Rutgers U. L. Rev. 127.

"Intentional torts are wrongs that the defendant knew or should have known would result through his or her actions or omissions. Negligent torts occur when the defendant's actions were unreasonably unsafe. Unlike intentional and negligent torts, strict liability torts do not depend on the degree of care that the defendant used. Rather, in strict liability cases, courts focus on whether a particular result or harm manifested.

"There are numerous specific torts including trespass, assault, battery, negligence, products liability, and intentional infliction of emotional distress. There are also separate areas of tort law including nuisance, defamation, invasion of privacy, and a category of economic torts." LII

Tortfeasor: A tortfeasor is one who commits a tort.

Unauthorized practice of law: Non-lawyers are not permitted to perform tasks that only lawyers can do, including but not limited to holding oneself out as an attorney,[4] giving legal advice that affects a person's rights, and representing clients in court.[5]

Unlicensed practice of law: Non-lawyers are sometimes permitted to engage in what might otherwise constitute the practice of law within limited spheres where they have specialized expertise, including but not limited to "... divorce, immigration, estate planning, mortgage lending, real estate, insurance, accounting, ... and others."[6]

---

4. *Matter of Contempt of the Supreme Court*, 673 N.E.2d 755, 757 (Ind. 1996).
5. *Matter of Thonert*, 693 N.E.2d 563 (Ind.1998).
6. Buhai, S. L. (2007). *Act Like a Lawyer, Be Judged Like a Lawyer: The Standard of Care for the Unlicensed Practice of Law*, Utah L. Rev. 88.

Index